RELATIONAL PSYCHOTHERAPY, PSYCHOANALYSIS AND COUNSELLING

Is therapy's relational turn only something to celebrate? It is a major worldwide trend taking place in all the therapy traditions. But up to now, appreciation of these developments has not been twinned with well-informed and constructive critique. Hence practitioners and students have not been able to engage as fully as they might with the complex questions and issues that relational working presents. *Relational Psychotherapy, Psychoanalysis and Counselling: Appraisals and reappraisals* seeks to redress this balance.

In this unique book, Del Loewenthal and Andrew Samuels bring together the contributions of writers from several countries and many therapy modalities, all of whom have engaged with what 'relational' means – whether to espouse the idea, to urge caution or to engage in sceptical reflection.

Relational Psychotherapy, Psychoanalysis and Counselling: Appraisals and reappraisals presents clinical work of the highest standard in a way that is moving and draws the reader in. The more intellectual contributions are accessible and respectful, avoiding the polarising tendencies of the profession. At a time when there has been a decline in the provision and standing of the depth therapies across the globe, this book shows that, whatever the criticisms, there is still creative energy in the field. It is hoped that practitioners and students in psychoanalysis, psychotherapy counselling and counselling psychology will welcome this book for its cutting-edge content and compassionate tone.

Del Loewenthal is Professor of Psychotherapy and Counselling, and Director of the Research Centre for Therapeutic Education at the University of Roehampton, where he also convenes Doctoral programmes. He is an analytic psychotherapist, chartered psychologist and photographer. He is founding editor of the *European Journal of Psychotherapy and Counselling*. He is chair of the Universities Psychotherapy and Counselling Association and former founding chair of the UK Council for Psychotherapy Research committee. His publications include *Phototherapy and Therapeutic Photography in a Digital Age* (Routledge, 2013), *Existential Psychotherapy and Counselling after Postmodernism: The Selected Works of Del Loewenthal* (Routledge, forthcoming) and, with Robert Snell, *Postmodernism for Psychotherapists* (Routledge, 2003), among numerous others. Del also has small private practices in Wimbledon and Brighton.

Andrew Samuels has, for 40 years, been evolving a unique blend of post-Jungian, relational psychoanalytic and humanistic approaches to therapy work. He is recognized internationally as a leading commentator from a psychotherapeutic perspective on political and social problems. His work on the father, sexuality, spirituality and countertransference has also been widely appreciated. He is a Founder Board Member of the International Association for Relational Psychoanalysis and Psychotherapy, past chair of the UK Council for Psychotherapy, and co-founder of Psychotherapists and Counsellors for Social Responsibility and also of the Alliance for Counselling and Psychotherapy. He is Professor of Analytical Psychology at Essex University and holds visiting chairs at New York, London and Roehampton Universities. His many books have been translated into 19 languages, including *Jung and the Post-Jungians* (Routledge, 1985); *A Critical Dictionary of Jungian Analysis* (Routledge, 1986); *The Plural Psyche: Personality, Morality and the Father* (Routledge, 1989); *The Political Psyche* (Routledge, 1993); and *Passions, Persons, Psychotherapy, Politics: The selected works of Andrew Samuels* (Routledge, forthcoming).

RELATIONAL PSYCHOTHERAPY, PSYCHOANALYSIS AND COUNSELLING

Appraisals and reappraisals

Edited by Del Loewenthal and Andrew Samuels

Routledge
Taylor & Francis Group
LONDON AND NEW YORK

First published 2014
by Routledge
27 Church Road, Hove, East Sussex BN3 2FA

and by Routledge
711 Third Avenue, New York, NY 10017

Routledge is an imprint of the Taylor & Francis Group, an informa business

© 2014 Del Loewenthal and Andrew Samuels

The right of the editors to be identified as the authors of the editorial material, and of the authors for their individual chapters, has been asserted in accordance with sections 77 and 78 of the Copyright, Designs and Patents Act 1988.

All rights reserved. No part of this book may be reprinted or reproduced or utilised in any form or by any electronic, mechanical, or other means, now known or hereafter invented, including photocopying and recording, or in any information storage or retrieval system, without permission in writing from the publishers.

Trademark notice: Product or corporate names may be trademarks or registered trademarks, and are used only for identification and explanation without intent to infringe.

British Library Cataloguing in Publication Data
A catalogue record for this book is available from the British Library

Library of Congress Cataloging in Publication Data
Relational psychotherapy, psychoanalysis, and counselling appraisals and reappraisals / edited by Del Loewenthal and Andrew Samuels.
    pages cm
  1. Interpersonal psychotherapy.   2. Psychotherapist and patient.
  3. Interpersonal relations.   I. Loewenthal, Del, 1947– editor of compilation.   II. Samuels, Andrew, editor of compilation.
RC489.I55R45 2014
616.89'14—dc23
                                                              2013046508

ISBN: 978-0-415-72153-0 (hbk)
ISBN: 978-0-415-72154-7 (pbk)
ISBN: 978-1-315-77415-2 (ebk)

Typeset in Times New Roman
by RefineCatch Limited, Bungay, Sufolk

Printed and bound in Great Britain by
TJ International Ltd, Padstow, Cornwall

CONTENTS

List of contributors viii
Permissions xiii
Acknowledgements xiv

PART I
Mainly celebrations 1

1 The magic of the relational? An introduction to appraising and reappraising relational psychotherapy, psychoanalysis and counselling 3
   DEL LOEWENTHAL

2 Democratizing psychoanalysis 12
   SUSIE ORBACH

3 Beloved 27
   JANE HABERLIN

4 The primal silence 39
   MARSHA NODELMAN

5 The intricate intimacies of psychotherapy and questions of self-disclosure 54
   WILLIAM F. CORNELL

6 Forgiveness – a relational process: Research and reflections 65
   JUDITH ANDERSON

CONTENTS

7   Mortality in the consulting room   80
    SUSAN COWAN-JENSSEN

8   Relational psychotherapy in Europe: A view
    from across the Atlantic   93
    LEWIS ARON

9   Commentary on relational psychoanalysis
    in Europe: How is this dialogue different?   107
    CHANA ULLMAN

PART II
Mainly critiques   119

10 The relational turn in psychoanalysis:
    Revolution or regression?   121
    ZVI CARMELI AND RACHEL BLASS

11 It's the stupid relationship   130
    IAN PARKER

12 Relational ethics: From existentialism to
    post-existentialism   140
    DEL LOEWENTHAL

13 Ordinary stories of intermingling of worlds
    and doing what is right: A person-centred view   152
    PETE SANDERS

14 Staying in dialogue with CBT   161
    TOM STRONG

15 Relational as theory? Relational as a principle?
    Relational as symbol of integration?   176
    HELENA HARGADEN

16 Shadows of the therapy relationship   184
    ANDREW SAMUELS

CONTENTS

17 A critical commentary on 'the relational turn' 193
   KEITH TUDOR

18 The relational: A postmodern meta-narrative 212
   ALISTAIR ROSS

19 Afterword: The personal equation 224
   ANDREW SAMUELS

   Index 228

CONTRIBUTORS

Judith Anderson is a Jungian Analytical Psychotherapist and Consultant Psychiatrist. She has a private psychotherapy practice working with adults and couples and draws on relational theory for her work. She chaired Psychotherapists and Counsellors for Social Responsibility for some years and is on the Steering Group of the Climate Psychology Alliance (judith.anderson@btinternet.com; www.leamingtonspapsychotherapy.co.uk).

Lewis Aron, PhD, is the Director of the New York University Postdoctoral Program in Psychotherapy and Psychoanalysis. He has served as President of the Division of Psychoanalysis (39) of the American Psychological Association; founding President of the International Association for Relational Psychoanalysis and Psychotherapy (IARPP); and founding President of the Division of Psychologist-Psychoanalysts of the New York State Psychological Association (NYSPA). He is the co-founder and co-chair of the Sándor Ferenczi Center at the New School for Social Research. Dr. Aron is one of the founders and is an Associate Editor of *Psychoanalytic Dialogues* and is the series editor (with Adrienne Harris) of the *Relational Perspectives Book Series* (Routledge). He is the Editor of the *Psychoanalysis & Jewish Life Book Series* (The Academic Studies Press); Author of *A Meeting of Minds* (The Analytic Press, 1996) and co-author, with Karen Starr, of *A Psychotherapy for the People: Toward a Progressive Psychoanalysis* (Routledge, 2013) (lew.aron@nyu.edu).

Rachel Blass (British Psychoanalytical Society and Israel Psychoanalytic Society) lives and practices in London where she is Professor of Psychoanalysis and of Psychology of Religion at Heythrop College, the University of London and a Visiting Professor at University College London. She is on the board of the International Journal of Psychoanalysis, where she is the editor of the 'Controversies' section. She has published and lectured widely on the conceptual, epistemological, and ethical foundations of psychoanalysis and their relevance to contemporary thinking and practice, focusing on Freud's work and its evolution in Kleinian psychoanalysis (r.blass@ucl.ac.uk).

CONTRIBUTORS

Zvi Carmeli is a clinical psychologist and a candidate at the Institute of Psychoanalysis of the Israel Psychoanalytic Society. He is the Head of the Department of Education at Herzog College and an Adjunct Lecturer at the Hebrew University of Jerusalem. He has researched and written on the underpinnings of the theory of mind of Relational Psychoanalytic theories and on the negative impact of introducing neuroscientific metaphors into psychoanalytic and psychological discourse (zcarmeli@gmail.com).

William F. Cornell, MA, TSTA-P, studied behavioural psychology at Reed College in Portland, Oregon, and phenomenological psychology at Duquesne University in Pittsburgh, Pennsylvania, following his graduate studies with training in transactional analysis and neo-Reichian body-centered psychotherapy. Since his formal training experiences, Bill has studied with several mentors and consultants within psychoanalytic perspectives. He has published numerous journal articles and book chapters, many exploring the interface between transactional analysis (TA), body-centered and psychoanalytic modalities, and has edited several books. He is co-editor of the *Transactional Analysis Journal*. He is the author of *Explorations in Transactional Analysis: The Meech Lake Papers* and the forthcoming, *Meeting in the Flesh* and *J'ai mal à ma vie. Les contradictions du soi* (wfcornell@gmail.com).

Susan Cowan-Jenssen is a UKCP registered integrative psychotherapist working in private practice. She is an EMDR Consultant specialising in post-traumatic stress and has an additional training in working with the seriously ill and bereaved from the Tavistock Clinic. She is a founder member of The Relational School in the UK and the London Psychotherapy and Trauma Centre. She has over 30 years' experience of working with individuals and groups both in the UK and in Scandinavia. She has published articles in books, journals and magazines on a wide range of psychological issues (suejenssen@blueyonder.co.uk; www.suecowanjenssen.co.uk).

Jane Haberlin trained with Arbours as a Psychoanalytic Psychotherapist. She has worked at the Arbours Crisis Centre and the Women's Therapy Centre. She is a founder member of The Relational School in London. She currently works as a therapist and supervisor in private practice and provides consultancy to organisations (janehaberlin@gmail.com).

Helena Hargaden, MSc, DPsych, is a training and supervisory transactional analyst, psychotherapist, writer, coach and supervisor. In collaboration with others she developed relational perspectives of TA and has been widely published and translated into a number of other languages. She lives on the English south coast by the sea where she has a clinical practice (helenahargaden27@hotmail.com).

Del Loewenthal is Professor of Psychotherapy and Counselling, and Director of the Research Centre for Therapeutic Education at the University of Roehampton

CONTRIBUTORS

where he also convenes Doctoral programmes. He is an analytic psychotherapist, chartered psychologist and photographer. He is founding editor of the European Journal of Psychotherapy and Counselling (Routledge). He is chair of the Universities Psychotherapy and Counselling Association and former founding chair of the UK Council for Psychotherapy Research Committee. His publications include *Phototherapy and Therapeutic Photography in a Digital Age*; *Post-Existentialism and the Psychological Therapies: Towards a Therapy without Foundations*; *Case Studies in Relational Research*; with Richard House, *Critically Engaging CBT, Childhood, Wellbeing and the Therapeutic Ethos* and *Against and for CBT*; with David Winter, *What is Psychotherapeutic Research?*; and with Robert Snell, *Postmodernism for Psychotherapists*. Del also has a small private practice in Wimbledon and Brighton (D.Loewenthal@roehampton.ac.uk; www.roehampton.ac.uk/staff/Del-Loewenthal).

Marsha Nodelman is a BPC registered psychoanalytic psychotherapist and a UKCP registered integrative psychotherapist and supervisor in private practice. She is a registered EMDR Europe Accredited Consultant specializing in post-traumatic stress and has worked as an honorary psychotherapist in the Traumatic Stress Service at the Maudsley Hospital. She has over 30 years of clinical experience working with individuals, couples and groups, and has taught at several training institutes. She has a special interest in trauma and couple work. She is a founder member of the London Psychotherapy and Trauma Centre and is the chair of the Education Committee of the Relational School of which she is a founder member (marshanodelman@btinternet.com; www.thelondonpsychotherapyandtraumacentre.co.uk/marsha-nodelman.html).

Susie Orbach chairs The Relational School in the UK. She has a practice seeing individuals and couples. She co-founded the Women's Therapy Centre in London and the Women's Therapy Centre Institute in New York. She has written many books including *The Impossibility of Sex*; *Bodies*; *Fat is a Feminist Issue*; *What Do Women Want?*, *Towards Emotional Literacy* and *Hunger Strike*. She has been a consultant at The World Bank and the NHS. She co-founded Psychotherapists and Counsellors for Social Responsibility and is convenor of the body activist organisation www.endangeredbodies.org. Her current research with colleagues from New York and the New School involves the transgenerational transmission of corporeality from mother to daughter and the development of the clinical instrument the © BODI. She regularly writes for the UK press and is a frequent commentator on BBC radio and TV on social, political and psychological issues. She gives at least 50 lectures and talks around the world and in the UK a year (sian@susieorbach.co.uk).

Ian Parker is co-director of the Discourse Unit (www.discourseunit.com), a practising psychoanalyst in Manchester, and author of *Lacanian Psychoanalysis:*

Revolutions in Subjectivity. He is currently Honorary Professor of Education at the University of Manchester and Visiting Professor in the Department of Psychosocial Studies at Birkbeck, University of London (ian.parker@manchester.ac.uk).

Alistair Ross is Director of Psychodynamic Studies, University Lecturer in Psychotherapy, and Dean of Kellogg College at Oxford University. Alistair is also Chair of the BACP's Professional Ethics and Quality Standards committee, reviews editor for *The European Journal of Psychotherapy and Counselling*, and a member of the editorial board of *Practical Theology*. Alistair's research focuses on the relationships between the sacred, spirituality, religion, psychoanalysis and psychotherapy. Recent books, lectures/articles include: 'Letters from Vienna: Freud and his friend Pastor Pfister'; 'Sacred Psychoanalysis' – the emergence of spirituality in contemporary psychoanalysis; 'Spiritual factors in therapy'; 'Harry Guntrip: an early relational psychoanalyst'; 'Grotstein's "Black Hole" and working with Borderline Personality'; 'Theological Reflections on Terrorism'; 'Winnicott's analysis of Guntrip revisited' and, with Dee Danchev, *Research Ethics for Counselling, Nursing and Social work* (Sage, 2014) (alistair.ross@kellogg.ox.ac.uk).

Andrew Samuels has, for 40 years, been evolving a unique clinical blend of post-Jungian, relational psychoanalytic, and humanistic approaches to therapy work. He is recognized internationally as a leading commentator from a psychotherapeutic perspective on political and social problems. His work on the father, sexuality, spirituality and countertransference has also been widely appreciated. He is a Founder Board Member of the International Association for Relational Psychoanalysis and Psychotherapy, past chair of the UK Council for Psychotherapy, and a co-founder of Psychotherapists and Counsellors for Social Responsibility and also of the Alliance for Counselling and Psychotherapy. He is Professor of Analytical Psychology at Essex University and holds visiting chairs at New York, London and Roehampton Universities. Andrew's many books have been translated into 19 languages, including *Jung and the Post-Jungians*; *The Plural Psyche*; *The Political Psyche*; and the award-winning *Politics on the Couch* (www.andrewsamuels.com; 12 MiHo Apartments, 565 Caledonian Road, London, N7 9RB, UK).

Pete Sanders retired after more than 30 years practising as a counsellor, educator and clinical supervisor. He has written several books, chapters and articles on counselling, psychotherapy and mental health. He is a trustee of the Soteria Network UK (pete@pccs-books.co.uk; Church Cottage, Discoed, Presteigne, Powys, LD8 2NW, UK).

Tom Strong is Professor of Counselling Psychology and Associate Dean Research at the University of Calgary's Faculty of Education. His interests are in the collaborative, critically reflective and generative potentials of counselling dialogues. He is the author of over 90 articles and chapters, the most recent books being *Discursive Perspectives in Therapeutic Practice* (Oxford, co-edited with Andy Lock) and *Social Constructionism: Sources and Stirrings in Theory and Practice* (Cambridge, with Andy Lock) (strongt@ucalgary.ca; Faculty of Education, University of Calgary, Alberta, T2N 1N4, Canada).

Keith Tudor is an Associate Professor at AUT University, Auckland, where he is also the Head of the Department of Psychotherapy and Counselling. He is a certified transactional analyst, a teaching and supervising transactional analyst, and a provisional member of the New Zealand Association of Psychotherapists. He has a small private practice in West Auckland. He is the series editor of *Advancing Theory in Therapy* (Routledge), the editor of *Psychotherapy and Politics International*, and the co-author of *Ata: Journal of Psychotherapy Aotearoa New Zealand*. He is the author/editor of over 250 publications, including 12 books, the latest of which, *Co-creative Transactional Analysis* (with Graeme Summers), is to be published by Karnac Books in 2014 (keith.tudor@aut.ac.nz; AUT University, Private Bag 92006, Auckland, 1142, NZ).

Chana Ullman, PhD, is a clinical psychologist, a training psychoanalyst and a faculty member at the Tel Aviv institute of Contemporary Psychoanalysis. She is a graduate of the Hebrew University of Jerusalem (MA) and of Boston University. She lives and practises in Rehovot, Israel. Dr. Ullman is a faculty member and supervisor at the relational track of the school of psychotherapy, Sackler school of medicine at Tel-Aviv University, and a supervisor at the school of psychotherapy at Bar Ilan University. She is the former chair of the Tel-Aviv Institute of Contemporary Psychoanalysis and a co-founder of the Israeli Forum of Relational Psychoanalysis and Psychotherapy. Dr. Ullman is a member of the board of the International Association of Relational Psychoanalysis and Psychotherapy and co-chairs the local chapters committee of IARPP. She is the author of *The Transformed Self: The Psychology of Religious Conversion* (Plenum press, 1989) and of numerous publications on relational theory, witnessing, political context and the psychoanalytic process (chanaullman@gmail.com).

PERMISSIONS

The following are reproduced with the kind permission of the publishers:

Chapters 2, 3, 4, 5, 6, 7, 8 and 9 are developed by permission of the publisher Taylor & Francis from articles that originally appeared in: *European Journal of Psychotherapy & Counselling*, Special Issue: Relational Psychology in Europe, Volume 9, Issue 1, 2007.

Chapters 1, 10, 11, 13, 14, 15, 16, 17 and 18 are developed by permission of the publisher Taylor & Francis from articles that originally appeared in: *European Journal of Psychotherapy & Counselling*, Special Issue: The Relational in Psychotherapy and Counselling – Cutting Edge or Cliché?, Volume 12, Issue 3, 2010.

Chapter 12 is developed from the book chapter 'From existentialism (and post-modernism) to post-existentialism: from Buber to Levinas' in *Post-existentialism and the Psychological Therapies: Towards a Therapy Without Foundations*, by Del Loewenthal (2011), with the permission of Karnac Books Ltd.

ACKNOWLEDGEMENTS

Del Loewenthal would like to thank all the contributors to this book for their helpfulness and commitment in bringing this project to fruition. He would also like to thank staff and students of the Research Centre for Therapeutic Education, Department of Psychology, University of Roehampton UK, for their enabling and delightful conversations; and in particular Catherine Altson, Betty Bertrand and Dawn Clark for their enthusiastic help in getting this book together. Last but not least, Del would like to acknowledge Andrew Samuels for his support and friendship, which goes back a long time, and, more recently, over the seven years we have been working on this relational project.

Andrew Samuels would like to thank friends and colleagues in the International Association for Relational Psychoanalysis and Psychotherapy and in the London Relational School for support, challenge and stimulation over many years. In particular, he would like to acknowledge the impact on his work of Susie Orbach, Jessica Benjamin, Muriel Dimen, Neil Altman, Irwin Hoffman, Lew Aron and the late Stephen Mitchell. It has been a joy to work with his old *compadre* Del Loewenthal, one of the most important figures in British and European psychotherapy.

We would both like to thank the people at Routledge – Kate Hawes, Kirsten Buchanan, Sally Mesner Lyons, Emily Pickett and Nigel Turner.

Part I

MAINLY CELEBRATIONS

1

THE MAGIC OF THE RELATIONAL?

An introduction to appraising and reappraising relational psychotherapy, psychoanalysis and counselling

Del Loewenthal

Is the 'relational turn' in psychoanalysis, psychotherapy and counselling something to celebrate? Half of the chapters and case studies in this book do just that. They show why there is now a widespread realization that the therapy relationship runs in both directions, is mutual, and involves the whole person of the practitioner.

The other half of the book consists of a set of respectful challenges to and critiques of the current consensus that relational therapy is definitely a 'good thing'. The uncritical reception of relational ideas is a growing problem for the field. Is it really a question of 'It's the relationship, stupid!'?

We hope the advantage of this unique book will be that it brings together in one volume both an account from British perspectives of the relational turn and also critiques and discussions of that turn. A special feature of the book is that two relational psychoanalysts (one from the US and one from Israel) comment in depth on the British authors in the Part I 'Mainly celebrations' chapters, and two relational psychotherapists (one from the UK and one from New Zealand) critique in the Part II 'Mainly critiques' chapters. Thus we aim for the spirit of tough-minded dialogue permeating the book.

There is a growing interest in relational therapy (Greenberg & Mitchell, 1983; Mitchell & Aron, 1999; Safran & Muran, 2000) as well as research on relating in psychotherapy (Birtchnell, 1999) and relational research (Loewenthal, 2007). For some, the 'relational' is most apparent in the psychoanalytic traditions of Freud, Klein and object relations theories as well as Jung; however, the increased interest in relational psychotherapy also includes a whole range of humanistic, existential, integrative and other approaches.

Importantly, there is growing international recognition of the research evidence (Beutler & Harwood, 2002; Luborsky & Auerbach, 1985), which suggests it is the relationship that is the most important factor in facilitating a successful outcome in psychological therapy. Furthermore, following the pioneering work of those such as Stephen Mitchell (1988), there is the emergence of such organisations as The International Association for Relational Psychoanalysis and Psychotherapy.

But what, then, of the different theories in the psychological therapies, regarding questions of the 'relational'? Do they make any difference? For example, do notions of object relations help or hinder? Is relational psychoanalysis really any different? Does the notion of learning relational skills just lead to further alienated inauthenticity in the name of authenticity? How can it be that, for some, interpreting the transference is a form of persecutory violence, whereas, for others, it's an ethical responsibility? Does naming a therapeutic modality as relational increase the possibility of a more human and fruitful approach or is it really an inappro-priate, unhelpful demand from the therapist, brought about from what is lacking in the therapist's own life? So, is it helpful to link psychotherapy with the name 'relational'? In particular, isn't there a danger of putting characteristics to the word 'relationship' and making it a technology where we talk about 'the' relational, 'relationality', etc.? Perhaps Heidegger's (1962) 'being with' is one alternative, if one could then stop it becoming a technology.

Yet, what I hesitantly term 'relational learning' does seem to have vital intrinsic qualities. How many readers' favourite, and their children's favourite, school subjects have consistently changed as their teachers have changed? What is it then about the relationship that makes the difference? Perhaps it's magic! Whatever it is, perhaps it needs to remain mysterious – for as Merleau-Ponty (1956) wrote, once you take away the mystery, you can take away the thing itself.

Does, potentially, Polanyi's (1983) 'tacit knowledge' come closest to describing what happens through the relational in therapy? If so, it is not something that can be taught and learned by either trainee psychological therapists or patients/clients. But might it be imparted and acquired? So, should we attempt a definition of the relational, or does its tacit, perhaps magical qualities make this too problematic? Hargaden and Schwartz (2007), who edited one of the two special issues of the *European Journal of Psychotherapy and Counselling* from which this book has evolved, identify what they consider to be key elements of relational psychotherapy:

- The centrality of the relationship
- Therapy as a two-way street involving a bi-directional process
- The vulnerability of both therapist and client is involved
- Countertransference is used, not merely as information but in thoughtful disclosure and collaborative dialogue
- The co-construction and multiplicity of meaning

Hargaden and Schwartz (2007) suggest that relational psychoanalysis usually tends to be regarded as a distinctive contemporary American contribution to psycho-analysis, emanating from the interpersonal (Washington) school of psycho-analysis associated with the psychiatrists Harry Stack Sullivan and William Alanson White. White in particular was instrumental, in the 1920s, in questioning the classical Freudian perspective, insisting that psychosis was capable of being treated psychodynamically with Freud's techniques. In the 1970s, a group of analysts (including Stephen Mitchell and Jay Greenberg at the William Alanson White Institute in New York) began to explore extensions of Sullivan's interpersonal psychoanalysis and what has become known as relational psychoanalysis emerged from this grouping.

Hargaden and Schwartz (2007) contend, however, that the relational perspective has in fact deep European roots that began with Eugen Bleuler, at the Rheinau Hospital for the Insane just outside Strasbourg. Bleuler maintained the possibility of relating to and understanding the utterances of the deeply disturbed people that he was to call schizophrenic. Hargaden and Schwartz (2007) see the tension between instinctual and relational approaches to mental distress as inherent in Freud's writings and, additionally, the work of Donald Winnicott, Ronald Fairbairn and John Bowlby is viewed as central to object relations and attachment theory – a development in Europe closely intertwining with the developing relational approaches in the US.

There is the belief that there are significant humanistic routes to relational psychoanalysis (Hargaden & Schwartz, 2007) including the work of Carl Rogers. Two films – *The Right to Be Desperate* and *Anger and Hurt* – show Rogers working with a man who was very ill and a victim of racism. In these films, Rogers works with a deep concentrated listening that is described as benign, yet intense and with a great warmth and depth of intellect. Hargaden and Schwartz (2007) regard this type of listening as very skilled and deeply empathic, whilst also retaining the therapist's subjective sense of self. This is viewed as the essence of a relational approach to working with clients.

If we then think that as psychological therapists we can actually be helpful by focusing on relationships, what are we actually looking at relationships between? Following Malan (1999), we might think it is the relationship between the patient/client and the psychological therapist; and/or the relationship between the patient/client and those around the client; and/or the relationship between the patient/client and significant others in their past.

However, if one were to return to William James (1890), a founding father of psychology (psychologists, never mind psychotherapists, might benefit in reading the original), one would find that he speaks about relationships in three different ways: first, the relationships between things, which would include the relationships between person and persons (this is 'intersubjectivity'); second, the relations between persons and materiality and environment (termed 'intermateriality') and third, what I would like to briefly explore here: the relationship between person and method (called 'intermethodology').

So, what may be particularly important is the relationship between the psychological therapist and their particular mode of working. For different modes of working probably evoke thoughts, feelings and behaviours of different orders. What James (1912) attempted to knock on the head was the traditional belief that methods usage only implicates the intellect by stating that passion, taste, emotion and practice cooperate in science as much as in any other practical affair. This radical empiricism is in contrast to the traditional belief that methods function independently of the total personalities who use them. This raises such questions as the potential suitability of the individual psychological therapist to carry out a particular therapeutic approach, as well as the effect of the professional training on the person.

With ideas of radical empiricism, developed from James, what is being suggested here is, first, an interest in the relationship of the person who is the psychological therapist with the particular method/school of psychotherapy they have chosen and what qualities it brings out in the therapist that are helpful and unhelpful for the therapeutic endeavour. Second, there is the question as to what else the particular modality method allows, perhaps despite itself, to percolate through beyond its self-contained, detached professional posturing. Here, we might see what the spaces between our method give rise to. In the case of psychological therapies, we attempt to give names to what happens in such spaces as 'transference' and 'countertransference', 'letting the other person know how they make us feel'. But what perhaps is being spoken about by 'the relational' appears in the nooks and crannies that the particular theory can't reach, beyond conceptual totalizing – and even beyond pluralism.

So, might we wonder what the relationship is between our distinguished contributors to this book and the methods they are putting forward; what qualities has it brought out in them which are helpful or unhelpful to their patients/clients and indeed themselves and to what extent do these methods allow something magical to happen? Also, to speculate to probably the extreme, is it possible that these different psychotherapeutic methods have really come about in order to deal with different types of 'psychopathologies' in people who are psychological therapists, enabling the therapist to be able to sit there for 50 minutes, minimising the damage their 'psychopathology' might do to the patient/client, whilst hopefully enabling something quite other to go to work and heal?

Perhaps a further advantage of having all these different approaches presented in this volume is that you, as the reader, may be able to modify your approach to the one that best suits your particular 'psychopathology'! Of course, here, as elsewhere, with so many different approaches provided in the psychological therapies, there is also the additional advantage of being able to project onto other approaches aspects of ourselves which we have not worked through, and which may not be able to be contained by our particular theorising!

What I have attempted to open up are questions regarding whether relational psychoanalysis, psychotherapy and counselling are 'cutting edge or cliché'. I think we are very fortunate in this book to have leading authorities in this field respond to such questions from different perspectives.

In Chapter 2, Susie Orbach discusses ways in which the complex shape of wanted (and feared) forms of relating by an individual analysand emerge in the therapy relationship. Orbach argues that in the reconfiguring of the meaning of the therapy relationship, the analyst is not an outsider, observing the impact of the analysand's various forms of longing and defences, but is inevitably drawn into and is an active participant in the relational field. Therapeutic neutrality and therapeutic stance are therefore reconceptualized, as are other issues that could be considered contentious, such as the blank screen, self-disclosure, the analyst's use of the countertransference, interpretation, power in the therapy relationship, dependency and money.

Following this, in Chapter 3 Jane Haberlin presents her clinical paper tracking episodes in a long, intensive therapy with a patient who felt haunted, both by her dead sister and by a part of herself, which led a parallel life. The chapter illustrates what relational therapy might look like in the consulting room through the lens of key themes such as bi-directional influence of patient and analyst, intersubjectivity and working with disassociation at relational depth.

Marsha Nodelman presents the case of Stephen in Chapter 4, 'The Primal Silence'. Marsha revisits her work with Stephen, a man in his mid-forties with cerebral palsy, to underline the significance of non-verbal analytic work as an essential vehicle for therapeutic action when the patient's dramatic birth history is enacted within the therapeutic relationship. The work with Stephen highlights the reciprocal processes of mutual influence and mutual regulation within the therapeutic dyad when altered and primitive states of consciousness cannot be formulated or communicated verbally.

In Chapter 5, William F. Cornell addresses the understanding of the analyst's/therapist's vulnerabilities within the therapeutic process and the intimate potential of the therapeutic relationship. The author stresses the awareness of the therapist's personal vulnerabilities in addition to the more common conceptualizations of countertransference. Case material is presented to illustrate the complex questions of self-disclosure and the intimate nature of therapeutic practice when viewed from a relational perspective.

Judith Anderson in Chapter 6 uses qualitative research based on interviews to explore how psychoanalytic practitioners may perceive forgiveness and argues that they see it as important, and sometimes at the heart of the psychoanalytic endeavour. In so doing, Judith acknowledges that forgiveness is a complex subject with cultural, religious and political associations and further explores how analytic thinking has enriched what is essentially a concept determined by religions and cultures. Judith concludes that the development of the capacity to forgive requires consciousness and empathy, for both self and other, and appropriate metabolizing of aggression.

In Chapter 7, Susan Cowan-Jenssen discusses the topic of mortality in the consulting room. Susan reviews some of the literature concerning how we make sense of our awareness of death and its place in our psyche. Through her exploration of how the ritual of the therapy hour can act as a defence against an awareness of death and a clinical vignette, Susan describes how the denial of her own anxieties about mortality kept her from fully understanding the depth of her client's terror of living and dying.

Chapters 8 and 9 are review chapters where international authors Lewis Aron and Chana Ullman comment on the European writers' chapters concerning European relational stances and dialogues in relational psychoanalysis.

Beginning Part II of the book, Zvi Carmeli and Rachel Blass commence the modality critiques in Chapter 10. They discuss the relational turn in psychoanalysis and argue that far from being revolutionary, as claimed, the adopted paternalistic attitude of the relational psychoanalyst can be considered regressive. They argue that in this 'new' form of therapeutic relationship, patients are subject to a corrective and suggestive relational process rather than the liberating one that is inherent to the Freudian revolution. Zvi and Rachel spell out the foundational claims of the Relational group over the last 25 years and its view that it has revolutionized psychoanalysis by bringing its relational potential to fruition. After clarifying these relational views, the authors explain why they think that the change introduced is misguided and not as revolutionary as it appears. The authors argue that counter to its self-perception, the Relational group in fact reverts to a pre-analytic conception of the person and to an authoritarian stance in relation to the patient. While presenting himself as liberal, unassuming and non-authoritarian in contrast to the traditional analyst, in his belief in his power to know what the patient is missing and to give it to him, the relational psychoanalyst, in effect, adopts a benevolent paternalistic dogmatism. It is here that the regressive move that actually lies at the heart of what has been referred to by some as the relational revolution in psychoanalysis is best exemplified.

Within Chapter 11, Ian Parker outlines how in contrast with Lacanian practice, where the analyst refrains from filling the gap left by the lack of knowledge and from interpreting the transference, the relational analyst aims for fullness and signification. Ian argues that relational psychoanalysis seems to force a choice between the 'Left' and 'Lacanian' sides of practice. He suggests this rubs at a sore point in Lacanian work, at a point of uneasy alliance between radical politics on the one hand and, on the other, the one-to-one frame of abstracted, individualized and limited horizons of change in the consulting room. According to Ian, this poses ultimately the crucial question of the direction of the treatment in relation to the broad context of politics versus the individual and the question of the end of analysis.

In Chapter 12, I write about post-existentialism and relational psychological therapies, asking if this is a return to 'me' in the context of a return to the subject. The chapter takes as its starting point recent trends in relational psychoanalysis and argues that a primacy should be given to practice rather than theory. There is some recognition of both contradiction in a relational approach based on knowledge and our search for meaning. I outline a practice-based approach termed 'post-existentialism' where the problematics of such a search for meaning might be helped by considering some implications of the ethics of Levinas, and what it means to put the other first. I argue that commenting on relational psychological therapies is best done from a Levinasian perspective, which is taken as being more post-existential than the existential ethics of Buber.

In Chapter 13, Pete Sanders claims that what he terms relationality is an inevitable and necessary condition of the therapeutic encounter. Unlike in manualized, normative psycho-technical approaches, in relational psychotherapy, therapists, as well as clients, take the risk of being changed by it. Pete presents anecdotes from psychotherapy literature and personal experience in support of the thesis that relational therapies are the evidenced, philosophical, ethical and moral rebuttal of mechanical psycho-technological therapies.

Tom Strong, in Chapter 14, considers Cognitive Behaviour Therapy (CBT) as a conversational, dialogic work-in-progress at the crossroads of many discourses. Referring to Mikhail Bakhtin's theory of dialogue, Tom's dialogic approach to CBT is described as involving a delicate negotiation of words and ways of talking, in contrast to manualized approaches where therapists hold clients and themselves to conversation through a CBT protocol. Instead, the kind of negotiated dialogue described invites reflections on clients' ineffective meanings, followed by collaborative efforts to overcome the 'linguistic poverty' of those meanings. CBT is thus recast in this chapter as Wittgenstein's conversational challenge of finding ways to go on together.

Helena Hargaden, in Chapter 15, argues that since the relational approach became more explicit at the beginning of this century it has had, broadly speaking, a beneficial influence on the psychotherapeutic professions. Helena proposes that the most important influence of the relational approach is that it has provided a principle of integration between different schools and modalities of psychological work. She considers how the term relational can also be understood as a symbol of the type of sensibility associated with the therapeutic task and explores the development of relational thinking within transactional analysis, describing its positive effects and identifying some potentially negative trends.

In Chapter 16, Andrew Samuels probes the shadow of the relational turn in psychoanalysis and psychotherapy, arguing that this turn in psychotherapy has led to moralism, conformism and hypocrisy on the part of many clinicians. Andrew explores how relationality cannot engage with the phenomenon of solitude in a satisfactory manner leading to a potential flight from the unconscious. Andrew also proposes that there is more than one therapy relationship to consider and that the key task is to hold their simultaneity in mind. He proposes a methodology by which this might be done. Furthermore, he argues that what is being discussed will be incomprehensible in terms of the various projects of state regulation of psychotherapy proposed over the years by the British Government.

In Chapter 17, Keith Tudor, one of the book's critical respondents of the chapters in Part II, comes from a person-centred perspective to explore the relational turn, interrogating its themes and pervasive nature.

Following this, in Chapter 18, Alistair Ross identifies common themes that form a relational postmodern meta-narrative, which he views as emerging from the thinking of eight authors who contributed to previous chapters in this book. Alistair comments that although these authors take on different perspectives, what they seem to agree on is that the relational is a vital subject and they identify the value of the 'other' within social and political contexts. The relational as intellectual discourse is discussed as having philosophical foundations expressed through overlapping narratives, where there is a desire for a distinctive identity for therapeutic modalities, whilst seeing the potential of the relational as an integrative symbol. Alistair argues, however, that there are areas where the relational does not sufficiently address issues of power or evil and that there are depths in us and our wider narratives that need to be confronted.

The book ends with an afterword from my co-editor Andrew Samuels in Chapter 19. Andrew reviews the human and personal aspects of practice and theory in the therapy field, touching on 'the personal equation' as somewhat neglected in the forging of people's professional positions. He also discusses aspects of the image of the Wounded Healer as these relate to the spectrum of thinking about therapy's relational turn. Wherever one situates oneself in the relational spectrum, Andrew highlights the problematic of 'the client' and issues of power, suggesting that the client's power in relation to the therapist, and the client's power in relation to themselves, both remain interesting topics to pursue.

As mentioned at the start of this chapter, relational therapy would appear to be of interest to counsellors, psychotherapists and psychoanalysts across all modalities (whereas other contemporary developments appear to generate more interest in specific modalities). You may currently think the emphasis on the relational is central, magical or misguided. For example, you might think the Lacanians are right in insisting that we should not directly interpret the transference relationship as this could be experienced as persecutory – like being told off by a parent. There again, you might think much of the privileging of relational schools is being brought about by therapists whose egos stop them taking the required place and instead need a rationalization for attempting to be forever more present! Wherever you are coming from, Andrew and I hope the book will help you rethink your practice and at the very least enable you, the reader, to understand more contemporary thinking regarding relational psychological therapies as well as, importantly, being able to consider their critiques.

References

Birtchnell, J. (1999). *Relating in psychotherapy: The application of a new theory*. Westport, CT: Praeger.

Beutler, L. E. and Harwood, T. M. (2002). What is and can be attributed to the therapeutic relationship? *Journal of Contemporary Psychotherapy, 32*: 25–33.

Greenberg, J. and Mitchell, S. (1983). *Object relations in psychoanalytic theory*. Cambridge, MA: Harvard University Press.

Hargaden, H. and Schwartz, J. (2007). Editorial. *European Journal of Psychotherapy & Counselling, 9*(1): 3–5. [Taylor & Francis Online]

Heidegger, M. (1962). *Being and time* (J. Macquarrie and E. Robinson, Trans.). Oxford: Blackwell.

James, W. (1890). *The principles of psychology* (Harvard edition, Vol. 2). New York: Holt.

James, W. (1912). *Essays in radical empiricism* (R. Barton Perry, Ed.). New York: Longmans, Green.

Loewenthal, D. (2007). *Case studies in relational research*. Basingstoke: Palgrave Macmillan.

Luborsky, L. and Auerbach, A. (1985). The therapeutic relationship in psychodynamic psychotherapy: The research evidence and its meaning for practice. In *Psychiatry update: The American Psychiatric Association Annual Review* (R. Hales and A. Frances, Eds.) Vol. 4, 550–561. Washington, DC: American Psychiatric Press.

Malan, D. (1999). *Individual psychotherapy and the science of psychodynamics* (2nd edition). Oxford: Butterworth-Heinemann.

Merleau-Ponty, M. (1956). What is phenomenology? *Cross Currents, 6*: 59–70.

Mitchell, S. (1988). *Relational concepts in psychoanalysis: An integration*. Cambridge, MA: Harvard University Press.

Mitchell, S. and Aron, L. (1999). *Relational psychoanalysis: The emergence of a tradition*. Hillsdale, NJ: The Analytic Press.

Polanyi, M. (1983). *The tacit dimension*. Gloucester, MA: Peter Smith.

Safran, J. Dd and Muran, J. C. (2000). *Negotiating the therapeutic alliance: A relational treatment guide*. New York: Guilford Press.

2
DEMOCRATIZING PSYCHOANALYSIS

Susie Orbach

The complex shape of wanted (and feared) forms of relating by an individual analysand emerges in the therapy relationship. In the reconfiguring of the meaning of the therapy relationship, the analyst is not an outsider, observing the impact of the analysand's various forms of longing and defences but is inevitably drawn into and is an active participant in the relational field. Therapeutic neutrality and therapeutic stance are therefore reconceptualized, as are other issues that could be considered contentious, such as the blank screen, self-disclosure, the analyst's use of the countertransference, interpretation, power in the therapy relationship, dependency and money.

Relational routes in (mainly) British psychoanalysis

From the 1930s to the 1970s, there was an extraordinary intellectual flowering within psychoanalysis. The Balints, object relations theory, Winnicott, Fairbairn, Guntrip, Bowlby and attachment theory, the work of R. D. Laing and his colleagues, the anti-psychiatry movement, all attempted to re-situate and re-cast what psychoanalysis had turned into. Then, members of the independent group such as Bollas and Rycroft, contemporary Freudians such as the Sandlers and Fonagy, the clinical and theoretical innovations of the Women's Therapy Centre, Nafsyat and other equally radical therapy initiatives, all these different tendencies focused on the actual experience of patients, their history and the ways in which intrapsychic development was an outcome of the internalizations of relationships they had experienced from the earliest moment of their entry into the world.

This emphasis on the actual has swept through nearly all psychoanalytic schools: Jungian, object relations, contemporary Freudian, Kohutian. It was always the basis, in the United States, of the work of the interpersonalists, the intersubjectivists and of latterly what has become known as the relational school.[1]

The emphasis on the actual has dovetailed with the work of infant researchers: Mahler, Bergman and Pine; Stern; Trevarthen; Beebe; and Steele and Steele, who have been demonstrating the very active, relationship-seeking requisites of the baby and the ways in which the character of parental responses structures the infant's relation to self. Beebe's work in particular, which scrutinizes mother–baby interactions frame by frame, shows the intricate play between mother and infant, the efforts the baby makes to engage the mother, the way the baby responds to the mother's initiatives and the emotional impact of failing attempts to engage with each other.

Routes to relational psychoanalysis from radical movements

Relational psychoanalytic practices reflect much of what Luise Eichenbaum and I were writing in the late 1970s and early 1980s about our work with women at the Women's Therapy Centre.[2] We were re-positioning both the mother and the psychotherapist not solely as the (failing) and fixed object of the analysand but also as subjects in the process of becoming (Eichenbaum & Orbach, 1982).

Stephen Mitchell (1988) published *Relational Concepts in Psychoanalysis* in 1988 and, although he recognized the analytic routes of his reconceptualization, particularly Fairbairn's work, he did not recognize developments that came from social movements such as feminism, the New Left and what is largely called radical therapy. These were movements engaging with psychoanalysis, group and individual psychotherapy, women's consciousness-raising groups, self-help groups for mental patients and so on, in order to contextualize the intrapsychic life of the individual as an outcome of relationship: relationship that was embedded in a set of classed, raced, religious, ethnic and gendered relations which was reflected in the particular nuances of psychological relations (Eichenbaum & Orbach, 1982, 2003; Orbach & Eichenbaum, 1995). Following Reich and Fanon, radical explorations of personality in the 1970s turned on an understanding of how we came to have the particular psychologies we inhabited. How was femininity fit for a patriarchal society? How might we describe the intrapsychic features that created women's experiences? How had racism become internalized by everyone in the West? What were the functions of 'othering'? How did class and class disavowal construct our various self-experience? How did women become heterosexual? And so on. These agendas became much excavated, at least in the therapist's head and in radical therapy-oriented study groups and seminars, engendering new theory and new ways of understanding and working clinically (Flax, 1978; Eichenbaum & Orbach, 1982; Samuels, 1989). Structures such as the Oedipus complex, penis envy and separation-individuation and so on were meanwhile challenged and re-thought to see what relevance they might have for radically oriented therapy. The confluence of these streams became relational psychoanalysis.

Democracy in the consulting room

Relational psychoanalysis has a democratic, co-created view of the therapeutic relationship. Instead of a sense of the patient as other, as the object of the therapeutic gaze, relational psychoanalysis always sees the person in therapy as an influencing and an influence-able subject. Similarly, the analyst is not a static figure on to whom the patient projects their transference but an active member of the therapeutic dyad who, as Lew Aron would argue, brings her or his subjectivity to the therapeutic relationship.

In relational approaches, the therapist's subjectivity is always present. If the analyst comes to feel uneasy when with a patient or thinking about a person they are working with, this feeling is scrutinized for what it might reveal about what is going on in the therapeutic dyad. The patient's behaviours and affects are not pre-described or interpretable according to a formula. What an analyst experienced during the course of a session – the countertransference material[3] – is never simply evaluated for what the patient 'did' or 'put into' the analyst. I mention this because, despite openness to one's analysands being a principle of all psychoanalysis and psychotherapy, in practice, within mainstream psychoanalysis in the UK there are rules about what to think about when an individual in therapy does an x or y that causes the analyst discomfort. Often the import of these 'rules' seems to be about deconstructing the individual's defence structure with the clinical aim of showing her or him the destructive nature of much of their internal world. This is a very different aim from that of relational psychoanalysis and I want to state quite clearly what I see as some differences between relational psychoanalysis and conventional psychoanalysis as regards therapeutic stance.

Example 1

I sit in on a seminar. I notice that the interpretation of an analysand's behaviour is carried on as though it were a sport. If a participant presents a case in which a patient brings flowers to the therapist, this solicits a set of attitudes from the assembled therapists about what the bringing of flowers means with the tinge that really the patient should not be doing so; she should know better, she is seductive. If the presenting therapist says these flowers were sent rather than presented, a series of interpretations about the invasiveness of the patient is then offered as though the patient were endeavouring to get under the therapist's radar screen which the patient would have known would have prevented the therapist from accepting the flowers in the first instance. Thus the patient is described as both sneaky and intrusive. The meaning of wanting to give is excavated to foster a particular result: that the patient does not know her/himself and must be shown the ways in which their initiative is an expression of the 'darker' side of themselves.[4]

The patient, when told these things, experiences shame as though she has transgressed. Interestingly, the therapist's discomfort is not explored but accepted as a simple consequence of the inappropriateness of the analysand's behaviour.

A hallmark of relational psychoanalysis is that there is no 'off the shelf' understanding of what is happening in the consulting room between patient and analyst. There is only a bespoke one – one that fits that particular analytic couple at that moment in that therapy. One could argue that, of course, this is what happens in any 'good' therapy. But experience at seminars where a flowers-type incident has emerged conveys a sense that 'good' therapy is infrequent, for this example has been offered many times in seminars and has invariably elicited the same type of interpretative response.

By contrast, the entry point to the relational analyst would be to register how the analyst herself feels about the flowers. There may be a complex of feelings in some cases or it might be quite straightforward in others. If the feelings were discordant, the analyst would inquire to herself about her own unease – to what extent the unease was personal to her: what kind of unease was it? Was it specific to being with this particular person? Was it a common feeling in this therapy or an unexpected and unusual one? On the other hand, if the analyst felt comfortable with the receipt of the flowers, she would also reflect on why she felt that way. If there was discomfort, the relational analyst would look to understand what was offered or attempted in the delivery of the flowers – why flowers, why now? Such questions, specific in space and time (why here? why now?), are posed from a neutral stance, a position of curiosity and interest: a something that might be comprehensible between the two parties but emphatically not an act with a given *a priori* meaning.

In the example cited, it was Rosh Hoshanna, the Jewish New Year, and the patient wished to send a gift to the analyst to arrive on the right day. The patient was not shamed by exploring why she sent the gift but was eager to talk about her desire to give and to have her giving received. The therapist then has to allow herself to receive and in the process she may have to explore her own conflicts or issues about receiving (Eichenbaum & Orbach, 1982, 1987).

Example 2

A colleague working with a child of Ethiopian refugees was very moved by the child's stories of missing animals. She felt a desire to take him to visit the zoo even though she knew this was inadequate to his loss. The child's home circumstances were dire and she felt sad for him. In supervision her desire to take the child to the zoo (which was something she kept to herself in the session) was interpreted as being invoked in her by the child's envy for what she had and could so easily give in her own middle-class parenting. Furthermore, the sadness she felt when thinking about this boy was, she was told, a response to what the child had put into her.[5]

The relational approach to the therapist's desire would start from an assumption of the child's desire to bring his two worlds together. What he may have evoked in the analyst might be understood as a sign of attachment in both therapist and child – that the losses experienced by the child were being brought to the therapy relationship.

Example 3

In various psychotherapy establishments, therapists walk around the hallways with their eyes addressed to the floor, lest they see or be seen by a patient. If one does see, or is seen inside or outside the building by a patient, this is not generally acknowledged. When I have asked about this I am told that it is for the patient to bring up the encounter. If I press further, I am told that it would be invasive, an imposition on the patient for the patient to be acknowledged. These responses strike me as peculiarly at odds with the often immaculate manners of these same colleagues in non-therapy settings. In trying to puzzle out why there should be this extraordinary difference in behaviour, I am led to believe that the patient is seen as an object rather than a subject, where the aim is to produce discomfort so that the normal niceties of daily life are removed and the defence structure is put under pressure.[6] In relational work, by contrast, there is little conflict about accidentally encountering the client as a subject outside the consulting room.

Finally, there is also a sense that for an analyst to feel close to his or her patients is simply not kosher therapy. (Of course we know that most practitioners do care very much for their analysands but the conceptualization around this is very much represented in forms one can only judge as confusingly bizarre.) The collaborative stance of relational psychoanalysis permits a relatively open exploration and experience of intimate feelings in the consulting room, rather than a frightened withdrawal or an authoritarian or distancing stance.

How we become human

The understandings of relational analysis start from the premise that the individual is born into a set of social and psychological circumstances. The human infant is a set of possibilities – not id based, not instinctually driven – but in order to become recognized as human, will need to attach. For those compelled by the notion of instinct theory, this was reframed in the 1940s by Fairbairn as a need for relationship and by Bowlby as a need for attachment. The nature of the relationships the child is exposed to, experiences and, of course, seeks to shape by her actions, is the template for that individual's self experience and relations to others. Relational psychoanalysis does not look to understand the structures in a reductionist way or by use of sociological tools. Its agenda is to understand how both the satisfactory and the problematic aspects of those profoundly influential relationships create the internal structuring of the individual. The relationship(s) also form(s) the sense of how the individual approaches the world: the ways she feels able to act upon it and in it, the aspects she fears, how she conceptualizes and experiences her relations to self and other. In addition, relational theory proposes a conflict-relational model. It does not propose that becoming is conflict free. It conceptualizes the struggle to be an individual as an inevitable dialectic conflict between the wish to connect and to experience one's distinctiveness while understanding that one can only connect with another if one is distinct and one's distinctiveness has been recognized.

Living as enactment

Being is constituted out of the enactment and living of both conscious behaviour and behaviour of which we are unaware. Transference or, to put it another way, the emotional imagos of early relationship incline us to see relationships in the present as resonating at a feeling level with structural aspects of those original relationships. Our present stance in relationship involves a foisting onto the relationship a template about historic relationship (be it authoritarian, benign, push–pull, withholding, merged or more commonly a combination of different elements). Our present encodes ways of being and experiencing which are less open than we might desire or think. We may see what is not there and miss what is. It is not so much that subjectivity is determined, but that longings and desires – those that we can be aware of and those longings and desires we interact with – are necessarily infused by the understandings and the experiences we have imbibed in the course of development. These understandings may be out of conscious knowledge and may operate in a conflictual manner with our longings. Being and becoming are processes. There is, from the perspective of relational psychoanalysis, no other way to understand and be. And it is a version of those internalized relationship as felt, understood and enacted by the individual that will precipitate and form a significant part of the experience of the therapy relationship.

Relational psychoanalysis recognizes that the individual is searching for relationship. An individual's defence structure may embody many impediments to relationship and those impediments will be brought to and lived out in the analysand's life as well as within the therapy relationship. Inevitably, relational psychoanalysis says, the desire for, fear of and complex shape of the wanted forms of relating will pull the analyst in. The analyst is not outside the field, observing and interpreting the impact of the patient's various forms of relating and thus sitting and interpreting. Of course, she is doing some of that (although I myself am very unhappy with the notion of interpreting).[7]

The analyst is inevitably drawn into and is an active participant in the relational field. Relational psychoanalysis does not see the analysand as doing things to the analyst, as putting things into the analyst, does not see challenging behaviour as acting out or as an attempt to draw the analyst in as though that were some kind of misdemeanour. Rather, we anticipate that the analyst will be drawn in to the relational field, for that is in the nature of relationship. We affect one another. We cannot not. We are not doing psychic surgery, dissecting and then shaking off the countertransference and describing it to the patient in some theoretically neutral or (accusatory) way. We do not believe that there is such a thing as therapeutic neutrality. There is engagement and this can be understood and related to in many different ways. But one form of engagement we reject is that which interprets the longing or desire of the patient as some kind of unacceptable demand on the therapist.

Therapeutic neutrality and the relational analyst

The therapist's stance is one in which we are co-participants in the therapeutic endeavour. Our job is to make ourselves available to the analysand: to absorb what is being said, the ways it is being said and what is not being said. Our minds make pictures out of the dilemmas we hear described and we ascribe various understandings to what we hear. But when I say available, I mean also that we are receptive to being affected and moved. What we hear and see in the consulting room reverberates in us. And, because this is an analytic setting, what we do with what we experience becomes part of the analytic field of study. We study ourselves and our analysands in the process of self-reflection.

Our emotional and intellectual availability is in the first instance something we 'talk privately with ourselves about' (Casement, 1985). We create a kind of split in our experience in which we are both present and observing and analysing the nature of our presence. This is, of course, a parallel process to what the analysand comes to do as well. We endeavour to have the same kind of curiosity towards our own responses that we hope that our analysand can have towards their own. When we encounter attitudes or emotions or are invited to participate in interactions we find difficult, even repellent, we hope not to send the repellent feeling back in a retaliatory way, or in a way that is personally idiosyncratic. The analytic space and the therapist's theoretical understandings provide the therapist with tools that allow her or him to act more thoughtfully and judicially than she or he might in ordinary social intercourse.

In making our interventions, we scrutinize what we believe is being conveyed to us in the feeling that we are experiencing (the countertransference). We examine how our countertransference may be an aspect of our personal defence structure. We hope to assess what might be useful in helping us to connect with the difficulties the individual we are seeing is experiencing. Let us say a patient starts to masturbate when she is in the room, we hope not to just stay stop that, we hope to be able to bear the discomfort of it sufficiently to be able to think about it beyond being alarmed. We slow time enough to notice and then formulate what is important to us in order to be able to interpret the quality of what we feel impelled to say or not say in a manner we hope is digestible and potentially transformative.

In working out the quality of what we feel, relational psychoanalysis goes beyond an understanding of the countertransference as exclusively a diagnostic tool. We take as given that what is expressed is a communication and that, because of how we understand ourselves when we are with this particular individual, we have a personal response that is an expression of our own subjectivity.

Harvey

For the past few weeks, Harvey, a 56-year-old man well employed in the arts, has been coming in talking like a cross between the National Front and the

Daily Mail. Furious, he rails about what has happened to his country, his England. The child of a quite cruel middle-class and prosperous father and a working-class turned middle-class inconsistent mum, he grew up in the suburbs around Edinburgh and was sent to a boarding school. When he got his A-levels, he came to London and became part of the generation who embraced alternative ideas. He welcomed the end of privilege and sexual liberation, and made his way through the cultural spaces that were opening up in London.

Harvey is both defiant and somewhat alarmed by the words that currently come out of his mouth. There is a comfort in his defiance having something to do with positioning himself with what he imagines is a growing majority position. He is now no longer a beleaguered but morally righteous left wing individual, fighting a minority battle against everyone. He is joined with his fellow countrymen who find themselves suddenly aware of being dispossessed from their England, an England that ceased to exist many years ago and indeed an England which he fought to disassemble himself, but an England nevertheless which he now fails to recognize.

While he loves the loosening of restrictions in everyday life, the greater sexual freedom, the liveliness of the restaurant, clothing and ethnic scenes, what he cannot come to terms with are the degraded work practices in his profession where product has replaced risk, demographics has replaced originality and where cost cutting and the destruction of the unions has broken the working practices of the unit he is in. People now work very long hours, feel they have less stake in the product and have little respect for the executives who are only concerned with churning out product.

Harvey does not recognize an England rife with poverty and with drugs, with a great divide between rich and poor. He does not recognize an England in which the dominant voice is not white and middle class, he does not recognise an England which has become a playground for the rich from other countries and he does not recognize an England which has become a place in which the tortured or disenfranchised from elsewhere seek to settle. His sentiments, which in more benevolent times would be expressed as a wish to change things towards what might be broadly thought of as an equality agenda, are turned now towards a populist sloganeering of the *Daily Mail* variety.

We are highly trained to reflect, to think, to listen and to understand inside the responses of my patient Harvey that yes, for a post-war baby, that stultifying Britain which they tore down with such a sense of personal and collective agency in the 1960s and 1970s has been transformed into a new culture greatly at odds with its post-war sensibilities and with the progressive sensibilities through a combination of Thatcherism, globalism, the demise of politics and the omnipresent offerings of consumerism and celebrity. By neither responding with a counter-polemic, nor simply concurring with our patients, we allow different sorts of thoughts to form. Harvey can explore his ideas but, in hearing himself doing so without external censure or concurrence, he enters into a study of his own subjectivity. He brings a third ear to himself and to his own polemical rant. He begins to be curious about his conclusions: why do the explanations that he is now offering himself have salience? He is not shamed by his responses. They cause him discomfort and in the therapy he can engage that discomfort. He does not have either to become defensive or to hide his new attitudes.

We talk about loss. The loss of something known, an England he recognized, an England he felt entitled to bash up and transform, an England in which he saw himself having a stake. By acknowledging loss, a space is opened for Harvey's displacement and his anger to find less targeted responses. He reflects on loss and the ways in which, in times of change, new circumstances can become sites of fear for him. The conversation between us moves on. We do not resolve his feelings in one session. We do not, as it were, reform him and the venality of his responses. Therapy is not a place for the exchange of one political coat for another. It is a place for deconstructing. It is a place for mixing up the easy, the commonplace, for adding texture, for being confused without fright, for exploring what we are feeling and what it means to think with complexity, with compassion towards self and with an understanding of defence structures that limit our capacity to actually address new situations rather than impose old emotional and psychic tableaux on them. But, of course, Harvey's story affects me deeply. I too have lived these times. I too experience confusion, delight, dismay about the changes the UK has gone through. As he talks, I am forced, if I wish to stay open to what he is struggling with, to explore my own prejudices, my own values, not just as a progressive, but also the ways in which a kind of nationalistic, 'Murdochized' heavy media has structured my responses to the social, economic and political, to the extraordinary social changes that have occurred since 1984. I have to find a way to engage with Harvey that denies neither my subjectivity nor his. I employ a version of analytic neutrality which is not about being a blank screen, but is marked by attentiveness and interest towards my responses to Harvey's utterances and feelings.

As it happens, this story has a happy ending. In time, Harvey was able to see how he squeezed his upset about not understanding Britain into a piece of rhetoric which gave him a temporary sense of belonging – a sense of belonging which had eluded him through his childhood, had briefly emerged in his twenties and thirties when he was part of the counter-cultural movement, but which had disappeared again in the past period where the values he held seemed once again at odds with the culture. Therapy helped him to understand the ways in which the longing to be 'part of' joined with the devilish psychological dynamic of adherence to historical emotional tableaux of identifying with the very set of emotional resonances which cause pain. Our past relationships, the ways in which we have internalized them and the positions which we have held in them form our individual relationship to the world.

Psychotherapy tells unequivocally that we cannot relinquish the power and dominance of past relationships in our psychic functioning until we accept them as they were. We increase our powerlessness to the extent that we are always railing against those who so affected us and are unable to come to terms with our relative powerlessness about what was. In the recognition of that powerlessness and the inner psychic battles we fought to deny that powerlessness, we endeavour to move towards acceptance and the ways in which we can have the past, be in the past, so that our present expresses our actual and potential power, rather than the victimized or angry stance of thwarted power.

The therapist's subjectivity

So what is Harvey's impact on the therapist's subjectivity and our impact on Harvey? Of course it is individual and particular to each therapeutic couple. We will all have different responses. We will have heard different parts of the story. We will not even have heard the same story for we will have stalled it, helped him enlarge it, or taken it in different directions. Our own responses to Harvey will encode our subjectivity, our interests and our views about what is psychologically and, explicitly in this instance, politically salient. The very endeavour of therapy will necessarily encode politics. What the politics are, where they lead the patient and the therapist, depend upon the political sensibilities of both parties but especially those of the therapist who can and does, both wittingly and unwittingly, focus the attention of the therapy in particular directions. We can imagine another therapist, with different politics and a different psychological theory, not looking at loss and conflicts over belonging, but focusing in another direction altogether: on what has been taken away, issues of rage about deprivation and a fear of spoiling the new.

In whatever ways we are drawn in, we will be responding to Harvey's longings for contact and understanding from our own response to the transferential field as well as with how Harvey's distress affects us. His isolation and agonies will necessarily stimulate our own. We might even anticipate that in the therapy relationship we might enact, without wishing to, the prohibiting, critical parental imago that Harvey has internalized and which he unconsciously anticipates we will take up, despite his wish to find a different, more embracing understanding. We can predict, too, that at one point or another, the therapist will enact some aspect of Harvey's world of inner relationships to confirm for him that he cannot be understood, he cannot belong. The therapist will in effect become disappointing. This for the relational analyst will not be judged as a failure of our personality or therapeutic fitness but as what is almost bound to occur at some point in the therapy relationship as a way of literalizing and enacting between the two of us what in Harvey's psychic structure holds him in positions that he finds disabling. The literalizing of the struggle between us does not emerge out of conscious intent. It happens because the therapy relationship is co-created between analyst and analysand. Our desires mutually, if asymmetrically, influence one another and the recognition of the bi-directionality of the therapeutic relationship is a crucial aspect of relational analysis. Working on what has been literalized is another therapeutic moment.

Therapeutic neutrality

This takes me back to the problematic of neutrality. Therapeutic neutrality has been idealized and fetishized. The idealization is a function of the distance the therapist wishes to take from the patient. It is an expression of the desire not to be influenced or be affected because it was thought that the analyst was a kind of psychic detective or surgeon. But I think we can accept today that relationship is influence and affect or it is not relationship. If we remain unaffected, we are quasi-'autistic' or constrained by our own splitting capacities. To be influenced and affected is not to give up our own agency or our own skills as analysts. It is to push to the centre stage of contemporary understandings of the analytic endeavour that what the patient is struggling with is 'being' and that the process of being involves the engagement of an other, a thinking, feeling other with whom to explore the difficulties of being. This endeavour will create space, impingements, psychic rearrangements. In democratizing the relationship, the analytic capacity to observe ourselves while being is deemed to belong to both of us. We can both become partially adequate and skilled at doing this and recognize the limitations we are bound to feel. To go back to the masturbating example, neutrality here means developing curiosity, a kind of 360-degree curiosity towards our own responses and those of the person who is causing us alarm or discomfort by their behaviour.

Self-disclosure

This brings me briefly to self-disclosure, one of the shibboleths by which relationality is criticized. If the analyst is a co-participant and co-creator of the therapeutic relationship, she or he is also disclosing who they are. The relational analyst does not walk into the room and don a psychological uniform. She goes in with her skills and theory, her emotional and intellectual availability, ready to engage. The forms of engagement that transpire will disclose much about who she is with this particular person. The way she is is disclosure. She is not concealing nor is she revealing intentionally. Her way of being is an expression of self and inevitably self-disclosing. This is not the self-disclosure of telling an analysand what I did in x situation. My experience of having been in x situation will be embodied in my engagement with her or him. I have a history and human agency which is as transformative (and struggles as much with repetitions) as that which I hope the analytic process can give her or him. Self-disclosure is not about saying or not saying. It is about an authenticity of being.

Dependency and recognition

I want now to discuss what for me is one of the most critical issues of relational psychoanalysis. Dependency and recognition, of course, have enormous implications for our institutional, class and gender arrangements. Relational psychoanalysis recognizes that, within the therapy relationship, issues of dependency and recognition will be central. Dependency is the term that Luise Eichenbaum and I have used. Recognition is that of Jessica Benjamin. Fairbairn's was mature dependency. In essence we are all talking about the developmental need for attachment, to be seen and to be accepted, and the defences that develop when dependency needs are not met and their not being met goes unacknowledged. Then the individual internalizes a sense that their desires, their longings, their dependency, their need for nurture and care and to be seen, in short, that which arises from inside of them, their very self, is wrong. They may express this 'wrongness' in many different ways from shame to insistence but behind the various defences will be a sense of unentitlement.

Within the therapy, this sense of unentitlement, of not daring to want or wanting so much (which is itself a variant of not being comfortable with wanting because there is no expectation that wanting leads to receiving) comes directly into the therapy relationship. It will form the explicit and the latent content of the therapy and it will shape the therapeutic relationship. Then too the therapist's own stance towards, and defences against, their personal dependency issues will challenge them in many ways. Within psychoanalysis, dependency has been a kind of dirty word, with women especially being described as overly dependent, clingy and needing to separate. Gender-conscious therapy brought to the fore the ways in which therapists' and patients' unconsciously shared fears of dependency needs meant that dependency needs within the therapy were collusively warded off by both parties. We suggested that looking at dependency – and not defending against it – is crucial. By looking we meant being able to invite and commit ourselves to grappling with dependency issues between the patient and therapist, including, of course, all the defences which range from being free of need for the therapist to feeling desperately and unreachably needy. These include defences which we ourselves embody. Just as in the analysand, these defences could be stirred up in us by the analysand (Eichenbaum & Orbach, 1982).

Autonomy can emerge only out of connection, what Luise Eichenbaum and I have termed 'separated attachments'. A sense of personal agency is intersubjectively located and arises out of dependency needs being addressed. Connection occurs through the capacity to see the other as an other as well as related to self and to experience oneself as both attached and separate simultaneously (Eichenbaum & Orbach, 1983, 1987).[8]

The democratization of fee structures

Money has always been problematic in the history of psychoanalysis. And, when it was distorted by the influence of private medicine in the United States, a theory was put in place stating that unless the patient paid, the therapy was not worth anything. From a European perspective, where indirect payment is as common as direct payment (as indeed it was in the States for a period of time when psychoanalysis was taken to a larger population base through free clinics, the

Veterans Administration and outpatient psychotherapy services), such a view appears anachronistic.

It has been disturbing to encounter an ideological position about the importance of direct payment, freighted down with interpretation about a patient's behaviour around money, when actually the majority of UK patients are seen without fee. The insistence – you must pay as an expression of valuing yourself and the therapy – of some clinics and clinicians becomes both tokenistic and totemic. The existence of the fee is then hailed as the site for the working out of issues about need, entitlement, contempt and so on. While such a rationale might have had general relevance in a model where the analyst was perceived to be a blank screen and the only directly analyst-personal material was to do with money and holidays, this is simply not the case in relational psychoanalysis, where the analyst offers her or himself for engagement within the session and where their subjectivity is in view and being struggled with (internally and interpersonally) rather than all challenges by the patient being referred back to the analysand's individual pathology.

So, for those in relational psychoanalysis who have absorbed the culture of mainstream psychoanalysis, it is necessary to excavate one's theories about fees and to think them through afresh. A tenet of practice at the Women's Therapy Centre in its first five years (1976–81) was a firm commitment to as little direct payment as possible.[9] We found absolutely no difference in terms of individuals' commitment to therapy whether they were paying directly or not. Indeed, certain clinical issues became particularly focused precisely because the fee was absent and they could not be sloughed away inside the fee. These issues were often around the theme of emotional receiving, of struggling with issues of dependency and attachment. Without a direct fee payment as carapace, the therapeutic couple had to confront and live through what was transpiring, being given, being risked and being received. Interestingly, with several of my own fee-paying people, there have been attempts to 'use' the fee almost to reverse the dependency issues in such a way that I come to be dependent on the people paying me.

Of course, indeed, therapists are dependent on fees financially. We need to be paid and we need to find humane and democratic ways to structure our financial arrangements with the people we see. We need to provide fee structures that work for us but I believe that a rigid fee structure is too inflexible for many people. The fees that rest on that idea of the analysand taking exactly the same holiday dates as the therapist and being financially responsible for sessions which are unattended because of half term or a need to travel seem, in today's climate, therapeutically indefensible. I, for instance, have a practice which is a combination. Individuals come week in week out for one, two or more weekly sessions in which their times vary only very occasionally. But I also see people who travel or who work in the theatre and cannot commit to a weekly or twice-weekly time despite their interest in coming. How then to structure fees?

Colleagues and I have always assessed our fees on a nominal 40 weeks a year basis (in our own minds). This may mean that one is charging marginally more per session, but it allows for people to take their half terms or go on a trek which might be wonderful for them, without it threatening the income of the therapist who then interprets such activities as 'an attack on the therapy'. Of course, each individual therapist has to have clear what she or he will work with. The therapist needs to think through for her or himself what she actually thinks about individuals who want to take their holidays when it suits them rather than suits the schedule of the therapist. A therapist also has to think through whether cancellation for illness is billable, and if so what kind of advance notice they require. None of this is to say that there will not be a particular individual in one's practice who is unable to take the therapy seriously without paying. This will sometimes be the case, but what relational psychoanalysis has to take on is that an idea of convenience for the therapist (regular income) does not become a false god of therapy or simply doing what one's own analyst did.

As therapists we are emotionally inconvenienced by the things we come to feel in our sessions. We are also dependent on the people we see. We do not necessarily hold them better by insisting on payment for when they go on holiday. Indeed, I think we may lose them. When we insist, I fear we are subverting the therapy for our own agenda; an agenda which may have made some sense at some point but is not justifiable today.

Conclusion

This account of relational psychoanalysis is not meant to exclude several main features of therapy: the finding of words to tell of experience previously unformulated or unheard, making narratives which can create new understandings of one's past and one's present, and linking up affect which has become separated off from the emotional circumstances which produced it so that in relinking one may digest the difficult feelings and increase one's emotional vocabulary. This is the ordinary activity of therapy. How it is done will be theory laden and in the case of relational psychoanalysis it will reflect a sense that psychoanalysis does not seek a truth, but many truths – truths that contradict one another, that change in time and are always perspectival and partial. Among its great strength for today's purposes is that we study people in the process of change and reflect on those changes as they happen to us and to our patients in the therapeutic couple.

Notes

1 Of course similar developments within humanistic psychotherapy were also occurring.
2 At that time we did not have a term we were happy with for what we were doing. The closest were social object relations theory and feminist object relations.
3 Although Aron (2001) would call this the analyst's subjectivity rather than the countertransference.
4 It reminds one of the old analytic cliché: arrive too early and one risks being labelled over-anxious; arrive late and one is controlling.

5 A relational analyst would more likely view her desire as a sign of attachment and the child's ability to want and perhaps to be able to receive after traumatic separation and loss.
6 If such an encounter occurs for a relational analyst, one respects the privacy of the individual with a discreet nod or hello and the follow-up to this, if not taken up by the analysand, would be brought up by the therapist.
7 Historically interpretation meant the analyst interpreting unconscious material. That was her or his function. Today we do not only 'interpret' and my unease stems from the reification of analyst's utterances being claimed as interpretations instead of simple interventions, attempts at understanding, connecting, sense making and so on.
8 The political implications of separated attachments and dependency are important in light of the ideological arguments on what constitutes a social, political and economic world in the last 20 post-Thatcherite years. We could see Thatcherism (and I include Blairism as a variant of Thatcherism) as the preparation for Britain's relation to globalism with its emphasis on pseudo-connection, the marauding of the other and the exploitation of complex economic dependencies. When we think about the forms of institutional arrangements and institution-to-institution arrangements, rethinking dependency issues, not to avoid them but to recognize and rebalance them, is crucial.
9 Unfortunately, because of funding difficulties, this could be offered only to people who were on social security and very low personal incomes.

References

Aron, L. (2001). The patient's experience of the analyst's subjectivity. In *A meeting of minds*. Mahwah, NJ: The Analytic Press.

Casement, P. (1985). *On learning from the patient*. London: Routledge.

Eichenbaum, L. and Orbach, S. (1982). *Outside in, inside out*. Harmondsworth: Penguin (revised, 1984 as *Understanding Women*).

Eichenbaum, L. and Orbach, S. (1983). *What do women want?* London: Michael Joseph.

Eichenbaum, L. and Orbach, S. (1987). *Between Women*. Harmondsworth: Penguin.

Eichenbaum, L. and Orbach, S. (2003). Relational psychoanalysis and feminism: A crossing of historical paths. *Psychotherapy and Politics International, 1*: 17–26.

Flax, J. (1978). The conflict between nurturance and autonomy in the mother–daughter relationship and within feminism. *Feminist Studies, 4*: 171–9.

Mitchell, S. (1988). *Relational Concepts in Psychoanalysis*. Cambridge, MA: Harvard University Press.

Orbach, S. and Eichenbaum, L. (1995). From objects to subjects. *British Journal of Psychotherapy, 12*: 89–93.

Samuels, A. (1989). *The plural psyche: Personality, morality and the father*. London: Routledge.

3

BELOVED

Jane Haberlin

This clinical paper tracks episodes in a long, intensive therapy with a patient who felt haunted, both by her dead sister and by a part of herself which led a parallel life. It illustrates what relational therapy might look like in the consulting room through the lens of key themes such as bi-directional influence of patient and analyst, intersubjectivity and working with disassociation at relational depth.

Some patients, like friends and lovers, enter one's life quietly; we look back at notes or diaries to retrieve a sense of how they first arrived. Others we meet for the first time vividly and the memory of that first encounter burns bright. My first meeting with Yvonne took place in a consulting room within a shared clinic. The waiting-room snapshot I formed of her was that of a young black woman, professional, hair intricately braided, expensive suit, huge briefcase. She had smiled warmly, extended her hand for me to shake and introduced herself with confidence. She was impressive. I led her down the corridor into the room and gestured towards the chair I wanted her to sit in. As she settled in the chair, she removed her glasses, closed her eyes and began to weep copious, thick, silent tears. She made no attempt to reach for the tissues; instead, she let the tears and the snot run down her face creating a network of rivulets which hugged the contours of her chin and neck. I found myself growing increasingly uncomfortable as the minutes went by, not so much with the silence or the mess, but by a visceral response in my own body about the irritation this salty, slimy mess would cause me – especially as I watched the stream slowly disappear into her cleavage. And yet I wondered about her lack of social inhibition, that she could bear to make this mess in front of me when it was so at odds with her polished exterior. After some minutes, she lifted her coutured arm and wiped her face and her chin on the sleeve of her jacket. This I noticed also caused a bit of a commotion inside me. She composed herself, took a deep breath, put her glasses back on and then began to speak. She told me that she had grown up in a care home and coming for help to an institutional setting, such as this clinic, was enormously distressing. She had vowed never to render herself vulnerable enough to need care again. She told me she had been taken into foster care and then a children's home at the age of four because her mother had killed her younger sister. In the care of the children's home she had been manipulated by some of the staff to perform sexual acts with other children. They were photographed and filmed and later a paedophile ring was uncovered and the home had been closed. She was then moved as a young teenager back into foster care, which she enjoyed and which she believes saved her life. She remains in close contact with her foster family.

I commented upon how she had just told me some shocking, painful events in her life in a most 'efficient' manner, almost as if I was being briefed. She smiled and went on to tell me that she was a management consultant and that it was a hazard of the job to deliver information in precise, clipped sentences: 'You give broad brush strokes first and then the finer detail later.' She worked for a prestigious consultancy with a reputation for headhunting excellent graduates. It became clear that throughout her turbulent childhood she had retreated into the sanctuary of her mind and had excelled at school. I made a note to myself that she was able to 'split off' from her body, sufficiently that she could let the tears flow without being affected by the impact they had on her skin, and that there was a marked disjuncture between the self-state that was flooded with feeling, frozen and unable to attend to her tears, and the self-state that could report the narrative of her distress with no affect at all. My countertransference chimed perfectly with this split as I felt repelled by the snotty messiness of her distress but the actual horror of her story I allowed in without upset.

Yvonne told me that she had become increasingly depressed since starting work. The most recent crisis, which prompted her to seek help, involved a 360° appraisal at work which had distressed and bewildered her greatly. She did not recognize the way she was being experienced by others at work and had been told that she had poor working relationships with her colleagues. The feedback at her appraisal was that she was contemptuous of co-workers, that she failed to listen to their viewpoint or to write up conversations and agreed actions accurately. She was deemed to be argumentative and dismissive. However, she was also described as a brilliant, skilled thinker, and a dynamic consultant who was highly valued by clients. When I asked her for her understanding of this feedback she said that she felt it was because her standards were exacting and she spoke the truth plainly. I was interested that she didn't mention any racial dynamic and acknowledged at this point our racial difference and asked how she felt about working with a white therapist. She dealt with this question in a perfunctory, supercilious manner:

P: Anything approaching love or nurturing which has been given to me in my life has come from white women; this doesn't mean I idealize them nor that I am filled with self-loathing for being black. Do I think you know how it feels to be in my skin? I doubt it. However, I also hope you have no idea how it feels to live knowing that your Mum killed your sister. I do hope you're not going to be politically correct with me; I've had my fill of social workers and their jargon. If I think you're being racially insensitive I will let you know, OK?

A: Is that an example of plain speaking?
P: I guess it is typical of my style of delivery, yes.

The tone and manner of her voice left me feeling slapped and I was in no doubt as to what her colleagues might have to contend with. Indeed the first two years of her therapy essentially involved trying to make sense of how mistrustful she was of others and of how difficult she found it to make relationships. She had had sexual relationships with both men and women but they were short lived. She felt she 'could not do intimacy', that she disappointed people; she was often accused of being hurtful, of leading people on, of not delivering. She felt unsure of her sexuality; she would often find herself in a sexual situation and then 'lose' any arousal. She allowed herself to be chosen rather than do the choosing and subsequently was unclear about what or who she desired. She would get into frequent fights with people usually because someone confronted her about being badly treated. What she could not appreciate was that behind their protest was a longing to be closer or more important to her; instead, she would escalate this conflict, unable to meet that person in their experience. She had limited capacity for reflection and was uninterested in seeing things from another's viewpoint.[1]

It would appear at times as though there was very little I could say that interested her; she refuted any observations or parallels I drew between her history, her life outside the room and the way she and I experienced each other. Any attempts to draw attention to the difficulties we had in relating were rebutted. She was consistently resistant to any transference interpretation and found it hard to give our relationship any status, snorting if I used any construction of words that hinted at something mutual developing between us. She was frequently late for appointments, always for some reason outside her control. If she was delayed at work she would never call with a warning or an apology. She would pay invoices extremely late or insist that she had already paid them. We would have bank statement and cheque-stub inspections in the session when she would eventually concede that she had 'thought' that she had paid – 'are you sure I didn't give you a cheque last session?', 'I remember specifically handing you a cheque'. The realization that this memory was unreliable seemed to cause her no concern. She would not miss a beat and would say: 'Oh well, sorry about that, let me write you a cheque now.' My invitations to look at what this might reveal to us about her inner world were met with mocking, scornful put-downs which positioned me as, variously, anal, grasping or prissy. I persisted in trying to draw her into some dyadic exploration of how interesting it was, and how useful, that the confusion around my bill, my needs, afforded us an opportunity to look at how relationships are co-constructed. I worked hard to convey that I did not think my experience was the truth or a superior version but instead wanted her to notice how she lacked curiosity about another's perspective. This perspective would be different from her own and thus potentially useful in helping her understand something of how she is in relationships. While I knew that this was her point of entry into relationships, that she both longed for closeness and yet feared connection with another, this rebuttal left me often exasperated, unsure if she really wanted psychotherapy at all. On occasion she would carry these feelings of failing; she wanted to do it right, to be an 'A' student, so that when I fed back this experience of us struggling to collaborate she would feel 'got at' and enormously ashamed. Her feeling ashamed would be accompanied by the kind of crying that I described in our initial meeting. I wondered how to draw out from the shadows the child who had been so abused and decided to make a tentative approach through talking about the manner in which she cried.

A: Yvonne, when you cry it's as if you think you must keep very still and not draw attention to your distress, not a sound, not a movement. It makes me think that you must believe yourself totally alone. I wonder how it would be if you could open your eyes and look at me. What would you see?

P: I'm too frightened to look. I think you're sneering. I think you're enjoying watching me be so humiliated . . . it's crazy, I'm sorry. I know you're not and yet I can't help thinking it.

A: I think when you feel ashamed about anything it provokes a memory of a time when you felt overwhelmed with feelings. A time when you were exploited, abused and horribly betrayed. I think that little girl finds it impossible to believe that there could be such an experience as compassion. If you opened your eyes you might begin to imagine the possibility of not being on your own, the possibility of someone bearing witness to your suffering rather than showing callous indifference to your distress.

And so we found a way to begin to speak of the legacy of the abuse she had endured and the detail of her time in the children's home.[2]

At times she felt it unbearable as memories came flooding back of humiliation and profound, aching loneliness. She remembered how sexualized she had become; how the children would often act out sexually when alone. She remembered how much comfort she took from masturbation and remembered masturbating openly at school, rubbing herself against the climbing frame during break time. She became furious and mortified that no one had intervened, that no one had seen this behaviour as a communication of profound distress, a communication that she was in trouble. She became angry about the care workers, social workers, cleaners, teachers, dinner ladies who had sat back 'not seeing' and her tears became hot and fierce. And then an incident occurred in which I enacted one of Davies and Frawley's (1994) eight transference/countertransference positions, that of the unseeing, uninvolved parent.

One weekend I turned on the national news to see coverage of a protest march involving the deportation of an illegal immigrant family who were being offered sanctuary in a church. The members of the church community had made a human shield and the police were reluctant to use force to cross it in order to deport the family. There at the front of the shield was Yvonne, she was interviewed by the camera crew and seemed to speak on behalf of the family; she sounded entitled, empassioned, involved and, most significantly for our work together, deeply distressed. My shock was that she had not mentioned this connection to the family or the church in our sessions or that this issue was building to such a crisis point. The Monday session arrived and I waited to hear of these events, but she did not mention the family, the protest or the TV interview and nor did I. My rationale at the time was that it was outside the analytic frame, that I should wait and see when and how she would bring it up. I think I went a little mad myself. I even found myself thinking: 'Maybe it wasn't her . . . maybe I was mistaken.' I knew something and yet I didn't acknowledge that I knew. Like the playground supervisors and the teachers and the care home staff, I did not see that she was in trouble.

Shortly after this time another event brought about a huge shift in the therapy. I was in the early weeks of pregnancy and began to have a bleed late on a Friday night. On arrival at the hospital, accompanied by my husband – dressed in pyjamas, coat and trainers – I encountered my patient sitting in the waiting room. We said hello to each other and then I was whisked away. I was deeply embarrassed to be seen in such a vulnerable state – as much by the inelegance of my appearance. Thankfully, the bleeding quickly stopped and because of the sedentary nature of our profession I was able to see her for our Monday session. I had been giving much thought to how to deal with her enquiry about what was wrong with me, of whether to acknowledge my pregnancy so early with her and what implications it would have. My patient arrived with her foot heavily strapped and with a cane and she began to tell me about the fall she had had while hill-walking on the previous Friday. She then segued into a story about a conversation she had been having with the friend she had been walking with and she went into a 10-minute vignette. I was aware that time was moving on and eventually said:

A: I don't feel comfortable continuing with the session without acknowledging that we saw each other on Friday night in A&E.

She stared at me with a look of complete bemusement.

P: No we didn't . . . What do you mean?

I repeated that I had seen her in the A&E department, named the hospital, and said that we said hello. She looked puzzled, her brow furrowed, and then her face relaxed again and she seemed to disengage from the matter.

P: Well, you may have seen me, but I didn't see you.

And that seemed to be the end of the matter for her. She began to speak of something different, eager to move on, but I drew her back by asking her to think about what it felt like to have this experience. I observed that she seemed eager to dismiss it and wondered why she did not think it a significant happening for the two of us. She became agitated at my insistence to stay with this absence of memory so I ventured: 'It seems as if it might be very frightening to think about this "not seeing" me or a "seeing me" but a forgetting of that meeting.' She became very still in the session and an atmosphere descended such that I felt myself holding my breath; as our time lapsed, I gently drew her back into the room, into the present. The session drew to a close with my mind full of many things; I was concerned about Yvonne and the fugue state she had entered and frightened about whether I was up to accompanying her through this next stage of her journey. I was also left doubting my own mind and sought my husband's confirmation that we had indeed seen someone in A&E to whom I had said hello. It was the look he gave me, as if the question were truly bizarre, that helped me to realize that the atmosphere that had descended in the room with Yvonne was as if a haunting were occurring; that I was talking about my seeing of her as if questioning whether I had seen a ghost (can I trust the workings of my own mind?) and that for Yvonne these sightings by others of her disassociated self-state must perturb her dreadfully and be why part of her defensive structure resists relating to others as subjects in their own right. Finally, I was struck by the complete absence of any curiosity on Yvonne's part as to why I should have been in the hospital.

At the beginning of the next session Yvonne reported that she had passed a very disturbed night and she drew her feet up onto the chair. She immediately looked much younger and the presentation of a businesswoman dissolved.

A: You seemed to go very far away yesterday; can you tell me what happened?

P: I was told by a key worker at my children's home that I was there when she died. But I don't remember . . .

A: Your sister. How did she die?

P: I have no idea. No one has ever told me. Have you read *Beloved*, you know, the Toni Morrison book? I read that book at university and it started me thinking about the fact that my mother killed my sister. I think that I have become muddled between that story and my sister's story . . . I can imagine my Mum smashing her head into a wall, and yet it's not an actual memory because my Mum looks old and drugged in the image, as she was the last time I saw her.

A: When did you see her?

P: I visited her at her home a few years ago. She had no idea who I was. She was completely out of it. Her eyes were dead. I never went back, what would be the point?

A: So you have an image in your head of a very sick, drugged woman, who you are told is your mother, and then in the last years there's been the horrific imagery conjured up in a book: *Beloved*.

She sat still, deep in thought, a quality of reverie about her appearance rather than fugue.

P: What happened in the hospital with you is always happening. People are always telling me that I said or did something I have no memory of. I think I have tunnel vision. You know like horses wear blinkers so that they can't see to the side or behind them. I think I must do that. I think I have the capacity to block things out. I have absolutely no memory of meeting you . . . and I feel really scared about what happens to me.

She then became still again and withdrew inside herself. This time I spoke to her after a couple of minutes.

A: Can you say what you see?
P: I can see my mother's naked back. I am lying next to her in bed. She is turned away from me . . . I must keep very still and not make a sound . . . I must be very good . . . That's it, that's all I remember.

In the course of the next few weeks our sessions were markedly different. We had always met for three sessions a week but now the sessions became linked to one another in Yvonne's mind, rather than existing as encapsulated discrete events as they had in the past, and we began to work at relational depth. She became curious about her self-with-other interactions (see Davies & Frawley, 1994). She reported with delight the newness of asking 'Why do you say that?' to a colleague or friend when they would make a comment about her which she did not understand. She began to want to own a narrative about herself and to map where there were big gaps in her knowledge. She retrieved no further memories from her early years with her mother or the events around her sister's death, but she was able to put words to the feelings she had about being taken into care, and the memories of that time came back fast and vivid. She would talk about feeling 'real', remembering the faces of the other children she had been friends with. The multiple losses of her life filled her with grief and yet she described the grieving as good. She had a history, an unusual, painful history, but this allowed her to be in her skin, rather than suspended outside herself.

Four months had now passed since we met in the hospital and I had to tell Yvonne that I was pregnant and would be taking a break. She stared at my belly for a long time and then closed her eyes.

P: You were with a man at the hospital. I do remember.

She began to breathe heavily as if she were panicking.

A: What else do you remember?
P: I remember that I was with a friend and I felt exposed, busted. I was panicked that you would come over and speak to me, tell my friend that you were my therapist.

A: You were terrified that I would be inappropriate, that I wouldn't hold the boundary, so that in that moment I became someone who would abuse your trust. You felt threatened.

She stared at me 'thoughtfully' and then, signalling with a nod of her head that something made sense, said:

P: I guess so. I can't believe I can hive off memories like that . . . Actually I think I might be able to believe it . . . understanding that it doesn't happen randomly helps.

In the following sessions we continued to speak about this disassociated self-state as someone who knows no other way of coping with overwhelming feelings, someone whose presence we need to acknowledge and look after and respect, someone who may have different feelings from her about the news of my pregnancy. As we worked in this way the memory of seeing her on television returned to me. I decided to share this memory and to offer it up for the two of us to understand what had been going on in my mind that I did not acknowledge seeing her. I compared my noticing but not commenting to the behaviour of the teachers and dinner ladies at her primary school who saw but did not comment on her masturbation. Her eyes grew wide and then she drew herself into a ball, and began to shake and whimper and finally cry noisily.

P: Oh God, I did do that, didn't I? I had completely split off from that day. It was awful. I was like a gatecrasher at a funeral, acting like the chief mourner. How disgusting.

She told me between sobs that she had become involved at university with an evangelical Christian group, most of whose members were white. She felt pressurized by them to become their representative whenever there was a racial matter; she felt under irresistible pressure to do as this group wanted and did not know how to extricate herself. She had agreed to go along to the church on that day and had been prepared to be part of the human shield. However, she had been pushed to the front by her church group and then 'found herself' speaking on camera. She did not know the family, nor did she know much of the detail of their claim to stay in the country, and yet she 'played the part with gusto'. The attention had been very exciting and she made a link for herself to the excitement of the sexual activity she was coerced into at the children's home. Only now can she see how it must have appeared to the genuine intimates of the family and she is filled with shame and embarrassment. The associations came in waves and she recalled that she had been seen by colleagues at work on the news and she had denied the reality of the event when they raised the subject at work. 'I must make people sick,' she said, and with that she thrust her hands between her legs and began to rock. It was a few minutes before I realized that she was masturbating. When I could no longer deny this to myself I asked her to look at me. She opened her eyes and held my gaze. She implored:

P: Help me, Look at the monster I am.
A: Not a monster, I see someone trying to deal with their agony . . . Can you stop rocking, can we find another way so that I can stay with you in your pain . . . I don't want to feel a pressure to look away . . . Tell me how you feel. Let's see if we can help you have these feelings and not get rid of them in a way which further distresses you.

She stopped rocking and threw herself violently back in the chair. She began to cry noisily, stamping her feet, thrashing at the chair with her arms. I felt a longing to hold her, to scoop up her flailing limbs as one would an overwrought child. I spoke to her softly, reassuring her that I was still there, and, when the thrashing did not subside, I asked her to open her eyes and look at me, and encouraged her to breathe. I handed her the tissues, something I had previously felt too inhibited to do in case the gesture was experienced as a communication of 'pull yourself together'. Her sobs continued noisily and yet she began to fill tissue after tissue, blowing her nose and throwing them in the waste-paper basket. By the end of the session the waste-basket was half full. Yvonne looked to the basket and then to me, her face swollen and full of feeling. We held each other's gaze, both understanding that something profound had occurred: what Stern (1985) called a moment of meeting in which there is mutual understanding, mutual acceptance, mutual intentionality, mutual receiving of the other: 'I know you know I know how you feel'. Something more active had occurred than that which we traditionally refer to as containment, in which the therapist acts as a containing vessel and it is key to working at relational depth; there are two interacting subjectivities and there is an interpersonal, mutually mentalizing space between us – we had together co-created and co-participated in a containing experience.

All this time I had been carrying a baby and we had been speaking about my maternity leave, about her feelings towards the baby in the room, about what fantasies she had about the baby. As the time moved closer for us to manage a separation she became furiously upset. While knowing it was right for her to vent these feelings, an achievement for her even to name them, I was shocked by how affected I felt by them. In one session, as she raged against the injustice of being abandoned, she began to work herself into quite a state and I experienced her words as crashing in on me. As she told me she could not stand it, she could not manage a break, that she wanted to be inside my body, she wanted to 'boot that baby out', I began to feel nauseous and light-headed. Instinctively, I put my hand to my stomach and, sensing that I might faint, asked her to stop speaking. Her demeanour changed immediately and she collapsed back into the chair looking very concerned. She blurted:

P: Are you OK? I'm sorry. Have I gone too far?

I took a moment to compose myself and then slowly, in small, bite-size pieces, said:

A: It's hard, isn't it? I think you need to know whether I appreciate the harm I am doing to you by leaving you at this point . . . Do I know that it feels as if I am neglecting you, abandoning you? . . . How can I leave you to care for another baby when you are so dependent on me? . . . Can I bear to carry these feelings of knowing that this feels life-threatening – my leaving you at this point, especially to care for my baby? . . . But I ask you to imagine that I do indeed know all of this and that I also feel very upset to have to leave you . . . I wonder if you can allow that to go in – an experience that this is a mutual if not symmetrical experience of loss . . . And that this is not abandonment but a break . . . That you and I will come back together and that our task is to hold the other in mind, not to kill the other off because the feelings of missing are too painful.

The following week, with only five sessions to go to our break, she asked at the end of the session: 'Can I feel?' and her hand moved towards my big round belly. Without conscious thought, I moved back and blurted out: 'No, I'm not comfortable with that.' Yvonne looked hurt, embarrassed, and rushed from the room, giving the front door an uncharacteristically heavy slam. My response was authentic, instinctive and immediate, without thought or reference to theory – I did not want her to touch my belly. I went through much reflection about why I refused her and I had to stay with anxiety about how this would affect Yvonne. In the next session she told me she could not believe her ears when I said no. She felt embarrassed and humiliated but then she said she noticed something new happening; she found herself thinking about why I might have said no. She wondered whether she freaked me out too much by the fantasies of 'booting the baby out' and that I might feel she would 'hex' the baby; she wondered whether it just felt too intimate for me; she wondered whether I 'wasn't allowed' to let patients touch me; but also, crucially, she wondered whether I had my own feelings about my body and maybe my reaction was not restricted to her. Finally, she reflected upon how she had never had role modelled for her how to say 'No, I don't want you to touch me' and that this was a profound experience for her. I acknowledged how far she had come that she could think in this way; that there were two people's psychologies in the room and that she could be curious about the goings on in another's mind. Recognizing me as a subject in my own right, as a being separate and different, with my own mind and my own inner world, was a profound achievement and through it she discovered her own subjectivity.[3] She would refer back to this moment in the therapy from time to time as the point in her life when she 'knew' that she could keep herself safe and that she would never be abused again.

So I took my maternity leave for sixteen weeks. On my return, Yvonne acknowledged that it had been difficult but she had managed to miss me; she had kept me alive in her mind. The development she presented was that she had approached the borough social services team whose care she had been under with a view to reading her file. She had had preliminary meetings with a social worker but had been waiting for my return before arranging an actual date. After much thought and preparation she went with her foster mother and read through her files. She found out that she had been fostered previous to the birth of her sister. Her mother was deemed well enough at this point to take back Yvonne but both children were on the 'At Risk Register'. Her sister had died of asphyxia at 17 months old. Yvonne had been with her mother and sister at the time of death but the scene was not the bloodbath imagined in *Beloved*. Her mother had been imprisoned and later diagnosed with schizophrenia. The neglect and the lack of effective intervention was the focus of rage and horrible, horrible grief. She went through the futile conjecture as to why she had lived (was it because she was older, quieter, less demanding, more compliant?) and she was left with the guilt of having survived. Finally, she wanted to rescue her sister from the ignominy of being buried in an unmarked grave and she had a small ceremony with her foster family at which a headstone was laid. The headstone was not inscribed 'Beloved' as the one in the book had been. It bore her full name, the dates of her short life, and 'Sister'.

I have a piece of calligraphy Yvonne had commissioned as a gift and gave to me at the time the headstone was laid. It comes from Toni Morrison's (1987) *Beloved*:

> *She is a friend of my mind. She gather me, man. The pieces I am, she gather them and give them back to me in all the right order. It's good you know, when you got a woman who is a friend of your mind.*

Notes

1 Fonagy and Bateman posit that there is little point in attempting to attend to the traditional aim of psychoanalysis, the promotion of insight, until the capacity for reflective functioning and mentalization has been instated (see Bateman & Fonagy, 2004; Fonagy & Target, 1997).
2 Like much of the paper this is a very condensed overview of the work and involved a fluid moving in and out of the different transference–countertransference configurations defined by Davies and Frawley (1994).
3 I have in mind here Benjamin's (1988) model of intersubjectivity as a developmental progression through key moments of transformation towards an imperfectly acquired capacity for mutual recognition. One of the riches of relational psychoanalytic theory is the recognition of the mother/analyst's subjectivity and the importance of supplementing the object relations metaphors of the mother/analyst as a container, metaboliser, holder of the baby/patient's experience with the need for the conscious recognition of the mother/analyst as a separate subject.

References

Bateman, A. and Fonagy, P. (2004). *Psychotherapy for borderline personality disorder: Mentalisation-based treatment.* Oxford: Oxford University Press.

Benjamin, J. (1988). *The bonds of love*, New York: Pantheon.
Davies, J. M. and Frawley, M. G. (1994). *Treating the adult survivor of childhood sexual abuse*. New York: Basic Books.
Fonagy, P. and Target, M. (1997). Attachment and reflective function: Their role in self-organisation. *Development and Psychopathology*, 9: 679–700.
Morrison, T. (1987). *Beloved*. New York: Knopf.
Stern, D. (1985). *The interpersonal world of the infant*. New York: Basic Books.

4

THE PRIMAL SILENCE

Marsha Nodelman

The case of Stephen, a man in his mid-forties with cerebral palsy, underlines the significance of non-verbal analytic work as an essential vehicle for therapeutic action when the patient's dramatic birth history is enacted within the therapeutic relationship. The work with Stephen highlights the reciprocal processes of mutual influence and mutual regulation within the therapeutic dyad when altered and primitive states of consciousness cannot be formulated or communicated verbally.

There is much more continuity between intra-uterine life and earliest infancy than the impressive caesurae of the act of birth would have us believe (Freud, 1926, p. 138).

Beginning

A colleague (herself a grandmother) whose mother had recently died related an insight she had had during the process of mourning. Although not ordinarily psychosomatic, she observed that since her mother's death different parts of her body had become physically symptomatic, making her feel anxious about her own mortality. But it was when she suddenly broke down in sobs that she realized that her bodily feelings were attached to the most primitive feeling, 'I can't live without her.'

We marvelled together at what is the most obvious and ordinary of facts; we inhabit and come from within our mother's body and our earliest relationship begins and is first established there.

This chapter is about an aspect of clinical work over a period of four and a half years with a man in his mid-forties who had cerebral palsy, although the observable evidence of the cerebral palsy was slight. What began to emerge and later dominate the work was Stephen's apparent regression to states of consciousness from a pre/postnatal period in his life, as Stephen latterly reflected, 'To a space where boundaries are not limited by conscious thinking. A place of no me, no identity.'

Stephen was referred to me because two decades earlier I had trained as a primal psychotherapist before my training as a psychoanalytic psychotherapist.

My former training emphasized the importance of preverbal states of mind/body and the implicit unconscious.

According to Stephen, his previous work had helped him to understand and work through much of what had been traumatic in both his childhood and adolescence. He presented himself as being 'in good psychological shape'. But he was returning for psychotherapy because he had 'never experienced being in love'. He put this down to a 'certain disconnectedness and uneasiness in getting really close'. He sensed this might be due to a disruption arising from a combination of birth trauma and his feeling of being different from others as a child.

When I asked for details about his birth, he had none because his mother had always refused to talk about it. He gathered it had been traumatic for them both and knew the cerebral palsy was a result.

Theoretical considerations

Winnicott (1949a) wrote that, with certain patients and at certain points in an analysis, the 'acceptance of birth material was crucial in and amongst other material'. He observed that when the 'birth trauma is significant every detail of impingement and reaction is, as it were, etched on the patient's memory' (1949a, p. 183).

There is a small volume of psychoanalytic literature that addresses the enduring effects of anxiety in clients as the result of the pre/postnatal experience/trauma. It is curious that there exists a paucity of literature when working/relating with the (dis)-embodied and sensory dimensions of traumatic experience from the period in development when the body was the absorbing 'sensory window' and container for all experience.

Alessandra Piontelli, from her now classic, pioneering observational studies using ultrasound scans of foetal life, has found remarkable consistencies in behaviour before and after birth and speculates that some rudimentary form of self–other differentiation begins in the womb. She describes what 'appears' to be 'pathological defensive phenomena' as a response to a 'dim realization of "me-not-me" sensations' (1988, p. 240).

I have observed in the consulting room with adult clients that, when there have been 'early' experiences of trauma, there appears to have been a precocious awareness of separateness, as in Stephen's experience: 'I was alone when there was no ego.' Significant trauma prematurely interrupts the illusion of symbiosis (Krystal, 1997) with the mother, breaking the 'protective shield' vital to a baby's sense of safety. The disruption of the state of primary undifferentiation threatens what Winnicott has described as the 'continuity of being'.

If the illusion of primary undifferentiation cannot be optimally continued by the mother/caregiver, the development of the infant's attachment and sense of self will be impaired. When the infant's self-unity cannot be safely maintained, primitive disassociative coping mechanisms are the most adaptive solution for preserving self-continuity (Bromberg, 1979) and defending against the fear of annihilation (Hopper, 1991).

Overwhelming anxieties relating to survival may have enduring effects that persist throughout life and may fuel existential anxieties and those concerning mortality, sometimes developing into psychosomatic disturbances (McDougall, 1989). Pre-symbolic dread may be a background source of anxiety, 'particularly in states of free-floating anxiety and panic disorder, where there is no clear focus for the anxiety' (Mollon, 2002, p. 15).

Pre/postnatal experiences have a profound effect on the infant especially when re-enforced by postnatal experiences. When a birth is traumatic and/or there are further complications, the impact on parents, especially the mother, is great. Most parents suddenly find they are on an emotional rollercoaster, bewildered and often in a state of shocked helplessness. Depending on the nature and severity of the situation the related stresses are often overwhelming and evoke devastating feelings. Many parents find forming an emotional connection and bond with their baby difficult and might be left with a sense of it all seeming unreal.

Complications to do with the health of the baby prolong the state of crisis. An incubator baby is taken straight away from his/her mother before she has held her baby in her arms. The effect of the separation and the barrier of the incubator can create psychological barriers to connection where the parents not only fear to touch the infant but also fear being touched emotionally by the newborn (Raphael-Leff, 2005).

When there are uncertainties regarding the infant's future developmental potential along with immediate and/or long-term separation of the infant from the family, parents may become paralysed, which makes forming a bond with the baby that much more difficult. If the survival of an infant is not yet assured and parents have to confront 'issues of life and death', they can protect themselves from fears of loss of their baby by splitting off from their feelings. Parents need encouragement to express and process their feelings during these traumatizing and sometimes relentless periods of crisis. In these cases therapeutic intervention should be made available to promote infant and parental health through secure attachment (Raphael-Leff, 2005).

Stella Acquarone observed in her psychotherapeutic work with a mother and her nine-month-old child with cerebral palsy:

> In the case of mothers and infants, where trauma is known to have occurred, it is of prime importance to cultivate skin-to-skin and eye-to-eye contact, as well as verbal contact with the infant. This helps to identify and integrate boundaries, image of self and self-with-others (object relations). All of these are required, to build a balanced inner world promoting emotional growth.
>
> (Acquarone, 1995, p. 56)

Stephen was well-dressed, attractive and had a relaxed and approachable manner. He held a professorship in physics having gained eminence in his field of research. He described the effects of his cerebral palsy as 'cosmetic' as there was no intellectual or motor impairment. The 'cosmetic' signs, although slight, were a continuing source of shame and embarrassment, which he always referred to as 'my disability'. The most distressing one was an involuntary tremor that ran along one leg and increased with stress and was noticeable when Stephen lay down. Stephen's negative feelings about being different were painfully attached to the shakiness of the tremor and any other visible evidence of the cerebral palsy. However, none of his intimate partners had ever found this displeasing. Stephen was ashamed of his body and perceived it as undesirable and unlovable. Although much of our work centred on these issues, they are not the present focus nor are they elaborated on in this chapter.

Stephen confessed that he had entertained the hope that by reliving/re-experiencing his birth experience in psychotherapy, the traumatic effects of his cerebral palsy might be ameliorated, although he acknowledged that this was more of a wish than an expectation. He had had a few intimate relationships but was not currently in one nor had he ever been married or in a long-term relationship. He had a number of friends but it latterly emerged that he did not feel, nor had he ever felt, deeply attached to anyone. He was sexually active but felt little emotional or relational connection to the women he saw.

We met twice a week for the first two years and once a week for the next two and a half years. Stephen lived a considerable distance away, which latterly influenced the frequency of our meetings.

Family history

Stephen was an only child and described his early childhood as good until the age of four, when his father was diagnosed and successfully treated for cancer. His mother became preoccupied with his father's illness and her hospital visits meant having to spend time away from Stephen for the first time, although not overnight. He was anxious about his father's condition but, as it was not part of his family's culture to talk about emotions, he was left alone with his anxieties. Not long after, he started school and became aware of the differences between him and the other children, which left him feeling self-conscious among his peer group. For example, on the playing field he could not run as fast as or coordinate the ball as well as other boys could and described himself as 'the child other children would not choose to sit next to or choose for their team'. Realizing that he could do well academically, Stephen retreated into his intellect. He knew he could not compete on the football field but succeeded in doing so in his studies and excelled.

Stephen's feelings towards his father were ambivalent. His father taunted him for the way he walked when he was young and had at other times behaved inappropriately towards Stephen. He described his mother as having a gentle nature and his early memories with her were of 'warmth and closeness'. He could recall sitting on her lap when he was small and playing in close proximity to her while she got on with her daily chores; however, his activities were usually solitary. Stephen preferred not to speak about his parents. He described his adolescence as lonely. He had a few friends but did not participate in any social or recreational activities with his peers. He busied himself with hobbies related to the sciences and later pursued these interests at university, where the absence of a social life painfully continued. It was at university that Stephen first sought out psychoanalysis because of 'separation anxiety' and he appreciated how much it had benefited him. This encouraged him to participate, over the next two decades, in a variety of workshops and courses to do with self-awareness and personal development. These activities provided a social context, which enabled him to engage intimately with others and develop a circle of friendships. He continued with these until midway into our work by which time he felt he had achieved enough and wished to utilize his time in other ways.

The work

Although I found Stephen's story touching, he himself was not. His manner was always pleasant and he described himself as 'sensitive' in friendship; however, I experienced him as aloof and emotionally detached. He often talked about his interest in 'self-awareness and exploration' although in our situation he appeared to lack the curiosity about self and other that I would usually have associated with self-interest and discovery.

During the first two or more years, when Stephen arrived for sessions, the customary recognition that commonly accompanies ordinary familiarity appeared absent. He would leave sessions similarly, as if we had never met. Latterly, I came to understand that this custom was partially acquired during his previous two analyses, where the culture between the analyst and Stephen was classically oriented toward the neutrality of the analyst.

I wondered what effect the abstinence of the analyst in this approach had had on Stephen, especially in relation to his feelings of insularity and disconnectedness. For this reason I adopted a style that was more facially expressive than was customary for me and frequently used eye contact as a means to engage and offer connection.

During the first year the quality of our relationship did not appear to develop into an ongoing sense of familiarity or intimacy. Early on he referred to interpretation as 'a dead kind of knowing, so maybe it's to do with mother or father, the knowing makes no difference.' He implied that his lack of interest in engaging in analytic exploration had to do with having twice done so before. I agreed that interpretation might not be useful, and wondered how I might be useful. Staying in the present moment did not alter Stephen's disappointment at not being able to access the traumatic material he came to process. His frustration resonated with my feeling of not getting anywhere and I was taken by surprise when Stephen claimed that he felt completely 'relaxed and comfy' with me and had done so from the very beginning.

I asked myself if 'relaxed and comfy' was similar to the 'close and warm' implicit relationship he remembered having had with his mother. And I wondered if it was the physical proximity that our bodies shared within an intersubjective space that was most meaningful about our encounter.

Much of Stephen's material and our work centred on the relational and interpersonal aspects of his body; however, during our exchanges Stephen communicated that he felt his 'body was left out of our equation'. And he did not elaborate. Despite his body image noticeably improving in the course of our work, he felt we were not getting anywhere. The 'where' he said he wished to be was 'connectedness'. Stephen hoped that if he could access his 'birth experience' he would be 'in touch and connected with his body'. He often referred to his mind as being split off from his body and in such a way that he could 'never really feel at rest or whole'. He located his mind in his head and often reported that it was this which kept him in what he referred to as 'being in work mode'. It left him feeling drained and with the view that his pursuits were without meaning and empty. Stephen had presented his body as his disability and the dwelling place he was unable to occupy.

When I asked what he imagined re-experiencing his birth might be like, he replied, 'A high-energy experience in my body, cathartic.' However, there were no bodily sensations to focus on. Having sifted through his verbal material for an idiomatic expression that might contain a symbolized trace of birth experience, like 'feeling stuck', 'trapped' or 'banging my head against the wall', there was nothing to decode. Nor was dream material available. My impression at times was that Stephen was simply awaiting the arrival of the big bang to jolt him into existence.

Towards the end of our first year a pattern began to emerge. Stephen usually began sessions talking about whatever was current in his thoughts. When responded to, he appeared to lose interest and characteristically expressed this with loud yawning followed by an apologetic smile and/or shrug. This interruption always occurred in the mid-flow of what I was saying. Because he often expressed disappointment about not getting anywhere and did so without affect, I experienced this as the negative expression of that frustration. In response he said he was probably just 'unwinding', adding that he would like to give therapy a chance but if, after a while, he was 'still not getting anywhere' he could not see the value in continuing. Aware that his journey time far exceeded the sixty minutes spent in a session, I expected the balance to tip in favour of his leaving.

Sessions fell flat and felt lifeless and I did not feel able to facilitate Stephen's interest, which I began to experience as my disability. It had occurred to me that his disappointment might relate to his disappointment at never having experienced 'being in love' because his feelings in intimate relationships 'inevitably fell flat'. Stephen found this meaningful and worthy of consideration and I felt I had bought some time. He continued with sessions yet appeared uninterested in our exchanges and detached from the process. His yawning increased in frequency and duration and always occurred in the mid-flow of whatever I was saying. For a time I wondered if it was the acoustic experience of my voice that was having a soporific impact upon him but later dismissed the idea.

I found his yawning curious but did not understand its meaning or the communication. My countertransferential feelings varied. It was irritating to be continuously interrupted by such loud yawning, which led me to wonder if Stephen was defensively neutralizing the dynamic tension between us while passively expressing his aggression by yawning his 'refusal' to participate in dialogue, like his mother's refusal to discuss his birth. I wondered what feelings his mother might harbour in relation to his birth and body and what Stephen's fantasies were about that which could never be openly discussed. He rarely referred to his parents and when he did, after a weekend visit, he commented that, 'it was boring, the atmosphere was dead and there was no lively exchange'. His description of being with his parents mirrored what I often experienced with Stephen and what I imagined was his experience.

Sessions felt like trying to jump-start a car with a flat battery and I began ashamedly to dread them. It was becoming difficult to retain reflective capacity. Our work appeared to have come to a standstill. At times of stuck-ness and impasse and/or when the analyst's preferred version of his/herself is in flux or being disrupted, it is easy to feel 'done to' (Benjamin, 2004), to be of the 'not me' state of mind and view 'client projections' as the spanner disrupting the work (Davies, 2004). It was my view during this period that it was Stephen's 'detachment' that was creating an impasse rather than the reciprocity of the projective identifications between analyst and client (Benjamin, 2004).

Stephen's yawning was continuous over many months and as he yawned his eyes would roll upward and disappear into his lids as if he were losing consciousness. In response I felt compelled to become more active in my effort to arouse him as the way to keep the relationship alive. This also applied to my capacity to think, which I was in danger of losing to drowsiness. In synchrony with Stephen, as he began to yawn my eyelids became leaden and my limbs heavy. I felt as if I was being anaesthetized and found it difficult to maintain focused listening. My concern was that I would become detached from the process as I was finding it difficult to sustain a sense of relatedness.

Paradoxically, it was the lack of engagement which had become engaging. The palpable lifelessness and lack of enlivened exchange in the consulting room evolved into an intense visceral anxiety that I began to feel before each session. My embodied anxiety was attached to the accompanying thought that I would 'lose' Stephen. My concern was that he would leave because he was not getting anywhere. The anxiety disappeared the moment Stephen began to speak and I realized he was not leaving. In this sense our relationship was anything but dead. As I had experienced this only with Stephen, I was aware that my body was holding something his could not. His inability to symbolize a sense of 'not having come alive' was being enacted in the lifelessness of our encounter. Waiting for him to speak at the start of each session reminded me of a parent anxiously watching a sleeping newborn to make sure he/she is still breathing. It was not enough to see if the sleeping Stephen was still breathing, I felt the urgency to arouse and stimulate and metaphorically keep him breathing, by talking.

My attempts and failures to arouse Stephen gave way to a painful memory from my early childhood, which evoked the embodied feelings of anxiety and grief from which I had become split off and had disassociated. As a 'replacement child' I had tried to enliven a mother who at times in her grief for her dead child was disconnected from me, her living one. It was my urgent need to elicit and preserve a connection and the attachment bond with my mother that was being (re-)enacted with Stephen. My enactment was defensive in that it was keeping me protected from a deep wound I myself had and my feelings of utter helplessness.

Retrieving a living strand of my history and the realization of my involvement was significant in creating an inner shift, which allowed the opportunity and 'freedom' (Symington, 1983) to understand the transference/countertransference dynamics and relational configurations being (re-)enacted. We were enabled therefore to shift from a stuck and polarized position of impasse (Ehrenberg, 2000).

I wondered with Stephen if the pattern of our sessions was more descriptive of his birth and early life than the 'big bang' he had anticipated. Because his mother again refused to talk about his birth when asked, I suggested that Stephen try and obtain his medical records from the hospital where he was born if he was curious about the details. Within a fortnight he returned with the documents. What I am able to recall is that Stephen had died at birth, and was resuscitated and placed in an incubator for a non-stated period of time. The loss of oxygen appeared to be the cause of the cerebral palsy. The attending paediatrician described him as 'the baby who could not be aroused'. The report did not specify how long he continued to remain unresponsive to environmental stimuli but I gathered it was for a considerable period. In a follow-up letter the paediatrician reported that he could not predict Stephen's developmental outcome given the severity of trauma and his lack of responsiveness.

The medical records appeared to confirm what my body had registered and felt in the countertransference and later understood. Neither Stephen's implicit affective states nor mine could have been made accessible through talking because the affects involved were not symbolized with words. Sensory experiences and implicit affective states, which remain unthought (Bollas, 1987), are preserved in enactive form (Lyons-Ruth, 1999) and are communicated and registered outside the analyst and client's awareness, co-creating a shared 'relational' unconscious (Gerson, 2004), regularly influencing emerging material with ongoing fluidity and mutuality. It is the 'affective interchange', which includes bodily sensations, that is the core of the analytic encounter (Renik, 1996, p. 510).

Orbach argues that:

> [A] mentalist stance can fail to sufficiently address the subjective experience of the body as a body and in doing so can miss crucial dimensions

of the patient's experience. Drawing on the countertransferential bodily experience of the analyst during specific therapies enables a fuller understanding of a person's bodily development.

(Orbach, 2004a, p. 1)

By the time the records of Stephen's birth arrived, I was no longer seeking 'actively' to engage him. I had realized that the effort to make contact with his 'isolationist, very unconnected self' (his words) was what was leading him away from 'self experiencing' and interrupting the internal processing of 'known, partly known and unthought known aspects of self experience' (Bollas, 1987, p. 259). Stephen later reported that all verbal communication had always felt inauthentic and left him feeling 'this is not me'. In that sense, perhaps Stephen's 'resistance' was some dissociated part that had been experiencing my words as disconfirming its existence (Bromberg, 1996).

Sessions changed. Stephen always began by talking but would soon 'freefall' into the interior dimension of his experiencing. He would go into what he called 'an altered state' and would refer to his mind as 'freewheeling'. As his eyes rolled upward he would enter the space he described as being between 'sleep and waking'. Many of our sessions over the next eighteen months were spent entirely in silence. At the end of each session Stephen often commented that the time had flown and that he now felt refreshed and was no longer in 'work mode'. Sometimes, he talked about what he had noticed in his altered state but mainly he did not. Occasionally, during sessions he might briefly open his eyes to make contact with mine as a way of maintaining proximity and connection. At first, Stephen broke his silence to report on a thought or image but it was evident that it was for my benefit or from habit and not from a genuine wish to communicate. Initially, it was necessary to encourage his 'freefall', and to assure him that 'unbroken' silence was fine. Stephen no longer expressed his frustration at not getting anywhere.

'Uninterrupted silence' was necessary as the medium for Stephen's intermediate experiencing. By medium, I mean to imply that the 'silence' was co-constructed with implicit meaning that was the result of analyst/client interaction. In the absence of words this secured the reassurance of analyst/client's continued aliveness (Slochower, 1992) and the holding-in-mind space that was the antithesis of detachment and defensive withdrawal. At any point in the work Stephen might have just asked for silence or say that I was placing him in a verbal straitjacket. Being alone in the presence of someone is based on the assumption that the other 'is available and continues to be available when remembered after being forgotten' (Winnicott, 1971, p. 47).

My countertransferential feelings during our work were informative of the bonding difficulties that must have seriously affected and afflicted the attachment relationship between Stephen and his parents and his sense of self and self with other. It is well documented that it is difficult for parents to bond to babies who as newborns are sleepy or drugged and slow to respond to their efforts when trying to engage and interact (Raphael-Leff, 2005).

At times, it seemed as if 'silence' in and of itself and/or my bodily presence represented a primary substance (Balint, 1968) that sustained and preserved for Stephen his continuity of being. It is in the relational and intersubjective context of our bodies that we begin to develop our sense of self. It was my 'presence' rather than 'my understanding' that enabled Stephen to make contact and connect with the pre-symbolic dimensions of his subjective experience.

At a most primitive level Stephen experienced my presence as the 'will to live', which at moments was as vital as a heartbeat. Towards the end of our work he named this experience the primal silence: 'The primal silence echoes an early stage, an infantile stage before values. Before the mortal coil. Before words, thought before words. It's about survival, one of my things . . . survival. The will to live is coming from you. You support the will to live.'

Winnicott wrote about an aspect of regressive work with a patient when there was no mind and no mental functioning:

> There had to be a temporary phase in which the breathing of her body was all. In this way the patient became able to accept the not-knowing condition because I was holding her and keeping a continuity by my own breathing, while she let go, gave in, knew nothing.
> (Winnicott, 1949b, p. 252)

Relationality and 'being with' the client on the most primitive level is fundamental to the process of the client's deep regression/experiencing as described by Winnicott above. Creating a reliable and 'relational environment' is a necessary condition for the client to be able to partially surrender the role of protecting his own ego stability because he feels safe enough to turn it over, in part, to the analyst. By doing so the patient allows the emergence of regressed states of experience, along with the intense re-enactment in the transference of early and sometimes developmentally fragmented modes of thinking, feeling, and behaving. The deeper the regression that can be safely allowed by the patient, the richer the experience and the greater its reverberation through the total organisation of the self (Bromberg, 1979, p. 199).

Towards the latter part of our work Stephen reflected on the facilitating nature of our relationship which, in his words,

> allowed me to metaphorically fall . . . because I could not go there when alone because of the anxiety that I would have no identity, dissolution, I was alone when there was no ego. Death anxiety. No firmament, no anchor. This space with you is safety. Surrender means no vigilance.
>
> It has been necessary to have the experience of being with another that is a security. The presence of another allows me to be able to let go, to a level deeper, to a pre-phobic, pre-fear state that doesn't require intellect to sustain it. This shows that it is possible to be in this state.

The texture of the silence and intersubjective space in sessions developed and evolved over time and my countertransference feelings changed in parallel with the changing atmosphere and quality of the silence. Initially, I experienced bodily sensations, which seemed to correspond to what Stephen described as 'falling', as if I too were falling, backwards down an abyss, a sensation like vertigo, which lasted moments at the beginning of sessions. It was like sleeping without dreaming. He rarely talked during or about his altered state(s). Stephen always commented on how quickly these sessions passed.

In her commentary on Philip Bromberg's (1991) chapter, 'On knowing one's patient inside out', Enid Balint (1991) challenged Bromberg's notion that a client's dissociated experience must be put into language in order for change to take place. Referring to the privacy of the self, she writes: 'Some of what the good parent/analyst provides is the freedom, precisely, to have experience in the presence of the other that is NOT recognised, not symbolised.'

It was only latterly that Stephen described the shifting landscape of his interior experience, occasionally speaking from it. It sounded as if his experiencing followed a developmentally sequential line. Finally, he described the state as one he was:

> able to recall as a baby/child, full of images, internal/external that come and go but not needing to make sense of them. It was before thought. A waking state the mind doesn't need to be in control of or in survival mode. Reconnecting. I have always felt that when I sink I might be in the domain of one side of the brain that I don't usually use. All work and interaction comes from one mind and this allows me to enter my other mind. I need to sink as a way to connect both sides of the brain.

Stephen talked about his 'mental life not having any depth' and said he 'lived in a higher brain always feeling mentally exhausted.' He said that our sessions were the only moments he had ever experienced 'rest' and could not access this state when alone.

In the last year of our work, in the middle of a session Stephen suddenly and excitedly exclaimed that our two bodies were in the same position. I had never seen him so excited or animated. Our arms and legs were crossed in a way that mirrored each other. He called this 'sharing an experience'. I was sure that in all the hours we had spent together this was not the first time our body posture mirrored one another. However, it was one of the first times an experience 'felt' shared because it was experienced as intersubjectively embodied. Stephen added that this meant we were of the 'same humanity', which he had felt excluded from because of his cerebral palsy. This session followed another that was key for him.

A couple of months earlier, Stephen brought in his laptop and asked if he could show me a portrait photograph of himself that a friend had taken. It was a good portrait having captured Stephen's likeness very well. He turned towards me and asked if I thought it looked like him. I told him my impression and his face lit up with joyful astonishment as he said, 'I thought so but wanted to be certain. I really like the face in the photograph. It's difficult to believe that that is how I look.' I laughed, re-confirming my impression. Stephen and I spent time gazing at his image. We were consolidating/celebrating something more than a surface likeness, it was a face, embodied with an identity and existence.

Developmentally, these two sessions illustrate that the humanity of Stephen's bodily self had been registered, recognized and engaged with by the analyst, which is crucial for those who have suffered early relational trauma (White, 2006). Our earliest and continuing relationship with self and other is a bodily one. '[W]e "learn" through our bodies, through the hands, faces and minds of significant carers and their bodily ministrations' (Raphael-Leff, 1995, p. 16). For analysts this implies the engagement of our 'own body narrative' with the other. Orbach argues that:

> Symbols are useful for symbolising but the body, struggling to come alive, struggling to be held, may well need more than symbols. It needs to be engaged with, struggled with, to feel welcomed, put upon, invaded, affronted, moved, turned on, and turned off by a body in the room. We psychoanalytic types can reprise an elaborate confirmation of disembodiment and prohibition in which defensiveness and false or dead bodies reign supreme.
>
> (Orbach, 2004b, p. 10)

Although sessions were experienced as 'restorative', Stephen latterly expressed a revived interest in 'reliving' his birth trauma and wanted to do a course of ten re-birthing sessions 'just to see what might come up'. He explained that it entailed breath work, assuring me that it would not interfere with our work. The practitioner he was going to see was eminent and had been practising in the field since the early 1970s.

After his first two sessions he reported that not very much had really happened until the third session. After the required breath work, Stephen 'blanked out'. The practitioner told Stephen that when he 'came to' he had turned blue, something the practitioner had not witnessed before. Stephen said the experience felt similar to those he had had in the 'primal silence' in our sessions. He found the 'blue' session very exhausting and decided not to complete the rest of the course.

My presence had provided Stephen with reassurance concerning identity and survival and the continuity of being. It enabled him to experience his isolation and separateness in the presence of another and thus paradoxically emerge from his isolation and into the mutuality of relationship. Towards the last year of our work, sessions again changed and Stephen spent more and more time talking. Silence during sessions was a rarity.

S: After our last session I was thinking how animated I felt about talking, how motivated.

M: Since you have been going into the space you are calling the primal silence you hardly utilize it now in sessions. You used to spend entire sessions in that space.

S: Reached it with you, I don't need to go into it.

M: Not just reached it with me but within you.

S: Birth equals a soporific experience. I wonder if this soporific space is my template – I suppose it's a familiar one – I tend to gravitate towards. I don't gravitate towards high-energy experiences, not as familiar. Experiencing this connectedness with you and to myself has allowed me what's important, my ability to connect more with myself and others.

It was only at this late stage in our work that I learned from Stephen that he had first sought out psychoanalysis because of 'separation anxiety', that he was psychosomatic and had attached much anxiety to his body, and that he was anxious to overcome his fear of flying. The fear of flying when explored was specific to the engine suddenly stopping. Similarly, his anxiety about his body was that his heart might suddenly stop. Indeed, as it once had. Until now I had no idea that anxiety had played a central role in his life.

Although he sometimes spoke from or about the primal silence and his mind 'freewheeling', the most significant change I noticed was that we began to talk to each other. And sessions flew by for me. A warm and reciprocal relationship emerged and our talks and explorations were mutually enjoyed and appreciated.

In one of our last sessions Stephen told me that one of his close friends had been in a near fatal car accident and was in a critical condition. Because he was staying with her at the hospital, we organised a telephone session in place of our meeting:

S: When I first heard [about his friend] I was shocked and very sad. Interestingly, I feel cheerful because it affected me, just how much my friend means to me, she's probably my closest friend.

M: You seem relieved to have feelings about it.

S: Absolutely right. In the back of my mind, do I have the capacity to love? The fact that I got upset because of my friend demonstrates I have love for my friend. Not that I walk in a pink haze. This obviously shows I have a deep connection that doesn't show in everyday life. I can get in touch with emotionality. It does exist. It was crushed out of existence for some reason.

M: This shows you you are alive.

S: Absolutely, exactly.

M: You've never mentioned this.

S: I regard myself as a cold fish.

M: You've always described yourself as a sensitive, caring friend.

S: Absolutely, but my sensitivity was learned behaviour rather than actual. This has shown me that it is genuine. Recently I have been thinking, am I capable of having a relationship that has a deep connection? Feeling in love? This has shown me it is possible.

Parting words

Stephen: 'Analysis will get you to a point where you have to get further. The talking cure will get you to the door but then you have to hand over to the other, to go through. Surrender is the opposite of vigilance. The final step is to surrender. Surrendering the ego to existence.'

Not long before our work drew to an end Stephen suggested that I should write about our experience, saying that a good title would be 'The primal silence'.

Postscript

On completion of this chapter I contacted Stephen by telephone to arrange to send him a copy. We had not been in contact since he left therapy three years previously. He greeted my call very warmly and was pleased to hear from me. He said he had been meaning to get in touch to let me know what has been going on in his life post therapy. He said:

> The reason I left therapy was to see if I could have the quality of relationship I had developed with you with someone out there in my life. It was extraordinary – very shortly after leaving I met a woman who I have been with ever since. We bought a house together a year ago. We're talking about long-term plans like growing old together. All good things have been happening. So I guess it's a happily ever after.

References

Acquarone, S. (1995). Mens sana in corpore sano: Psychotherapy with a cerebral palsy child aged nine months. *Psychoanalytic Psychotherapy*, 9(1): 41–57.
Balint, M. (1968). *The basic fault: Therapeutic aspects of regression*. London: Tavistock.
Balint, E. (1991). Commentary on Philip Bromberg's 'On knowing one's patient inside out'. *Psychoanalytic Dialogues*, 1: 423–30.
Benjamin, J. (2004). Beyond doer and done to: An intersubjective view of thirdness. *Psychoanalytic Quarterly*, 73: 5–46.
Bollas, C. (1987). *The shadow of the object: Psychoanalysis of the unthought known*. London: Free Association Books.
Bromberg, P. M. (1979). Interpersonal psychoanalysis and regression. *Contemporary Psychoanalysis*, 15: 647–55.
Bromberg, P. M. (1991). On knowing one's patient inside out: The aesthetics of unconscious communication. *Psychoanalytic Dialogues*, 1: 399–422
Bromberg, P. M. (1996). Standing in the spaces: The multiplicity of self and the psychoanalytic relationship. *Contemporary Psychoanalysis*, 32: 509–35.

Davies, J. M. (2004). Whose bad objects are we anyway? Repetition and our elusive love affair with evil. *Psychoanalytic Dialogues, 14*(6): 711–32.

Ehrenberg, D. B. (2000). Potential impasses as analytic opportunity. *Contemporary Psychoanalysis, 36*: 573–86.

Freud, S. (1926). Inhibitions, symptoms and anxiety. *SE:* 20.

Gerson, S. (2004). The relational unconscious: A core element of intersubjectivity, thirdness and clinical process. *Psychoanalytic Quarterly, 73*: 63–98.

Hopper, E. (1991). Encapsulation as a defence against the fear of annihilation. *International Journal of Psychoanalysis, 72*: 607–24

Krystal, H. (1997). Desomatization and the consequences of infantile psychic trauma. *Psychoanalytic Inquiry, 17*: 126–50.

Lyons-Ruth, K. (1999). The two-person unconscious. *Psychoanalytic Inquiry, 19*: 576–617.

McDougall, J. (1989). *Theatres of the body*. London: Free Association Books.

Mollon, P. (2002). *Remembering trauma* (2nd edition.). London: Whurr.

Orbach, S. (2004a). How can we have a body: Desires and corpreality. For the William Alanson White Conference. Longing: Psychoanalytic Musings on Desire. New York.

Orbach, S. (2004b). The body in clinical practice, part two: When touch comes to therapy. In *Touch, attachment and the body* (K. White, Ed.). London: Karnac.

Piontelli, A. (1988). Prenatal life and birth as reflected in the analysis of a two-year-old psychotic girl. *International Review of Psycho-Analysis, 15*: 73–81.

Raphael-Leff, J. (1995). Imaginative bodies of childbearing: Visions and revisions. In *The imaginative body: Psychodynamic therapy in healthcare* (A. Erskine and D. Judd, Eds.). London: Whurr.

Raphael-Leff, J. (2005). *Psychological processes of childbearing*. London: Anna Freud Centre.

Renik, O. (1996). The perils of neutrality. *Psychoanalytic Quarterly, 65*: 495–517.

Slochower, J. (1992). A hateful borderline patient and the holding environment. *Contemporary Psychoanalysis, 28*: 72–88.

Symington, N. (1983). The analyst's act of freedom as agent of therapeutic change. *International Review of Psycho-Analysis, 10*: 283–91.

White, K. (2006). There's always something missing inside: A response to Elaine Arnold's paper 'Separation and loss through immigration of African Caribbean women in the UK'. *Attachment & Human Development, 8*(2): 175–78.

Winnicott, D. W. (1949a). Birth memories, birth trauma, and anxiety. In *Collected papers: Through paediatrics to psychoanalysis*, 174–93. London: Karnac.

Winnicott, D. W. (1949b). Mind and its relation to the psyche-soma. In *Collected papers: Through paediatrics to psychoanalysis*, 243–54. London: Karnac.

Winnicott, D. W. (1971). Playing: A theoretical statement. In *Playing and reality*, 38–52. New York: Basic Books.

5

THE INTRICATE INTIMACIES OF PSYCHOTHERAPY AND QUESTIONS OF SELF-DISCLOSURE

William F. Cornell

This chapter addresses the understanding of the analyst's/therapist's vulnerabilities within the therapeutic process and the intimate potential of the therapeutic relationship. The author stresses the awareness of the therapist's personal vulnerabilities in addition to the more common conceptualizations of countertransference. Case material is presented to illustrate the complex questions of self-disclosure and the intimate nature of the therapeutic endeavour when viewed from a relational perspective.

> The analyst's role is not defined by invulnerability ... but by a special (though inconsistent) willingness, and a practiced (though imperfect) capacity to accept and deal with her vulnerability.
> (D. B. Stern, 2004, p. 216)

The cancer scare now seemed to be over after several weeks of Ben and I anxiously awaiting the results of a series of tests. Many around Ben waited with him, proclaiming variations of 'Oh, it's probably nothing ... Everything will be OK.' These were intended as statements of comfort, but Ben experienced them as dismissive and placating. Other than his session with me, there seemed no place where Ben could express his feelings of anxiety, shock and a bereft anticipation of leaving his young children fatherless.

Ben talked for most of the session about his relief with the positive results, feeling a bit foolish about his level of anxiety while awaiting the results but eager to stay more and more fully engaged in life. I was deeply relieved. I have a deep regard and affection for Ben, and the thought of losing him to cancer was horrifying to me. As I had imagined the possibility of his being ill, I had been wondering silently if I would be capable of seeing him through the treatment process.

As he prepared to leave the session, Ben said, 'Well, we won't have to talk about cancer any more.' I responded, 'I think it is something that we will need to

THE INTRICACY OF THERAPY AND SELF-DISCLOSURE

come back to for some time, as the possibility of being seriously ill or dying has stirred up many important things that we need to continue talking about.' 'I think we can let it go,' said Ben. 'And besides, I don't feel I have the right to keep hurting you.' Hurting me? I had no idea what Ben was talking about. I pointed out that he had every right to say things that might hurt me, that it was my responsibility to deal with whatever feelings our work and relationship might stir in me, but I had no idea how he felt he had been hurting me during this period of the cancer scare. Ben explained, 'Virtually every time I used the word cancer, it was like a shadow came over your face. Sometimes you looked like you were going to cry. I don't want to cause you pain.' I was dumbstruck. His words made instant sense to me. He had seen something in my face that I was not even aware of feeling, let alone showing. I was deeply touched by his noticing and his expression of concern. 'I have some idea what you may have been seeing, Ben, and it's important we come back to this next week.'

For the next week, I struggled with what, if anything, to say to Ben about the meaning of what he saw on my face. I was stunned and rather embarrassed that something had been evident on my face but not to me. I knew, as soon as Ben spoke, that the sadness he was seeing on my face was there; it was not a projection on Ben's part. My mother died at 40 of cancer, when I was in my late adolescence, my brother and sister in early adolescence. Her young death left deep, unmanaged scars, and my father died ten years later of an intentionally untreated cancer. I could not stand the thought that Ben, who was just discovering the pleasures and satisfactions of his life, could have his young life taken away by this disease, that his kids might lose their father so early in their lives. My admiration and affection for Ben deepened in response to his caring and honesty with me. I knew that if I spoke of my parents' deaths, I could probably not do so without crying. What would it mean to Ben, who had grown up with a determinedly depressive mother and a father who converted all affect into rage, to see his therapist in tears?

In the next session, I told Ben that what he'd seen on my face was undoubtedly a deep sadness that came from my own life. I would talk with him about it if he wished to know and if it would support his therapy. I suggested he take a week to think it over. He replied immediately that he did not think it was 'his place' to know something so personal. I assured Ben it was 'his place' to know something of me if he so chose, especially about something that had entered our relationship unbidden and unplanned. The question I wanted him to consider was whether my speaking of myself would support his therapy.

McLaughlin has stressed that 'whether we are analyst or patient, our deepest hopes for what we may find the world to be, as well as our worst fears of what it will be, reflect our transference expectancies as shaped by our developmental past' (2005, p. 187). More than half a century earlier in his remarkable, though long unpublished, clinical diaries, Ferenczi noted that through the:

> unmasking of the so called transference and countertransference as the hiding places of the most significant obstacles to the completion of all

analyses, one comes to be almost convinced that no analysis can succeed as long as the false and alleged differences between the 'analytical situation' and ordinary life are not overcome.

(1988 [1932], p. 212)

For both Ferenczi and McLaughlin, the inevitable humanness and vulnerability of the analyst were potential sources of, simultaneously, trouble, insight, impasse and/or mutual influence and understanding.

Ferenczi also observed a certain merging of psychic realities in the analytic couple that brings affective vitality to the analytic endeavor:

The emotions of the analyst combine with the ideas of the analysand, and the ideas of the analyst (representational images) with the emotions of the analysand; in this way the otherwise lifeless images become events, and the empty emotional tumult acquires an intellectual content (?) [sic].

(Ferenczi, 1988 [1932], p. 14)

Ferenczi follows this statement with a question mark in parentheses. What does this question mark mean? Does Ferenczi question his own perceptions? Is it a question of what does one do clinically with this observation once it has been made? Is it a question to the reader to take up? Ferenczi's awareness of his own emotional limits and entanglements with his patients led to his experimentation with mutual analysis and his open acknowledgement of his mistakes and misunderstandings with regard to his analysands (Aron & Harris, 1993; Ferenczi, 1988 [1932]; Thompson, 1964). McLaughlin's (2005, pp. 75–6) response to his own awareness of what he called hard spots and blind spots interfering in the relations with his patients was to remove himself temporarily from the transference pressures to the privacy of his woodshop, his 'transference sanctuary', entering a period of reverie and self-analysis, so that he could return to his patient in a more open state of mind and affect (McLaughlin, 2005, pp. 114–16). He seldom reported the content of his private self-analysis to his analysands; he used it, instead, to bring himself back to the analytic work, the relationship and the mutual transferences with a clearer sense of self that would enable a more open engagement.

Poland, in a chapter delivered in recognition of McLaughlin's contributions to psychoanalysis, mirrors Ferenczi's observations about the psychic impact of the patient upon the therapist's being. He wryly observes, 'Positions of subject and object flow subtly and interchangeably. No matter how it seems on the surface, below the surface traffic is always two-way' (2005, p. 18). Poland (2005, p. 16) outlines four areas of danger and vulnerability for the analyst:

1 countertransferential fears provoked by the patient;
2 fears idiosyncratic to the analyst's character that emerge during the course of some analyses;

3   those fears and vulnerabilities intrinsic to the analytic process (object attachment and loss; resistance and relentless negativism on the part of the patient); and
4   those [fears] resulting from the human condition, from the analyst's vulnerability to the demands of reality and fate even when working best.

Poland writes in a deeply personal and self-revealing fashion, and concludes (in contrast to Ferenczi and in accord with McLaughlin):

> A word about self-disclosure. The agonizing personal introspective strife in which I was engaged as part of this woman's analysis was my own task, not to be carried out by my burdening my patient with the details of my private inner work ... Nonetheless, it was important that I try to resolve my own issues in myself, using them to facilitate but not to complicate the patient's work. My aim was to unburden the patient's analysis, not to burden it with my private labors. The analyst's fear may be triggered or even caused by the patient; the analyst's task is to sort out private issues privately.
>
> (Poland, 2005, p. 20)

While I admire the clarity and integrity of Poland's position, I would see the choices regarding self-disclosure as variable, dependent on context and the place in time in the evolution of the therapeutic relationship. Would I burden Ben with self-disclosure at this point in his work with me? What kind of disclosure might be most appropriate and therapeutic? These questions are complex, not readily answered by any single theoretical position (Aron, 1991, 1996; Bollas, 1989; Davies, 1994; Maroda, 1991; McLaughlin, 2005; Slavin & Kriegman, 1998; Searles, 1959, 1979; Stern, 2003, 2004). Questions of analyst/therapist self-disclosure have been, and continue to be, controversial (Bonovitz, 2006; Eagle, 2003; Gediman, 2006; Greenberg, 1995; Hartman, 2006; Hoffman, 1998; Renik, 1993, 1999; Slochower, 2006). I considered several possibilities as to what, if any more, to say to Ben should he ask. I might acknowledge to Ben that the shadow he had seen on my face was a shadow cast by my own history and simply ask for his associations and fantasies. I wondered whether, if I did not disclose anything further about myself, it would hold open the space for Ben's own experience, conflicts and choices as to whether or not to explore this terrain further. Could further self-disclosure on my part foreclose Ben's experience of himself? I might say something like, 'This is a frightening place I know something about from my own life, so I know something of its importance and am willing to stay there with you in this fear and anxiety.' I thought that perhaps my telling something of my own life's losses and feelings toward those I have loved might offer a kind of model and permission for Ben to move into territory that has been forbidden and shameful. I considered telling him more about my feelings for him and his children without telling him anything about my own life. Each seemed like a valid choice.

Over the days between sessions, I found myself thinking particularly about Aron's article 'The patient's experience of the analyst's subjectivity' (1991) and re-read the article with Ben in mind. Aron describes the need of children to reach into the inner worlds of their parents and of patients' desire to know something of the interior lives of their analysts, and proposes that this knowing of the other's interiority is an essential developmental achievement in the capacity to think psychologically. I realized that for Ben, his father's internal world was a black, forbidding and forbidden box. It was not to be known. In kind, Ben's internal world was of no interest to his father. Any expression of Ben's feelings was subject to ridicule and assault (in adulthood as well as childhood). Early in treatment, Ben had told me that as a child he planted a fruit tree in the yard every year on his birthday. On his 15th birthday, he stopped planting trees because 'by the time the tree bore fruit, I would be an adult, and I knew that once I was an adult, nothing would taste sweet any more. There would only be bitterness.' Ben learned to live a solitary and silent life. It was 'not his place' to expect truly to know someone else or expect to be known.

Much in my own life and development had taught me that those closest to me, in a kind of benign neglect, were most content when I managed myself by myself (Corrigan & Gordon, 1995; Shabad & Selinger, 1995; Winnicott, 1975 [1949]). Ben, too, had learned to take care of himself and expect little but trouble and judgement from others. From the very beginnings of our work, I had felt an identification with Ben. Our fathers had both fought in the Second World War and had been deeply scarred. My father came back deeply withdrawn and silent; Ben's father came back self-pitying and violent. As sons, we each grew up with fathers whose internal worlds were deeply disturbed and sealed off. We each lived much of our own internal lives in silence. I decided, should Ben ask me to say more, it was time to tell him something of my own life, to let him learn directly something of my own subjectivity.

The following week, Ben did ask me to speak of the meaning of the sadness he had seen on my face. I told him the story of my parents' deaths and the impact on me of my fantasies of what might happen to his children should he die so young, and of my admiration for his taking the early warning signs seriously and immediately pursuing help. I did cry. Ben listened to me with tenderness and interest, and something shifted in the shame he has often felt in the face of his own sadness and vulnerability, which he had always seen as 'weak'. He did not experience me as weak as I spoke frankly with him. Here, at this moment, it was my speech rather than that of the client, my openness and vulnerability, that served both Ben and me.

Time passed, and this interchange faded into the background of our sessions. When invited to write about these matters, I thought immediately of this experience with Ben and decided to write about it. Early in our work, Ben had given me a couple of his published chapters to read. He is very accomplished in his field but had great difficulty with writing about his work. He asked me to read some of his chapters both to understand more about what he does and to help him deal with his writing blocks. I found his work fascinating (though difficult to comprehend), and we were able to address his writing blocks quite productively. In a further step of self-disclosure, I decided to give Ben the first draft of this chapter to read for his perspective and also to ask for permission to publish something about him. He was deeply moved by the chapter, touched that the encounter between us had meant something to me as well as to him. Ben said, 'I've always known you were a thoughtful therapist, but reading the chapter has shown me something of how you think. I learned a lot.' He gave me permission to publish what had happened between us.

I could sense that something had shifted in Ben at least in part as a result of this exchange about the shadow over my face. Ben re-established contact with his father after a couple of years of silence following a particularly nasty fight. His father's behavior had not changed, but Ben began to sense that his father was anxious inside, as well as gruff, belligerent and argumentative. When his father had to be hospitalized for a serious illness, Ben called regularly, and his father was able to express appreciation for Ben's concern. Once he recovered and left the hospital, Ben's father returned to his usual mode, but Ben found himself more accepting of his father's way of being and was pleased that he, Ben, had been able to offer his father something different that at least for a little while had been received.

Recently Ben asked if the chapter (then a paper) had been accepted for publication. I told him that it had. He said he admired me for writing something so honest and personal and that he thought it signaled a change in my profession that it had been accepted. Ben had once been in a psychoanalysis which he described as 'trying to talk to a stone wall in a dark room', so he thought it was strictly forbidden for a therapist to say anything personal about himself. I asked how the experience I had written about has stayed with him. He said that it has had numerous effects for him, that first of all my sharing myself with him had made me 'both more human and more professional' in his mind. My decision to share the draft of the chapter with him was 'sweet and respectful'. Most important for himself, he learned that 'to show my vulnerability was OK, healthy, that it makes me feel closer'. He said that, while I had encouraged his vulnerability on many occasions, he did not trust it, but that when he saw mine, he could feel what had been only an idea before. 'I had always been ashamed of my withdrawal. But reading the chapter I could see that you understood it, and that you withdraw sometimes, too, so that really made it OK.'

A second vignette illustrates a very different experience of an unexpected self-awareness and unwanted vulnerability. Charlie and I had struggled for years. Unlike the growing closeness and affection I felt for Ben, my years of involvement with Charlie were marked by determination but also bounded by caution and a wary self-protection. Charlie was nearing 50, had never married, had no friends at the start of treatment and wandered from job to job working always 'beneath his potential' and his academic training.

Over the course of therapy, his job status improved and tentative friendships were in the making. But our relationship seemed forever at the edge of fraying and unraveling. Charlie constantly underscored my failure really to 'get him'. In my failures I joined a multitude of others who never seemed to 'get' Charlie. I would quietly steam, wondering if it ever occurred to Charlie that, were he to 'get' someone else's experience, he might have a few friends, maybe even a wife and family.

I was acutely aware of the painful developmental history of Charlie's life with relentlessly self-involved parents who seemed to see him as a not very attractive piece of furniture that had been delivered, unwanted, to their living room. They just stepped around him. I knew what he felt he needed of me, and I despaired of my capacity (or willingness) to give it to him. I could barely stand how he treated me, or others, and there seemed no room to address this with him. I careened between feelings of irritation and urgent anxiety that he would never get a full life for himself and a sense of guilt that I was not more helpful. Regular consultation helped me manage my countertransference and do technically competent work, but in some fundamental way I could not open myself to Charlie in a way that would truly allow me to 'get' him with my being, as well as my head.

Gerson (2003) describes the transferential relationship as the medium through which unconscious desires can begin to emerge and be articulated, while constantly shadowed and intertwined with memories (and anticipations) of failure, the bedrock of deadly and deadening anxiety and defense. And yet, Gerson (2005) argues, 'we constantly seek others as transformational objects to make something about ourselves more available to ourselves'. The impasse between Charlie and me, the deadlock of our mutual, negative transferences, repeatedly foreclosed our experiences of ourselves rather than making something of ourselves more available to ourselves or each other.

Charlie and I fell constantly into the shadows, the urgency of desire seeming to be a source of irritation and frustration, rather than being hopeful and enlivening. I recall some old song about a mutual admiration society; Charlie and I had formed a mutual irritation society. Then one day, quite unexpectedly, a high school acquaintance, a woman in whom Charlie had had considerable adolescent interest, was back in the city for a funeral. She gave Charlie a call, and they met for lunch. In session, Charlie was uncharacteristically bereft and, also uncharacteristically, upset with himself, rather than being upset with the world and everyone in it. 'What's wrong with me, Bill? She has a family, a marriage, not the greatest but not so bad. I might have had a life with her. What is it I do wrong? I must do something wrong. You must help me see what I'm doing.' I was quiet. I listened. I could feel my wariness yielding, my chest opening. I was afraid to say much of anything, as though I would break this magical spell.

Near tears by the end of the session, Charlie was standing to leave: 'She was here for a funeral. If it had been me who'd died, would she have come? Who would have known to tell her I died? If I died tomorrow, who would come from out of state to be at my funeral? No one. Who would there be to call? No one. If I died tomorrow, there would not be enough people who cared to be pallbearers for my casket.'

He left.

I stood there, barely able to breathe. I felt nauseous and thought I was going to collapse. What Charlie had just described as the fear for his death was the reality of my father's death and funeral. After my mother's death, my father had become so withdrawn, isolated and increasingly bizarre that by the time he died ten years later, there was no one in his life, there would be no pallbearers for his casket, only his mother, brother, two sons and a daughter to attend his funeral. I had to go to a real estate company where he had worked briefly and, very unsuccessfully, ask the staff to be his pallbearers. I began to understand my urgency, my irritation and my inability to open to Charlie, and my self-deadening in the face of his unsocialized behavior and his relentless despair.

The session haunted me the rest of the day. I had to will my attention to my other clients. I went home that night and turned to my personal 'sanctuary of transference': music. Bob Dylan, Neil Young, Joan Baez, music that carried me back to my Dad in bitter compassion. I cried, this time in private. I felt the collapse of my Dad's life and the impact of his choices on me. I could feel how deeply, unbearably and unconsciously I had merged Charlie with my father. I could feel the beginnings of a willingness, an openness, a capacity to undo the knots between us. I did not tell Charlie what had happened to me in that moment when he spoke of his imagined funeral with no pallbearers. Unlike with Ben, I had no impulse to be personal with Charlie. I recalled a time when I did share a personal experience with Charlie in an effort (rather desperate and un-thought-out) to make a link with him and feel some identification. Charlie responded, 'That's really irritating. I don't pay you to hear about your life. I pay you to listen to mine. Please keep your life to yourself. Or pay somebody else to listen to you.' Unlike with Ben, for Charlie, given his character and where we were in our developing relationship, such self-disclosure would have been an intrusion, a burden, to use Poland's phrase. At another time in the course of treatment, this might not be the case.

A personal self-disclosure to Charlie would not have facilitated our work or his self-understanding. What was possible for me, however, as a result of my self-encounter and realizations, was to return to Charlie with openness, patience and, for the first time, hope. I have no doubt that he felt the difference, though he never spoke of it. He, too, was in a different place after his lunch with his high school girlfriend. He began to question himself, and I was able to engage with those questions without pressure or irritation.

The vulnerabilities and psychic conflicts centered in the tragic deaths of my young parents were within me, and deeply affected my work with these two men. The same history inhabited me quite differently with these two very different men. With Ben, probably not coincidentally a father, like me, and self-blaming, like me, my own history of loss facilitated a deep regard and positive identification with him. With Charlie, my history and vulnerability unconsciously evoked in his presence fostered a defensive identification and a relentless wariness. The decisions I made in the context of my work with these men were, therefore, quite different.

Over the past quarter-century, various relationally based models of psychoanalysis and psychotherapy have gradually informed one another, though each had been evolving in relative separation from the others from the 1930s until the 1980s. Ferenczi may not have been the first psychoanalyst to notice that the patient was not the only troubled and vulnerable person in the analytic couple, but he was the first to try to work with it clinically and write about it publicly. His experiments with 'mutual analysis' may have been brilliant failures, but his emotional honesty inspired many, some of whom emigrated to the United States, offering an alternative to the more classical analytic position dominant in the US before and after the Second World War (Thompson, 1950; Rudnytsky, Bokay & Giampieri-Deutsch, 1996). Ironically, several of the innovators in relationally oriented models struggled in relative isolation and solitude – Ferenczi in Budapest, Fairbairn in Edinburgh, Sullivan in Washington DC, and McLaughlin in Pittsburgh. Others, like Klein and Winnicott in London and Greenberg and Mitchell in New York, had the advantage of major urban centers of psychoanalytic thinking and a sense of a following of like-minded colleagues, though, as one reads their work, one can see that they, too, were not always met with open arms by their more classically oriented colleagues. In the United Kingdom, so often isolated from Europe, a different mode of relational psychoanalysis – object relations – was developing. In the object relational mode, the trouble and vulnerability within the dyad was seen as centered in the client; disturbances within the analyst were seen as products of the affective and infective impact of the patient, through splitting, projection and projective identification. In the United States in the 1930s, Harry Stack Sullivan was laboring mostly alone but coming to his own conclusions about the inevitability of mutual influence in the therapeutic dyad. His work, together with that of Clara Thompson, Erich Fromm and Frieda Fromm-Reichman, among other European émigrés, evolved into the school of interpersonal psychoanalysis.

It took several decades after the war for these models to reshape psychoanalysis in the US. Jay Greenberg and Steven Mitchell's *Object relations in psychoanalytic theory* (1983) and Mitchell's *Relational concepts in psychoanalysis: An integration* (1988) were the first major efforts to integrate interpersonal and object relational models into American psychoanalysis, giving birth to what is now known as 'relational psychoanalysis'. During that same period, McLaughlin was writing a series of important chapters exploring the use of the analyst's countertransference and the mutuality of influence within the therapeutic dyad. These emerging models stressed the importance of the analyst's own subjectivity within the psychotherapeutic endeavor.

From the perspective of classical, ego psychological and object relational models of psychoanalysis, the desires, disturbances and resistances under study are those within the patient. Within the relational sensibility (although there are many variations of this paradigm), it is understood that both therapist and client bring aspects of their unformulated, unconscious experience into the consulting room, that the unconscious pressures of the desired and the prohibited exist in both members of the dyad (Stern, 1997). Hence, at times, there will be the inevitable vulnerability of the analyst that may well affect the work with the patient but does not necessarily come from the patient. How to make use of countertransference and the therapist's human vulnerability varies from model to model, and practitioner to practitioner. The relational models share a rough consensus that the nature of unconscious experience and the work of analysis are not only the retrieval of rejected and disavowed drives and infantile attachment needs, but a process of unconscious unfolding and discovery of emerging possibilities.

As can be seen from the perspectives of Ferenczi and McLaughlin, two analysts of relentless curiosity and experimentation, who wrote with unusual candor, as well as from the clinical vignettes, a therapist's willingness to experience and inhabit their own vulnerabilities can deepen the therapeutic endeavor and be of compelling benefit to their clients.

References

Aron, L. (1991). The patient's experience of the analyst's subjectivity. *Psychoanalytic Dialogues, 1*: 29–51.
Aron, L. (1996). *A meeting of minds*. Hillsdale, NJ: The Analytic Press.
Aron, L. and Harris, A. (1993). *The Legacy of Sandor Ferenczi*. Hillsdale, NJ: The Analytic Press.
Bollas, C. (1989). *The forces of destiny*. London: Free Association Books.
Bonovitz, C. (2006). The illusion of certainty in self-disclosure: Commentary on paper by Helen K. Gediman. *Psychoanalytic Dialogues, 16*: 293–304.
Corrigan, E. G. and Gordon, P.-E. (1995). The mind as object. In *The mind object: Precocity and pathology of self-sufficiency* (E. G. Corrigan and P.-E. Gordon, Eds.). Northvale, NJ: Jason Aronson (pp. 1–22).
Davies, J. M. (1994). Love in the afternoon: A relational consideration of desire and dread in the countertransference. *Psychoanalytic Dialogues, 4*: 153–70.
Eagle, M. N. (2003). The postmodern turn in psychoanalysis: A critique. *Psychoanalytic Psychology, 20*: 411–24.
Ferenczi, S. (1988) [1932]. *The clinical diary of Sandor Ferenczi* (J. Dupont, Ed.; M. Balint and N. Z. Jackson, Trans.). Cambridge, MA: Harvard University Press.
Gediman, H. K. (2006). Facilitating analysis with implicit and explicit self-disclosures. *Psychoanalytic Dialogues, 16*: 241–62. Reply to commentaries, *16*: 305–16.
Gerson, S. (2003). The enlivening transference and the shadow of deadliness. Paper given to the Boston Psychoanalytic Society and Institute, 3 May.
Gerson, S. (2005). Ghosts from the stage to the consulting room: The family unconscious in classics of 20th-century theatre. Paper given to the Western Pennsylvania Forum for Relational and Body-Centered Psychotherapies, Pittsburgh, PA, 6 November.
Greenberg, J. (1995). Self-disclosure: Is it psychoanalytic? *Contemporary Psychoanalysis, 31*: 193–205.

Greenberg, J. and Mitchell, S. (1983). *Object relations in psychoanalytic theory.* Cambridge, MA: Harvard University Press.

Hartman, S. (2006). Disclosure, dis-closure, diss/clothes/sure: Commentary on chapter by Helen K. Gediman. *Psychoanalytic Dialogues, 16*: 273–92.

Hoffman, I. Z. (1998). *Ritual and spontaneity in the psychoanalytic process: A dialectical constructivist view.* Hillsdale, NJ: The Analytic Press.

McLaughlin, J. T. (2005). *The healer's bent: Solitude and dialogue in the clinical encounter* (W. F. Cornell, Ed.). Hillsdale, NJ: The Analytic Press.

Maroda, K. (1991). *The power of countertransference.* Chichester: Wiley.

Mitchell, S. (1988). *Relational concepts in psychoanalysis: An integration.* Cambridge, MA: Harvard University Press.

Poland, W. (2005). The analyst's fears. Chapter presented at Generativity: Honoring the Contributions of James T. McLaughlin conference, Pittsburgh, PA, 15 October.

Renik, O. (1993). Analytic interaction: Conceptualizing technique in the light of the analyst's irreducible subjectivity. *Psychoanalytic Quarterly, 62*: 553–71.

Renik, O. (1999). Playing one's cards face up in analysis. *Psychoanalytic Quarterly, 68*: 521–39.

Rudnytsky, P. L., Bokay, A. and Giampieri-Deutsch, P. (1996). *Ferenczi's turn in psychoanalysis.* New York: New York University Press.

Searles, H. (1959). Oedipal love in the countertransference. *International Journal of Psycho-Analysis, 40*: 180–90.

Searles, H. (1979). *Countertransference and related subjects.* New York: International Universities Press.

Shabad, P. and Selinger, S. S. (1995). Bracing for disappointment and the counterphobic leap into the future. In *The mind object: Precocity and pathology of self-sufficiency* (E. G. Corrigan and P.-E. Gordon, Eds.). Northvale, NJ: Jason Aronson (pp. 209–28).

Slavin, M. and Kriegman, D. (1998). Why the analyst needs to change: Toward a theory of conflict, negotiation, and mutual influence in the therapeutic process. *Psychoanalytic Dialogues, 8*: 247–84.

Slochower, J. (2006). The psychoanalytic other: Commentary on chapter by Helen K. Gediman. *Psychoanalytic Dialogues, 16*: 263–72.

Stern, D. B. (1997). *Unformulated experience: From dissociation to imagination in psychoanalysis.* Hillsdale, NJ: The Analytic Press.

Stern, D. B. (2003). The fusion of horizons: Dissociation, enactment, and understanding. *Psychoanalytic Dialogues, 13*: 843–73.

Stern, D. B. (2004). The eye that sees itself: Dissociation, enactment, and the achievement of conflict. *Contemporary Psychoanalysis, 14*: 197–237.

Thompson, C. M. (1950). *Psychoanalysis: Evolution and development.* New York: Thomas Nelson & Sons.

Thompson, C. M. (1964). *Interpersonal psychoanalysis: The selected papers of Clara M. Thompson* (M. R. Green, Ed.). New York: Basic Books.

Winnicott, D. W. (1975) [1949]. Mind and its relation to the psyche-soma. In *Through paediatrics to psycho-analysis.* London: Karnac (pp. 243–52).

6

FORGIVENESS – A RELATIONAL PROCESS

Research and reflections

Judith Anderson

Through qualitative research based on interviews, I describe how psychoanalytic practitioners perceive forgiveness, a complex subject with cultural, religious and political associations. They see it as important, and sometimes at the heart of the psychoanalytic endeavour. Analytic thinking has enriched what is essentially a concept determined by religions and cultures. The development of the capacity to forgive requires consciousness and empathy, for both self and other, and the need for appropriate metabolizing of aggression.

Introduction

In considering such an important subject in the context of psychotherapy, a relational perspective determines that the subjectivity of the therapist is an important focus of attention. I explore how forgiveness is defined, how the capacity to forgive comes about, what processes are linked with forgiveness, what reservations psychotherapists have about it and what wider cultural or spiritual perspectives are relevant.

The subject became the focus of my attention when I was asked to give a paper on it (Anderson, 2004a). Reflecting on practice, I realized that clinical experience had made me cynical about forgiveness in my work, largely from knowing patients who had been encouraged to forgive prematurely by well-meaning religious advisers. As Eliot (1920) wrote, 'After such knowledge, what forgiveness'. Inevitably, such a universal subject raises questions of personal applicability; I could relate to Klein's notion of moving through hostility to forgiveness in the process of my own analysis. I was at a stage of life where a re-examination of the past seemed to call. What did I need to forgive? For what did others need my apology? Would they forgive me?

I held three major themes in mind during the research (Anderson, 2004b): the wider cultural/religious context, the possible neglect of forgiveness by psychoanalysts and forgiveness as part of a multifaceted complex including repentance, atonement, revenge and betrayal, a psychological dynamic in which one part cannot exist without the others, although only one aspect may be in focus.

Literature review

Religion and culture

Within society, and therefore within the mind of the psychotherapist, forgiveness is likely to be linked, consciously or unconsciously, to specific religious or cultural definitions and ideas, for example, the Christian phrase, 'Forgive us our trespasses, as we forgive those who trespass against us.' Religious writing may give clues about psychological processes. Jung suggests that 'religious statements are psychic confessions which in the last resort are based on unconscious i.e. on transcendental processes' (1952, para. 555).

Religions that specify self-awareness or insight as a major aspect of forgiveness, such as Hinduism and Buddhism, bear witness to one route we discover in the consulting room. The teachings of monotheistic religions have a relational aspect. The forgiveness of sins is a prominent feature of Christian theology (Snaith, 1950, p. 86) with connections made between God's forgiveness and the forgiveness of others. Jewish rabbinic sources (e.g. Blumenthal, 1996) define two types of forgiveness. The most basic kind is 'forgoing the other's indebtedness' (*mechilá*). Only if the offender has sincerely repented ('done *teshuva*') should the offended person offer *mechilá*, forgiving the debt of the offender and relinquishing any claim against him. This is not a reconciliation of heart or an embracing of the offender; it is reaching the conclusion that the offender no longer owes anything. The crime remains; only the debt is forgiven. Then there is *selichá*, an act of the heart achieving empathy for the offender, that he, too, is human, frail and deserving of sympathy.

In Islamic teaching, in a parallel with the Christian parable of the Prodigal Son, the generosity of God's mercy is described as follows: 'As soon as my servant makes a step toward me, I make two steps toward him; as soon as he comes to me walking, I come to him running.' In Christian teaching, this aspect too is emphasized, with the radical call to forgive 'seventy times seven'. In his book about 9/11, Williams challenges the passivity that we might suspect:

> The peasant looks at the soldier and speaks to him, saying, 'I choose to go the other mile.' The world of the aggressor, the master, is questioned because the person who is not supposed to take initiatives suddenly does. As Gandhi discovered this is very frightening for most of those who exercise power.
>
> (Williams, 2002, p. 28)

Carmichael (2003) examines changing contemporary definitions of sin and forgiveness. She sees the cases of Myra Hindley, James Bulger, Mary Bell and Sarah Payne as modern stories of sin and guilt. She discusses the shift from individual sin to structural sin, such as poverty, slavery, violence and war, in which many are implicitly involved.

'Liberation' theologians take up this theme. 'We shall concentrate on the great sin of the continent [Latin America], which shapes its whole social and historical reality, which crucifies and kills majorities and whole peoples. In this context we have to ask what it means to forgive the sin and forgive the sinner' (Sobrino, 1986, p. 46). Distinguishing between forgiveness and reconciliation, some writers argue that it is possible to have reconciliation without forgiveness, others that forgiveness is a prerequisite for reconciliation and others that it is possible to forgive but not be reconciled; these variations seem situationally determined.

Derrida addressed the notion of forgiveness thus:

> [all definitions] refer to a certain idea of pure and unconditional forgiveness, without which this discourse would not have the least meaning; which, in order to have its own meaning must have no meaning, no finality, even no intelligibility. It is the madness of the impossible.
> (Derrida, 2001, p. 53)

He concluded: 'Yes, there is the unforgivable. Is this not, in truth, the only thing to forgive? There is only forgiveness, if there is any, where there is the unforgivable' (ibid., p. 40).

Psychoanalytic writing

As Wangh (2005) also found, forgiveness is neglected by psychoanalysts. Freud did not write about 'forgiveness' explicitly, mentioning it five times in his entire writing, compared with 253 mentions of 'punishment' (Akhtar, 2002, p. 176). Even contemporary psychoanalysts who write of the spiritual barely mention it. There is one comprehensive psychoanalytic review on the subject (Akhtar, 2002). A few authors give it extensive consideration: Steiner (1996) 'Revenge and resentment in the "Oedipus situation"'; Cavell (2003) 'Freedom and forgiveness'; and Gottlieb (2004) 'Refusing the cure: Sophocles's Philoctetes and the clinical problems of self-injurious spite, shame and forgiveness'. There is one psychoanalytic book on the subject, by the American self-psychologist Durham (2000). The main British text is by integrative psychotherapists Ransley and Spy (2004).

The processes of forgiveness that are described are those of the inner world, to do with the development of a general capacity to forgive, rather than forgiving a particular offence. Akhtar (2002) suggests that forgiveness is active and comprises two mental operations: a changed attitude and the resolution of an unpleasant angry emotion within, the change in affect preceding that in relationship.

Despite their brevity, the references in Melanie Klein's and Winnicott's work suggest that they value the capacity to forgive as an important indicator of psychological health. In Klein's paper 'Love, guilt and reparation' (1937), she defines forgiveness as a change in affect, resulting from a full appreciation of psychic wounds, 'frustrations we had to bear', which leads to the capacity for self-love and then the capacity to love others. Also implied is that the capacity for forgiveness in a broader sense derives from this fundamental capacity to forgive early caregivers. There is a clear suggestion that forgiveness becomes possible through the working through in analysis of hate and guilt. Akhtar (2002, p. 187) emphasizes the importance of the earliest relationships, particularly the parental role in metabolizing aggression.

Other psychoanalytic authors describe similar processes without the word 'forgiveness'. For example, Balint's description of working with patients at the level of what he calls 'the basic fault' (1968, pp. 182–3), where he emphasizes the role of the therapeutic relationship in mediating internal change.

Often the psychoanalytic literature refers to self-psychology, especially Kohut's work on narcissism, to understand the difficulties in achieving forgiveness. Patton finds Kohut's (1972, 1984) work on defensive rage helpful in his pastoral counselling:

> The shame-prone individual does not recognize the person who injured them as a centre of independent initiative with whom he happens to be at cross-purposes. He is experienced only as an offended part of the shamed person's self . . . The transformation of this defensive rage does not take place by directly attacking it, but by relating empathically to the defending person.
>
> (Patton, 2000, p. 288)

Reviewing Patton's (1985) work Anderson concludes: 'We are most able to forgive those who have offended us when we become aware – because of our common human plight – that we are not in a position to forgive' (1986, p. 173).

Kernberg writes about forgiveness in couple relationships:

> Authentic forgiveness is an expression of a mature sense of morality, an acceptance of the pain that comes with the loss of illusions about self and other, faith in the possibility of the recovery of trust, the possibility that love will be recreated and maintained in spite of and beyond its aggressive components. Forgiveness based on naïveté or narcissistic grandiosity has much less value in reconstructing the life of a couple.
>
> (Kernberg, 1995, p. 103)

Cooper and Gilbert (2004), integrative psychotherapists, writing of their couple work, cite Buber (1966 [1923]) before drawing on the idea of 'whole object relating'. Like Kernberg, they link the problems with forgiving that bring a couple to therapy with failures in an underlying capacity to forgive: 'In order to achieve full forgiveness, the person "forgiving" will, in our view, need to practice "inclusion", defined by Buber as the capacity to be grounded in one's own experience and at the same time enter the world of the other.' They add that it may not be possible for some people to forgive 'until they have been able to repair their fractured early object relationships. In such cases couple work may not be the intervention of first choice' (Cooper & Gilbert, 2004, pp. 75–6).

Steiner writes about recovery from 'a psychic retreat based on resentment and grievance', which arises from Oedipal wounds. 'The patient comes to fear that the relinquishment of the grievance would lead to collapse and catastrophe and it seems to provide a sense of integration and protection from breakdown' (1996, p. 433).

I would suggest that research studies on early relationships may also inform an understanding of the developmental origins of the capacity to forgive. In the Strange Situation Test (Ainsworth et al., 1978), 'secure' infants protest on separation but can be pacified on reunion and return to exploratory play. Perhaps an early prototype of the capacity to forgive is the experience of a world where repair is possible. Beebe (2000) suggests that breaks and recoveries in vocal rhythm co-ordination between mothers and four-month-old infants occur even in second-by-second unconscious bodily attunements, and those in the mid range of co-ordination predict secure attachment eight months later. In other words, secure infants had early experiences of bearable cycles of disruption and repair.

Both Akhtar (2002) and Gottlieb (2004) refer to Fonagy's work on mentalization (e.g. Fonagy & Target, 1997). Fonagy's psychoanalytic perspective on the psychological concept of 'theory of mind' may prove another fruitful paradigm for understanding inner psychological processes creating the capacity to forgive.

Forgiveness in the consulting room

Stolorow describes introducing the idea of forgiveness to a patient in a state of rage with him. This had a powerful positive effect:

> When forgiveness is not experienced as a possibility, then hate is felt as absolute, totally engulfing . . . The possibility of forgiveness renders hate finite and temporary . . . hate cannot annihilate but can only temporarily anaesthetize the loving part of the self in relation to the hated person.
> (Stolorow, 1971, p. 102)

Akhtar (2002) writes of differing perspectives on whether the therapist should ever apologize to the patient, quoting case material where he found it productive. He notes Kernberg's (1976) idea of the patient requiring the analyst's forgiveness and Winnicott's (1947, p. 202) statement that, at the end of a long analysis that has burdened the analyst, the patient should know how much the work has cost.

Samuels (1989) writes of forgiveness in the consulting room and in society. He distinguishes between original morality and moral imagination, to be held in tension when coming to ethical decisions. Original morality holds moral certitude, whereas moral imagination contains intuitive and psychological understandings (ibid., p. 203). He suggests that the most important point is that forgiveness introduces a new element to a situation (ibid., p. 210).

Psychology, neuroscience and evolution

The main clinical psychology text (McCullough, Pargament & Thoresen, 2000) examines various stages in the process akin to mourning (Malcolm & Greenberg, 2000, p. 179) and different types of forgiveness. Mullet and Giraud (2000) review research by Enright, Santos and Al-Mabuk (1989) that links these to developmental stages in the perception of justice. Other researchers link the ability to forgive with personality traits, religious beliefs and aspects of the relationships in which forgiveness takes place.

Forgiveness is the subject of neuropsychological research. Farrow et al. (2001) used functional MRI to locate specific regions of the brain activated by empathic and forgivability [sic] judgements, contributing to social cohesion. Harris (2003) reviews MacLean's work (1985a, 1985b, 1990) on 'looking with feeling toward others' as a basic element in empathy. Neuro-imaging studies of social cognition, mother–infant communication, moral behaviour, forgiveness and trust are consistent with particular brain systems, particularly mirror neurons, being activated. An evolutionary perspective suggests forgiveness developing when the advantages of joint social action outweigh self-interest (Akhtar, 2002).

Forgiveness – positive or negative?

The idea of forgiveness as 'good' is implicit in much of the literature reviewed so far. Psychoanalytical theorists view the capacity for forgiveness as positive, emotionally mature and healthy. For example, Rey (1986), says: 'Only when the super-ego becomes less cruel, less demanding as well of perfection, is the ego capable of accepting an internal object which is not perfectly repaired, can accept compromise, forgive and be forgiven, and experience hope and gratitude' (cited in Akhtar, 2002, p. 30).

Much non-psychoanalytical writing also privileges forgiveness. The extensive self-help literature (e.g. Griffin, 2003) seems based on the assumption that failures to forgive are damaging to the individual. Most religious writing sees forgiveness as self-evidently positive and physiological research emphasizes the health benefits (Lawler et al., 2003; van Oyen Witvliet, Ludwig & van der Laan, 2001).

In a political context, forgiveness is acclaimed as an important ingredient in the recovery of individuals and societies that have suffered deeply. While recognizing a moral aspect of revenge, Henderson (2002) speaks of a new matrix created by forgiveness. Tutu (2004, 1999) writes of principles of restorative justice being rooted in the African concept of *ubuntu*. 'We are made for togetherness, to live in a delicate network of interdependence. The totally self-sufficient person is subhuman for none of us comes fully formed into the world . . . For *ubuntu*, the greatest good is communal harmony' (Tutu, 2004, pp. 4–5; concept also described in detail in Tutu, 1999, pp. 34–6). *Ubuntu* was one of many ideas behind the Truth and Reconciliation Commission in South Africa. In other writing (Tutu & Allen, 1994), Tutu emphasizes different perspectives on forgiveness. At Biko's funeral in 1977, he spoke of the importance of equal rights before reconciliation could take place. To church groups he refers more to Christian ethics of forgiveness and the need for apology. Holloway (2002, p. 86) says that there are some deeds so monstrous that they will drive us mad if we do not forgive them, because no proportional reparation is possible, no just accounting, nothing that makes any sense.

In contrast to a positive perspective, some writers reject the polarity between forgiveness and resentment. Ransley (2004), while accepting that bitterness is personally corrosive, does not believe forgiveness is always possible or appropriate and prefers the more ambiguous phrase 'letting go'. Safer (1999) believes that there is moral unforgiveness where justice is privileged above forgiveness and describes reformed unforgivers, who have forgiven too easily and then choose not to. Samuels also questions the forgiveness/blame dichotomy, describing 'a middle position in which I partly blame the malefactor or bad part of myself and partly forgive him or it' (1989, pp. 203–4).

Akhtar identifies and analyses eight psychopathological syndromes involving forgiveness. Some religious literature discusses with great sensitivity the struggles between forgiveness and justice, often referring to Wiesenthal's writing (1998). Particularly impressive is the symposium *After-words: Post Holocaust Struggles with Forgiveness, Reconciliation and Justice* (Patterson & Roth, 2004).

An important strand in the trauma literature emphasizes that demands for the victim to forgive can be entirely unjust. In Fortune and Marshall (2002), various authors analyse the way in which powerful organizations act unethically. Horsfield (2002) notes, of working with women abused by religious ministers, how often they are criticized for their failure to forgive, for 'holding a grudge':

> One should be alert to signals from survivors of assault that they cannot forgive . . . If one views forgiveness as an ethical issue, and women as moral agents, their action can be seen in a totally different light. It is not that the women are holding a grudge, but rather that they take seriously the values by which we are urged to live. The individual is placed in a situation where they cannot forgive without either denying their own worth or truth, giving in to the violence, denying the value of that which has been violated, or dehumanizing the assaulter.
>
> (Horsfield, 2002, p. 62)

Forgiveness and revenge

Many writers, such as Steiner (1996) and Gottleib (2004), include reflections on revenge when they write of forgiveness. Hillman writes of our desperate attempts to avoid the pain that results from betrayal – adopting strategies of revenge, denial, particularly of the meaning of the other, and cynicism. He states that trust in the real world must always contain the possibility of betrayal and, therefore, forgiveness (1964, pp. 78–9). Phillips reminds us that revenge gives us something to do and keeps hope alive (Phillips, 1998, cited in Holloway, 2002, p. 67).

Research methodology

The research paradigm was qualitative with heuristic, phenomenological and hermeneutic elements. Heuristic research has an introspective quality, and I began with reflections on my own practice and continued to reflect throughout the research. I was interested in the phenomenon of forgiveness as an important component of human relating in general, how it emerged in the psychoanalytic consulting room and its recent more frequent emergence as a topic in psychoanalytic, psychological and political discourse. The hermeneutic element was present in examining my research findings in detail to see if further interpretations could be made and ideas developed. I was also interested in moments in the research interviews where I, as researcher, made interpretations to the subject.

An approximately hour-long semi-structured interview, which would be recorded, was devised, based on literature reviews, personal reflections on practice and collegial discussions (Anderson, 2004a). The research was in two stages. In stage one I interviewed three psychoanalytic psychotherapists and three professional 'experts' in forgiveness – a hospital chaplain, a couple therapist and a forgiving survivor of political torture.

The following were the themes for the stage-one interviews:

- Definitions
- Relevance in the consulting room
- Concepts that stand in for the same phenomenon
- Theoretical understanding of why/how patients are/are not able/willing to forgive
- Practitioner's knowledge source, e.g. religious understanding, previous professional experience
- Inclusion in training
- Who forgives whom in the consulting room?
- Theory that gets in the way of thinking about forgiveness versus theory that facilitates it
- Myths/stories/images.

For the interviews with the experts, I asked similar questions, including how their work involved forgiveness and their understanding of the phenomenon and its importance.

From the analysis of the first stage, and further reflections, the semi-structured interview was revised and adapted. I then interviewed four psychotherapists – three psychoanalytic and one integrative.

These are the resulting additional themes for the stage-two interviews:

- Perception of the place of forgiveness in human relationships
- Perception of the place of forgiveness in intimate human relationships
- How are consciousness and forgiveness linked?
- Why might psychotherapists find it difficult to think about forgiveness in the consulting room?
- Why might psychotherapists have a resistance to using words that have a religious connotation?
- Questions to challenge a narrow/broad view of forgiveness.

For both stages an analysis of both form and content was made of both the written transcription and the audio version of the interviews. This allowed themes to emerge. The research had ethical committee approval.

Results

Most psychotherapists found forgiveness hard to define. They turned to dictionaries, or their knowledge of etymology. It seemed easier to say what forgiveness was not. They used descriptive terms like letting go, release, accepting, taking ownership. There was a sense of knowing what forgiveness means.

Without exception all psychotherapists thought forgiveness a vital aspect of human relating, particularly close relationships, and all thought the subject was relevant in their work. For most, this was an opinion they had come to before the research. Others were more cautious. One discovered its importance within the interview: 'When you asked me the question about how forgiveness is relevant in the consulting room, my spontaneous reaction was "no". Now I think it's what the whole thing is about in a way.'

My findings echo those of Ransley and Spy in *Forgiveness and the Healing Process: A Central Therapeutic Concern*. In my research, however, I did not encounter the immediate aversion to the topic that Ransley found in some practitioners: 'no such thing', 'yuk', 'dubious Christian notion' (2004, p. 53).

There were considerable overlaps between concepts that are common currency in the consulting room and the idea of forgiveness, of a specific offence or the development of the broader capacity. Psychological processes most mentioned were:

- The development of consciousness or insight
- The achievement of empathy and the ability to listen

- The development of the 'stage of concern'
- The move from the paranoid-schizoid to the depressive position
- An experience of being forgiven, perhaps self-forgiveness
- Owning one's part in a situation
- Similarity with grieving process
- Links with the capacity to feel compassion, perhaps through the experience of the therapist's compassion.

The psychoanalytical project was seen as allied to the task of 'love your neighbour as yourself'. In therapy, patients learned to love and forgive themselves and others, and might develop the capacity to understand more fully, and come to some negotiation between, different parts of themselves.

One psychotherapist spoke more about the difficulty of recognizing the need for forgiveness. The capacities both to be forgiven and to forgive required a sense of being in a world where repair was possible and it was possible to do something to create that repair. It was important to notice the unforgiving state as the person's emotional truth at the time.

Forgiveness was also seen as negative, conjuring up unhelpful ideas of sin; most patients felt bad enough already. All therapists had some examples of this. 'Forgiveness creates a situation of a surrendered acceptance of something that is fundamentally unacceptable and therefore de-potentiates possibilities for change, or makes people compliant with situations or circumstances that are problematic.'

Three psychotherapists mentioned the 'Ealing Vicarage case', where a priest 'forgave' the burglar who had raped his daughter; they could not see how this was forgiveness. It was premature and 'over his daughter's head', an example of omnipotent forgiveness without proper process and with little respect for the person who had been injured (see Kernberg's [1995] comments on forgiveness based on narcissistic grandiosity). Feelings of outrage and revenge might be an integral part of a developmental move to forgiveness. 'If you forgive too soon, you're stuck.' Some spoke of the interpersonal in the case of specific acts or omissions, the need for acknowledgement, in some cases apology, and for some patients the need for rituals of forgiveness and absolution.

With one exception, forgiveness had not been mentioned in analytic trainings. Psychotherapists spoke about it from their clinical and their life experience: 'I think the only way I've thought about it is when I've thought about it for myself.' Some had a religious background. Only one was formally practising faith.

None could cite the (few) major psychoanalytic references on forgiveness, but they did mention authors writing of allied processes, such as Winnicott, Gilligan (1999), who had written of shame as a major factor in violent offences, and Cox (1998), who had written about the subject of remorse. Apart from various religious texts, there was mention of novels, myths and films.

Most therapists could identify forgiveness occurring in the relationships inside and outside the consulting room. A therapist with experience of prison work spoke particularly of self-forgiveness. I was told clinical examples were given of forgiveness between patient and therapist, with the acknowledgement that being attacked by the patient was part of the experience of being a therapist as was the need to hold on to a non-retaliatory stance, yet not avoid the truth of the emotional encounter. Couple psychotherapists spoke of modelling repair and forgiveness between them in their own dialogues.

In discussing the relevance of different psychoanalytic theories, one therapist thought Freud's approach was muddled; an example was his accusation that Dora 'preferred revenge over love' (1953). Theories that emphasized only the dark side of human relating may not allow for positive aspects such as forgiveness, but also it was important to work with destructiveness and hatred. There might be hubris in psychoanalysis 'taking over' ideas such as forgiveness.

Conclusions

I am cautious about being authoritative in my conclusions because of the capacity for dogmatism on the subject to be unhelpful.

Forgiveness occurs when truth has broadened, in contrast to the 'narrow-mindedness of vengeful states' (Brenman, 1985). There is the capacity to bear complexity and ambivalence, where I am both good and bad; you have offended and hurt me but you have your good parts too, or your badness can be understood, and above all we are both part of the human race.

Forgiveness can free up relationships. Perhaps there is a freedom to be intimate or not; the unforgiving person may be bound in a particular kind of relating.

Is forgiveness passive or active? Much emerged from clinicians about what has to be given up, anger which might energize, a particular identity, the seductive simplicity of a story and more, which might suggest passivity. Nevertheless, there is also activity, things to do, repairs to be made.

What lies in the territory between vengeance and forgiveness? Even the most sophisticated psychoanalytic writers seem to polarize, equating lack of forgiveness with revenge. In moving papers like those of Gottleib (2004), Steiner (1996) and Brenman (1985), it is still as if there were no states between. The research practitioners, by contrast, recognized the nuances of states of unforgiveness. In my view, psychoanalytic writing needs to reflect this understanding, recognising that in some situations not to forgive is the healthier psychological state, and does not represent lack of emotional maturity. Holding outrage may provide a valid structure to the personality and to groups seeking justice in particular situations. Individuals may give up vengeance and the victim position, may develop empathy for the 'offender' and yet in certain situations not find it possible or appropriate to forgive. We need to engage our capacity to live with complexity.

Forgiveness cannot be an aim of psychoanalytic practice. Nevertheless, our theories, properly applied, can re-order and re-invigorate the concept. Above all the psychotherapist needs to be aware of their subjectivity in this area, both in general and when working with specific patients.

A personal benefit of the research in my clinical work was paradoxical, a greater capacity to understand situations in which patients remain in states of outrage and unforgiveness. I began to understand more about possible resistances to the idea in the consulting room and became less cautious about using the word 'forgiveness' where appropriate. My initial scepticism has moved to a greater understanding of the complexity of the subject and the need to take note of its contemporary social use.

Benjamin's idea (1988) that healthy human relating involves breakdowns from the recoveries to what she calls 'mutual assertion and recognition' were frequently on my mind in working with this subject.

Acknowledgements

Interviewing the survivor of political torture raised the idea of forgiveness as a gift. Working on this research was a gift and I am grateful to colleagues who took part in the research, and, in particular, to Dr Jacques China, my supervisor. This paper is dedicated to David Ervine, a Northern Ireland politician who died aged 53 on 8 January 2007. He was more of an 'expert' in practical forgiveness and reconciliation that most of us will ever be.

References

Ainsworth, M. D. S., Blehar, M. C., Waters, E. and Wall, S. (1978). *Patterns of attachment: A psychological study of the strange situation.* Hillsdale, NJ: Erlbaum.

Akhtar, S. (2002). Forgiveness: Origins, dynamics, psychopathology, and technical relevance. *Psychoanalytic Quarterly, 71*: 175–212.

Anderson, H. (1986). Human forgiveness is possible. *Journal of Pastoral Care and Counselling, 40*: 173–9.

Anderson, J. (2004a). Forgiveness: a singular achievement? Paper given at West Midlands Institute of Psychotherapy Conference 'After such knowledge – what forgiveness?', Leamington Spa, 3 April.

Anderson, J. (2004b). Exploring forgiveness within the psychoanalytic encounter. Guild of Psychotherapists and University of Hertfordshire. MA dissertation.

Balint, M. (1968). *The basic fault: Therapeutic aspects of regression.* London: Routledge.

Beebe, B. (2000). Systems models in development and psychoanalysis: The case of vocal rhythm coordination and attachment infant. *Mental Health Journal, 21*: 99–122.

Benjamin, J. (1988). *Bonds of love: Psychoanalysis, feminism and the problem of domination.* New York: Pantheon.

Blumenthal, D. R. (1996). Repentance and forgiveness. In Crosscurrents. Retrieved from http://www.aril.org/blumenthal.htm

Brenman, E. (1985). Cruelty and narrow-mindedness. *International Journal of Psycho-Analysis, 66*: 273–81.

Buber, M. (1966) [1923]. *I and Thou* (W. Kaufman, Trans.). New York: Touchstone.

Carmichael, K. (2003). *Sin and forgiveness: New responses in a changing world.* Aldershot: Ashgate.

Cavell, M. (2003). Freedom and forgiveness. *International Journal of Psycho-Analysis*, *84*: 515–31.
Cooper, J. and Gilbert, M. (2004). The role of forgiveness in working with couples. In *Forgiveness and the healing process: A central therapeutic concern* (C. Ransley and T. Spy, Eds.). Hove and New York: Brunner-Routledge.
Cox, M. (1998). *Remorse and reparation*. London and Philadelphia, PA: Jessica Kingsley.
Derrida, J. (2001). *On cosmopolitanism and forgiveness*. London: Routledge.
Durham, M. S. (2000). *The therapist's encounters with revenge and forgiveness*. London and Philadelphia, PA: Jessica Kingsley.
Eliot, T. S. (1920). Gerontion. In *The Collected poems of T. S. Eliot*. London: Faber.
Enright, R. D., Santos, M. J. D. and Al-Mabuk, R. (1989). The adolescent as forgiver. *Journal of Adolescence*, *12*: 95–110.
Farrow, T. F., Zheng, Y., Wilkinson, I. D., Spence, S. A., Deakin, J. F., Tarrier, N., Griffiths, P. D. and Woodruff, P. W. (2001). Investigating the functional anatomy of empathy and forgiveness. *Neuroreport*, *12*: 2433–8.
Fonagy, P. and Target, M. (1997). Attachment and reflective function: Their role in self-organisation. *Development and Psychopathology*, *9*: 679–700.
Fortune, M. and Marshall, J. (Eds.) (2002). *Forgiveness and abuse: Jewish and Christian reflections*. New York: Haworth Press. Also published as *Journal of Religion and Abuse, 4*.
Freud, S. (1953). Fragment of an analysis of a case of hysteria. In *The Standard Edition of the Complete Psychological Works of Sigmund Freud* (J. Strachey, Ed.) Vol. 7, 7–112. London: Hogath Press (original work published 1901).
Gilligan, J. (1999). *Violence: Reflections on our deadliest epidemic*. London and Philadelphia, PA: Jessica Kingsley.
Gottlieb, R. M. (2004). Refusing the cure: Sophocles's Philoctetes and the clinical problems of self-injurious spite, shame and forgiveness. *International Journal of Psycho-Analysis*, *85*: 669–89.
Griffin, K. (2003). *The forgiveness formula: Why letting go is good for you and how to make it happen*. London: Simon & Schuster.
Harris, J. C. (2003). Social neuroscience, empathy, brain integration, and neurodevelopmental disorders. *Physiology & Behavior*, *79*: 525–31.
Henderson, M. (2002). *Forgiveness: Breaking the chain of hate*. London: Grosvenor Books.
Hillman, J. (1964). Betrayal. Lecture 128, Guild of Pastoral Psychology, London. In *Loose ends: Primary papers in archetypal psychology* (J. Hillman, Ed.) pp. 63–81. New York and Zurich: Spring Publications, 1975.
Holloway, R. (2002). *On forgiveness: How can we forgive the unforgivable?* Edinburgh: Canongate.
Horsfield, P. (2002). Forgiving abuse: An ethical critique. In *Forgiveness and abuse: Jewish and Christian reflections* (M. Fortune and J. Marshall, Eds.). New York: Haworth Press. Also published as *Journal of Religion and Abuse, 4*.
Jung, C. G. (1952). Answer to job. In *Collected Works* Vol. 11 (H. Reed, M. Fordham and G. Adler, Eds.). London: Routledge & Kegan Paul.
Kernberg, O. F. (1976). *Object relations: Theory and clinical psychoanalysis*. New York: International Universities Press.
Kernberg, O. F. (1995). *Love relations: Normality and pathology*. New Haven, CT and London: Yale University Press.

Klein, M. (1937). Love, guilt and reparation. In *The writing of Melanie Klein: Love, guilt and reparation and other works 1921–1945*. London: The Hogarth Press.

Kohut, H. (1972). Thoughts on narcissism and narcissistic rage. In *The search for the self: Selected writings of Heinz Kohut* (P. H. Ornstein, Ed.) Vol. 2, pp. 615–58. New York: International Universities Press.

Kohut, H. (1984). *The nature of the psychoanalytic cure*. Chicago, IL: University of Chicago Press.

Lawler, K. A., Younger, J. W., Piferi, R. L., Billington, E., Jobe, R., Edmondson, K. and Jones, W. H. (2003). A change of heart: Cardiovascular correlates of forgiveness in response to interpersonal conflict. *Journal of Behavioral Medicine, 26*: 373–93.

McCullough, M. E., Pargament, K. I. and Thoresen, C. E. (2000). *Forgiveness: Theory, research and practice*. New York: Guilford Press.

MacLean, P. D. (1985a). Evolutionary psychiatry and the triune brain. *Psychological Medicine, 15*: 219–21.

MacLean, P. D. (1985b). *The triune brain in evolution*. New York: Plenum.

MacLean, P. D. (1990). Brain evolution leading to family, play, and the separation call. *Archives of General Psychiatry, 42*: 404–17.

Malcolm, W. M and Greenberg, L. S. (2000). Forgiveness as a process of change in individual psychotherapy. In *Forgiveness: Theory, research and practice* (M. E. McCullough, K. I. Pargament and C. E. Thoresen, Eds.). New York: Guilford Press.

Mullet, E. and Giraud, M. (2000). Developmental and cognitive points of view on forgiveness. In *Forgiveness: Theory, research and practice* (M. E. McCullough, K. I. Pargament and C. E. Thoresen, Eds.). New York: Guilford Press.

Patterson, D. and Roth, J. K. (2004). *After-words: Post Holocaust struggles with forgiveness, reconciliation and justice*. Seattle, WA and London: University of Washington Press.

Patton, J. (1985). *Is human forgiveness possible? A pastoral care perspective*. Nashville, TN: Abingdon Press.

Patton, J. (2000). Forgiveness in pastoral care and counselling. In *Forgiveness: Theory, research and practice* (M. E. McCullough, K. I. Pargament and C. E. Thoresen, Eds.). New York: Guilford Press.

Phillips, A. (1998). *The beast in the nursery*. London: Faber.

Ransley, C. (2004). Be cautious about forgiveness. In *Forgiveness and the healing process: A central therapeutic concern* (C. Ransley and T. Spy, Eds.). Hove and New York: Brunner-Routledge.

Ransley, C. and Spy, T. (2004). *Forgiveness and the healing process: A central therapeutic concern*. Hove and New York: Brunner-Routledge.

Rey, J. H. (1986). Reparation. *Journal of the Melanie Klein Society, 4*: 5–35.

Safer, J. (1999). Must you forgive? *Psychology Today*, July–August.

Samuels, A. (1989). *The plural psyche: Personality, morality and the father*. London and New York: Routledge

Snaith, N. H. (1950). Grace. In *A theological word book of the bible* (A. Richardson, Ed.). London: SCM Press.

Sobrino, J. (1986). Latin America: Place of sin and place of forgiveness. *Concilium, 184*: 12–21.

Steiner, J. (1996). Revenge and resentment in the 'Oedipus situation'. *International Journal of Psycho-Analysis, 77*: 433–43.

Stolorow, R. S. (1971). On forgiveness. *American Journal of Psychoanalysis, 31*: 102–3.

Tutu, D. (1999). *No future without forgiveness*. London: Rider Press.

Tutu, D. (2004). The Longford lecture. London, 16 February. Retrieved from: http://www.prisonreformtrust.org.uk/pdf%20files/LngfordLectTutu.pdf

Tutu, D. and Allen, J. (1994). *The rainbow people of God*. London, New York, Toronto, Sydney and Auckland: Doubleday Press.

van Oyen Witvliet, C., Ludwig, T. E. and van der Laan, K. L. (2001). Granting forgiveness or harboring grudges: Implications for emotion, physiology, and health. *Psychological Science, 12*: 117–23.

Wangh, S. (2005). Revenge and forgiveness in Laramie, Wyoming. *Psychoanalytic Dialogues, 15*: 1–16

Wiesenthal, S. (1998). *The sunflower: On the possibilities and limits of forgiveness* (H. J. Cajus and B. B. Fetamine, Eds.). New York: Schocken.

Williams, R. (2002). *Writing in the dust: Reflections on 11th September and its aftermath*. London: Hodder & Stoughton.

Winnicott, D. W. (1947). Hate in the countertransference. In *Collected Works: Through paediatrics to psychoanalysis*. London: The Hogarth Press and the Institute of Psychoanalysis, 1987.

7

MORTALITY IN THE CONSULTING ROOM

Susan Cowan-Jenssen

Human beings are the only creatures aware of their own mortality. In this paper, I review some of the literature about how we make sense of our awareness of death and its place in our psyche. I explore how the ritual of the therapy hour can act as a defence against an awareness of death, for both the client and the therapist. A clinical vignette describes how the denial of my own anxiety about mortality kept me from fully understanding the depth of my client's terror of living and dying.

> All the arts and sciences have their roots in the struggle against death
> (St Gregory of Nyssa, 4th century)

Mortality is a topic that many of us, therapists included, want to avoid. It was not until my mother died, aged 93, that the full inevitability of death hit me. None of us escape, not even me, and it was going to happen one day whether I accepted it or not. Since then I have wondered about my earlier blindness, or perhaps it is better called 'denial'. It is not as if I did not worry about the death of those dear to me. Loved ones seemed to be terrifyingly mortal, but somehow not me. Was there something here that needed to be addressed, a question mark to be raised over my apparent immortality?

Paradoxically, I am even something of a specialist on the subject, having lived with the threat of a potentially fatal illness within my own family, as well as having done an additional training on working with the dying and bereaved. But this has not made me an expert on my own death and the area I write about is the unwelcome, almost disassociated, knowledge that 'none of us escape'. Human beings are the only animals that consciously know about their own death. How does that knowledge impact on us? How easy is it for us to pick up the coded anxieties of our clients and the subtext of death when we are not that keen to look at this issue ourselves? This article is about the discovery of my own blind spot regarding my mortality and how it impacted in the consulting room.

First, though, I want to outline my exploration of the literature, which helped me to identify and understand that we all live with the knowledge and fear that we must die. One of the first known texts on the subject of death was written some

4,000 years ago in the Babylonian epic Gilgamesh. The author speaks of the death of his friend Enkidu and his realization that he too will die. 'Now what sleep is this that has taken hold of thee? Thou hast become dark and canst not hear me. When I die shall I not be like unto Enkidu? Sorrow enters my heart, I am afraid of death' (cited in Heidel, 1946).

Yalom (1980) noted the relative dearth of literature in psychotherapy on the subject of death or rather on how each of us, individually, comes to deal with the reality of our own mortality. Irwin Hoffman (1998) made the same observation nearly twenty years later. There are exceptions to this of course. Harold Searles (1961) wrote of his own death anxiety and his belief that it is a profound, disintegrating fear of death that fuels psychosis. Recently the Italian psychoanalyst Franco de Masi (2004) has written about our anxieties in the light of death. His work hopefully indicates a change, since until now the clinical literature, with the exception of the existentially orientated psychotherapists, seems to give the subject of mortality a wide berth. There have been a variety of explanations for this. One reason given is that Freud uncharacteristically had no clear theory on death anxiety (Baumann, 1992; Becker, 1973; Lifton, 1979; Yalom 1980). For Becker, Freud got lost when he talked of 'death instinct' and not 'death fear'. He believed that Freud used the idea of a death instinct to shore up a libido theory that was proving inadequate as an explanation of human motivation.

The 'death instinct' tries to explain man's capacity for destructiveness in the language of instinct, rather than the language of relationship. For Freud, the death instinct represented the organism's desire to die and to return to a former state of non-being. This can be avoided by the outward direction of this instinct so that the desire to die becomes the desire to kill. Thus evil and violence can be explained as arising from the instinctual. Rank (1972 [1936]) had a more relational perspective. He saw violence arising from fear, from knowing terror for one's own life, and thus that fear of one's own death can be reduced by violence against the other: 'the death fear of the ego is lessened by the killing, the sacrifice, of the other; through the death of the other, one buys oneself free from the penalty of dying, of being killed.' It would follow that the greater the anxiety, the greater would be the temptation to allay that anxiety through brutality. What we know about how soldiers behave in war situations would seem to bear this out.

Freud, living through the First World War, wrote, perhaps not surprisingly, on our ambivalence and confusion about death:

> We showed an unmistakable tendency to put death on one side, to eliminate it from life. We tried to hush it up . . . it is indeed impossible to imagine our own death; and whenever we attempt to do so we can perceive that we are in fact still present as spectators. Hence the psychoanalytic school could venture the assertion that at bottom no one believes in his own death, or, to put the same thing another way, that in the unconscious every one of us is convinced of his own immortality.
> (Freud, 1915, p. 289)

He ended his paper with the words: 'We recall the old saying: *Si vis pacem, para bellum*. If you want to preserve peace, arm for war. It would be in keeping with the times to alter it: *Si vis vitam, para mortem*. If you want to endure life, prepare yourself for death' (Freud, 1915, p. 300).

Freud did not place the fear of death at the core of primary anxiety since he believed there was no place for the reality of death in the unconscious. Therefore, despite his words on the importance of acknowledging death, he could not put death at the heart of our psyche. He argued that it was impossible for us to conceptualize our own non-being. It seems a weak conclusion for such a central subject. For Freud the two primary causes of anxiety are loss of mother (separation anxiety) and loss of the penis (castration anxiety). He believed that the fear of death was analogous to the fear of castration: 'Castration can be pictured on the basis of the daily experience of the faeces being separated from the body or on the basis of losing the mother's breast at weaning. But nothing resembling death can ever have been experienced' (Freud, 1926, p. 130). However, it is not really convincing to argue that loss of faeces or weaning are more powerful signifiers than our innate sense of non-being. What both castration and abandonment surely signify is death. An abandoned infant will die and castration is the annihilation of the continuity of the species.

Melanie Klein wrote of her disagreement with Freud's conclusion: 'The fear of death reinforces castration fear and is not "analogous" to it . . . since reproduction is the essential way of counteracting death, the loss of the genital would mean the end of the creative power which preserves and continues life' (1948, p. 117). However, she used the concept of the death instinct and pushed it further. She argued that, if there is a universal unconscious death instinct, then, if humans are to survive, there would also have to be a terror of this instinct:

> I would also think that if we assume the existence of a death instinct, we must also assume that in the deepest layers of the mind there is a response to this instinct in the form of fear of annihilation of life. The danger arising from the inner working of the death instinct is the first cause of anxiety.
>
> (Klein, 1948, p. 116)

However, Klein still operated within an instinctual rather than a relational model. The anxiety is generated from within, rather than from without. Schwartz (2000) argued that what Klein was observing, when she described fears of disintegration and annihilation, was toddlers in distress who were experiencing acute separation anxieties that were the result of failures in their early attachments. The work of Fairbairn, Winnicott and Bowlby would show that, above all, we humans are relational and, when the outside world is not safe enough, i.e. when parenting is not 'good enough', then the infant will be prey to devastating and overwhelming feelings. This is not to say that anxieties about mortality are not inevitably part of living, but arguably the ability to deal with them, without disintegration, ultimately depends on having had adequate stable attachments when young and vulnerable.

One of the few psychoanalysts who developed a theory on mortality and the human condition was Otto Rank. He posited an existential view, which differed from Freud's instinctual oppositions. For Rank the conflict was not between instincts and society but between the wish for the lost symbiosis of the womb and the need for the ego to grow into its own uniqueness (Rank, 1972 [1936]; Menaker, 1982). However, in the journey towards individuation man comes to know his own finiteness. To be born is to know death and this is a basic fact of human life. The relationship between life and death is expressed in Rank's idea of the 'will' phenomenon and the paradox at the heart of human existence. We need closeness and love in order to survive and equally we need to separate for development. Too much closeness stifles us and Rank calls this the 'death' fear since it crushes individuation and development. Yet too much distance can lead to fear of abandonment and isolation and Rank equates this fear with the 'life' fear. Thus the fear of separation is matched by the fear of merger:

> The neurotic must punish himself ... This is not merely because he can only grant himself this or that pleasure satisfaction thus, but because he must bribe life itself, for which, according to Schopenhauer's deep insight, we all pay with death ... The neurotic then is a man whom extreme fear keeps from accepting this basis of life, and who accordingly seeks in his own way to buy himself free from his guilt. He does this through a constant restriction of life (restraint through fear); that is, he refuses the loan (life) in order to escape the payment of the debt (death).
> (Rank, 1972 [1936], p. 126)

Searles says something similar when describing the difficulty schizophrenic patients have in feeling alive: 'One need not fear death so long as one feels dead anyway; one has, subjectively, nothing to lose through death' (1961, p. 495).

Rank talked of 'will' and guilt. To 'will' is to individuate, and to separate from the other and to live one's own unique destiny. It requires a healthy ruthlessness and, as we separate and leave the other behind, we feel guilty. It means choosing to live, to stand out even if others are in retreat. What strikes me about this idea of guilt is how it can exist only because of our relationship to others. It occurs because we are creatures who above all are 'object seeking', and guilt arises not principally from hateful feelings but from loving feelings. This is very different from the Freudian and Kleinian view and marks the beginning of a relational psychology.

Rank also identified the guilt of not living one's life, of failing to individuate, of retreating from relationships. This is a failure to fulfil one's potential. Thus guilt is inevitably part of the human condition because we love and need but have to separate and as we experience separation so we will know anxiety. This is the significance of the birth trauma, for in the act of birth lies the imprint of the separation trauma. For Rank, the human dilemma was not the Freudian conflict between the sexual and the social but a conflict between the longing to merge and remain the child and the need to emerge and become the adult in one's own life.

Fully living in the present requires the acceptance that life is finite. We might not want to think about it but without death our lives would be experienced very differently. This is beautifully captured in lines from Berhman's adaptation of Giraudoux's *Amphitryon 38*.

> Jupiter, the immortal god, takes on the physical and mortal form of Amphitryon in order to make love to his exquisite wife. He talks to his fellow god Mercury about the experience and how he felt a distance between them when she used expressions such as 'when I was a child' or 'when I'm old'. He says of the gods, 'But we miss something, Mercury – undoubtedly we miss something – the poignance of the transient – the intimation of mortality – that sweet sadness of grasping at something you cannot hold.'
>
> (Giraudoux, 1938, pp. 40–1)

Traditionally, religious beliefs and practice have helped us to understand and bear the fact of our mortality. Rituals have developed that serve both to express and to contain the pain of death. The anthropologist Hocart (1954) studied the role of ritual in primitive culture. The role of ritual is to take control over the material world and establish what is in fact an illusory consistency. The priest was the person in charge of meaning and understanding. Becker (1975), a cultural anthropologist, argued that all cultural forms are sacred in that they seek the perpetuation and redemption of human existence, and the therapeutic endeavour is no exception. It cannot be denied that the therapy process is replete with ritual. The practice of maintaining a 50-minute hour, at the same time and in the same place, creates a ritual that is not open to change. If therapy is to be an alive, engaging experience then it seems to me that we also have to consider our use of ritual in the therapy process. Hoffman (1998) discusses, from a relational perspective, the dialectic between ritual and spontaneity in therapy and how there is a need for both. Excessive ritual deadens but excessive spontaneity can lead to lack of containment, irresponsibility and little space for reflection. A useful therapy experience would require both elements.

How do we work with issues surrounding death when both patient and therapist struggle with their feelings of mortality and the wish to deny the painful reality of their mortality and ageing? How do we walk the tightrope between ritual and openness when, arguably, one of the roles of ritual in therapy is to keep the reality of uncertainty and mortality at bay? The use of the therapy frame becomes crucial in this drama. Does the security of the therapy hour provide the safety needed to face our terrors or does it provide an illusion of consistency that distracts us from our painful fears? Do we think adequately about the necessity and meaning of endings?

Lacan and Langs have both written about the need to confront death in the course of therapy, but they reach opposing clinical conclusions about the role of the therapy hour. Yet neither of them appears to acknowledge the priest-like role they have allotted to themselves. Lacan believed that sessions should have no fixed time limit so that the patient would be made aware of the fact that there were no certainties in life. Stuart Schneiderman wrote a humorous account of his analysis with Lacan, whom he admired enormously. He describes coming to a session full of anticipation, eager to communicate his thoughts:

> You want the analyst to hear this because it is really important. But no sooner have you broached the topic, no sooner have the words identifying it passed through your lips, than Lacan all of a sudden rises from his chair and pronounces the session to be over, finished, done with ... When it's over it's over, no appeal, no going back, no revising or reconsidering.
>
> (Schneiderman, 1984, p. 132)

While this might seem an intriguing idea, it gives the analyst enormous power. Lacan warns against colluding with the patient's wish that the analyst takes the role of the 'one who is supposed to know' but he seems to have relished the role of the 'one' who knows when it is time to end a session. The 'anti-ritual' stance of no set time for the duration of a session still allows only one person to be timekeeper. The lack of negotiation seems to be a real danger for the patient. The analyst might be mirroring the inevitability of death where there is no compromise, but he/she does not possess divine power and moreover is no more powerful than the patient as regards mortality.

Langs (1997) proposes a different way of confronting death anxieties in his patients but I think, like Lacan, he 'deifies' the analytic frame and thus the analyst as guardian of the frame. He believes that the therapist's own defences against death can prevent this issue being properly addressed in therapy. Asking questions and active engagement with the patient are approaches that he sees as 'designed to eliminate or minimize death-related derivative or encoded expressions'. Anything that dilutes the analytic rigour is a distraction. Since this would condemn any notion of 'relational' psychotherapy, it is interesting to look at this further. He argues that the frame of the therapy is non-negotiable. Indeed he says of frame modification that 'I have offered abundant evidence that therapists' frame breaks are unconsciously experienced by their patients as seductive, assaultive, and murderously destructive'. Langs would argue that by making the frame non-negotiable you are faced with something like death. Therefore it will provoke death anxiety, which would need to be interpreted. But the sacrosanct nature of the therapy hour is an illusion; it is an artefact created by the mortal therapist and like any ritual it is an attempt to master what cannot be mastered. The therapist here is like a priest who has deified the therapy frame as greater than both therapist and client. While Langs's position is quite extreme, the sanctity of the therapy hour is often held up as an ideal in classical psychoanalysis. A highly regarded Kleinian analyst, when asked recently what she felt most proud of in her long career, replied that she was most proud of having held the integrity of the analytic frame.

The time allotted to a therapy session is inevitably limited and each ending is also telling us that nothing lasts forever. Does it need to be elevated to a sacred 50 minutes or imperiously shortened? We hope our patients are able to reflect with us on the content of the material they bring to the session. But are we open to the notion that the setting we provide could also be reflected on and questioned. And, if not, why not? I think the great challenge for therapists when faced with death and death anxiety is not to retreat behind the frame and take refuge in ritual and authority. The therapist is in a more powerful position than the patient. One of the reasons that power is so attractive is that it makes us feel special. The more power one has, the more special one can feel, and the more special one feels, the more immortal one is in fantasy. The authority and power of being a therapist, however benign, is enormously comforting and protective. For our patients we are indeed special and thus it is crucial to keep the power balance in therapy under scrutiny and open to discussion. Working within a relational framework means being willing to surrender power when it is necessary. Only by staying with our mutual humanity and mortality can we really be in touch with our patients. While this is an ideal, the following clinical vignette is an example of how tempting it can be to use power in the form of therapeutic distance to keep discomfort at bay.

Peter was a mature student in his late twenties who came for therapy suffering from depression and social anxiety. He put this down to his having suffered from Irritable Bowel Syndrome (IBS) for the previous eighteen months. His irritable bowel had been extensively treated but with limited success. He had gone to both conventional and alternative doctors and had been told he was intolerant of certain foods. As a consequence, his diet had become very limited, which also contributed to his social unease in the company of others.

He blamed his IBS for most of his anxieties but it soon emerged that his social and work problems predated his IBS. He was a lonely man who still lived at home with his parents when he was not at university. He was studying Greek civilization and was finding his studies immensely demanding.

His father was Greek, and had moved to the UK as a young adult; his mother was English. The father had come from a very poor family and had worked incredibly hard to make good. Peter's mother helped in the business they created, and both parents had to spend a lot of time working away from home. At the age of 13 Peter went to boarding school. It was not a success. Although he was good academically, he was very miserable at school, missing his home and feeling isolated. Pleas to his parents to take him away were not heeded. Peter had two younger sisters who were educated locally. He felt rivalrous with both, not helped by the fact that he felt they were favoured as more lively and interesting. One of his sisters has a serious alcohol problem.

His relationship with his father had never been close. His father was a chronically anxious man who was intensely ambitious. Nothing his son achieved was ever quite good enough. Peter was a very talented swimmer and his father pushed and interfered and spoiled his son's enjoyment of the sport. He felt closer to his mother who sounded as if she was permanently exhausted from working in the family business and raising children. An elderly aunt came to live with the family in order to help out, and Peter felt close to her. He described his mother as controlling and sarcastic. She could fly off the handle and rage at Peter for being 'useless', especially in his teenage years. Although she gave Peter more emotional support than his father did, she could be very unreliable. A theme to which Peter often returned was her chronic lateness. She was unable to get him to school on time, and he would get into trouble with the teachers. More disturbing was her lateness when she was visiting him at boarding school. She could be several hours late. He would hide outside the school grounds, terrified that his friends should see that his mother was late. He felt mounting anxiety for her safety and increasing distress at her carelessness. He felt an immense sense of shame.

When I started seeing Peter he was studying at university but felt very isolated. He had little contact with the others in his department. His social anxieties were preventing him from making friends. They centred on him being in situations where people might find him boring or awkward. He would not know what to say. He blamed his IBS for all his problems because he felt too ill or exhausted to go out or to do his academic work.

He found his symptoms distressing and all-absorbing. It was as if the closest relationship he had was with his bowel tract. We spent a long time looking at different aspects of his social anxieties and his bowel symptoms, but he was always very concrete in his conclusions. His IBS was the reason he was having problems and his irritable bowel was due to food intolerances. He could be obsessional about his symptoms and he would ruminate on them for hours at a time. Thomas Szasz, in *Pain and pleasure* (1957), explored the idea of the use of the body as an object. The body and its symptoms can be related to and thought about as a way of defending against loneliness and despair. In lieu of helplessness, a fantasy control is established. Feelings of helplessness that are expressed psychosomatically are generally seen in psychoanalysis as originating in the early child/mother bond.

Joyce McDougall, in her book *Theatres of the body* (1989), writes of understanding infant experiences as being registered on a body that does not 'think' with words. Intense emotions, which can be felt as life threatening by the baby, are experienced physically. Thus a somatic symptom like IBS can represent a trauma with its roots in the early child/mother relationship where the mother, for whatever reason, has not been able to provide the containment needed to help the infant digest its emotional turmoil. Mara Sidoli (2000) expresses something similar in her idea that psychosomatic clients use their bodies as containers and signifiers.

It is not clear what did happen in Peter's early years but he did learn that his parents had to get married because of his conception. His parents had to move around in the early years due to his father's work, and his mother, young and inexperienced, had to live in strange places with a small baby. What became apparent was that he did not have an internal experience of a mother who was soothing; on the contrary he had identified with a highly critical, anxious parent.

Peter suffered physical symptoms as an expression of distress from an early age. When he was ten years old he was bullied at school and developed tummy ache. The family doctor diagnosed this as depression but Peter's mother found this difficult to comprehend. Physical ailments were recognized and accepted but the family culture seemed quite blind to emotions. In his sessions with me, he found it very difficult to get beyond the 'legitimate' physical symptoms. He expressed anxiousness, loneliness and a sense of failure but somehow always came back to his bowels.

Even when his symptoms got increasingly better, through a surgical procedure, he was still overwhelmed by a sense of failure and shame, which he continued to link to his illness. At times it felt as if we were like two deaf people shouting at each other. I was trying to uncover the meaning of the symptom and he experienced my attempts to introduce possible interpretations for his symptoms as unhelpful and lacking in empathy. I felt increasingly removed, exasperated, unhelpful and unempathic.

Additionally, an erotic and hostile element started to emerge in the transference. Peter often had a slightly superior smile on his face even when talking about sad issues. He would make jokes about older women but deny that there was anything significant in the joking. In one session, he had tears in his eyes because he was thinking that one day I would be old and unattractive. I felt perplexed and unmoved by the tears; this felt to me like hostility masquerading as concern. Over time he did acknowledge that he was angry that he found me attractive and in his mind I triumphed in this knowledge at his expense. He even feared that I might joke about him with colleagues. His desires felt humiliating and he was able to link this to his painful relationship with his ambivalent and very sarcastic mother.

Yet little seemed to be changing for him in therapy. Some sessions seemed very productive but then he would return to making inappropriate smutty jokes and complaining that I did not understand his symptoms. He desperately wanted intimacy, yet feared it with equal intensity. He felt a mixture of rage and despair when around women he found attractive and, feeling persecuted by these feelings, he retaliated. I wondered about my own reaction to his 'jokes'. Finding him intrusive, I wanted to push him away. I thought of this in terms of 'role-responsiveness' (Sandler, 1976), feeling like his mother, who seems at times to have felt greatly exasperated with him but who was also a source of comfort. Try as I might to give a meaning to how I experienced him and our relationship, he found it hard to see that I was not just humourless, rejecting and cold. He would at times admit to his anger and longings to be close to me but essentially he believed that if I was nicer and understood his bowel symptoms better all would be well. I was thinking his therapy was going nowhere: He had irritable bowels, albeit much improved, and I was just irritable. Like him, I was stuck, somewhat at a loss but in this situation he was at a disadvantage. At times like these it is hard not to pathologize the client as a way of letting oneself off the hook. Lacan's view is that the 'inability to sustain a praxis in an authentic manner results, as is usually the case with mankind, in the exercise of power' (1979 [1958]).

Peter was trying to communicate something that I was not hearing and he felt powerless. He knew that he was making me angry but could not stop himself. Betty Joseph describes something like this process in her paper 'Addiction to near-death': 'These patients will try to create despair in the analyst and then get him to collude with the despair or become actively involved by being harsh, critical or in some way or another verbally sadistic to the patient' (1982). This could describe what Peter was doing and how I was feeling but it clearly puts all the onus of the pathology onto him. As a subjective participant in the process, what was I bringing to the table? In my 'clinical detachment', I kept the upper hand, trying to resist whatever he was trying to draw me into. With this position, I was hanging on to both my safety and my authority but this hindered me from really understanding what he was struggling with. I was not open to the subtext of his terror of living and dying, his panic at living with an unreliable body. He was right: I did not understand the meaning of his symptoms for him. He needed to know whether I could live in an ageing body that would one day fail me and thus help him with his own vulnerable body. He needed to feel he had a future even in a mortal body.

Matters eventually came to a climax when he made one more seemingly innocuous remark about how come I had had children at such an old age. (He had phoned me at home to cancel a session and by chance had spoken to my son and realized he was young.) I suddenly felt furious. He again claimed this was a meaningless, jocular remark. Suddenly I said, almost without thinking, that I wondered what he was getting out of therapy. If he felt I was helping him, then I was happy to continue working, but if it was not helping him, then I thought he could probably find someone else who could be more useful. I was quite shocked at myself delivering this ultimatum. I repeated that I was not saying I would not work with him but I wanted him to think about whether the process we were engaged in was of any real help. If it was, we would continue but if it was not, we should stop.

I thought hard about my response and worried that the ultimatum was a bullying tactic, i.e. 'behave or go'. There was certainly that element there but, in retrospect, I think he experienced my therapeutic distance as far more punitive than my anger. At least now I had shown him how I was really feeling. Was this what Winnicott called 'objective hate'? In his paper 'Hate in the countertransference' (1949), he explores the inevitability that, along with love, the 'mother hates her infant from the word go'. He is also describing what happens in therapy, the levels of feelings, often fear and hate, that coexist with love. Slavin and Kriegman (1998) write: 'The fear and hate that Winnicott finds central to human relating seem to arise from what we see as the "psychic undertow" that operates between any two distinct beings who are attempting to interact in an intimate way.' The client risks much more emotionally than the therapist and has to discover if it is worth the risk of fully engaging in this relationship.

Through adaptive probing, patients may palpably sense how they can influence (deconstruct) us. They can sense that, when faced with this challenge, we put ourselves back together (in a somewhat different way) in the context of our particular relationship with them:

> A genuine renegotiation, reintegration (an increased experience of 'realness') is far more likely to occur when our patients see what happens when – tapping into the faultlines of our identity, our conflicts – they take us someplace that is obviously hard for us to go. But we go there and often change in the process, because having a relationship with them requires it.
>
> (Slavin & Kriegman, 1998, p. 279)

The next day Peter telephoned, anxious to say that his life at university was really very terrible and lonely. He felt like a complete failure in all aspects of his life. He admitted that he had been 'pissing about' and deliberately provocative but did not know why. We looked at this over the next months and I had to acknowledge, both to him and myself, that his personal remarks had got to me. I had a considerable investment in my own ability 'to roll with the punches', as it were, and my owned vulnerability opened up the possibility that he too could explore the failure he felt in virtually every aspect of his life. This in turn helped me more fully to comprehend the horror and shame he felt around his body.

Yet it still took me some time to make the connection between his fear of ageing, of death, and my own anxieties. It took the death of my mother to put me in touch with my own mortality and fears of decay. I suddenly realized that the points where I felt most angry were all to do with getting old. His sadness for when I would be old and unattractive, his comment about having children late, a question about whether menopausal women enjoyed sex. (The chill that entered my voice when he asked that question could have refrozen ice caps.) Yes, they were aggressive, intrusive and sadistic, but he was also asking me about bodies. How did I live in an ageing body? How did I keep a sense of future when I had a body that was decaying and would die? Rank believed that sexual conflict is universal because it represents an anxiety about a lived-in, fragile body. Therefore, for a child, questions about sex can also be questions about ageing and death.

Dodi Goldman (2003) wrote that, for some people, 'there is nothing more shameful than the contingency and finitude of human life, the intractability of our limits.' Hoffman (1998) describes this as an existential affront. Human life is a poor substitute for an imagined life that does not get snuffed out so arbitrarily. We are not consulted about our conception and we are not consulted about our death.

He uses the wonderful expression that 'we are all adult endurers of the ongoing abuse of the human condition.' For some, like Peter, it is a narcissistic wound.

Our relationship continued to change and a greater sense of trust was established on both sides. He began writing me a letter that would arrive on the day of the session. In this way, he was keeping our work in mind in the interval between our sessions. Although he was much more open, he still found it difficult in my presence to be fully vulnerable. The letter was a way of letting me know what was happening and what he was feeling between sessions. It provided a physical as well as a psychic link.

He still feared for his health and wrote that 'I'm worried about my future survival.' He wanted closeness but admitted he could feel disgust at people's bodies. 'I've become aware that the rest of humanity seems repulsive to me.' In another letter he said, 'I've been aware recently that I find it difficult to make connections with people. I don't seem to feel much warmth for other people.' But he admitted feeling that if he did let people close they might expect something from him. He spent hours daydreaming and then hated himself for not concentrating on his work. Gradually he could admit that to relinquish his world of fantasy, his lonely relationship with his body, and enter the real world of active engagement felt terrifying.

Just how lethal and murderous he felt his bowel symptoms to be was clear to both of us when he gave voice to the illness in one session. 'I am killing you. I control you totally. You are in my power. I have power of life and death over you. I was stronger than you and maybe I can be stronger than you again. I can make you stop being human.' I wondered why he thought he had merited such cruelty. He answered that it had happened because he was bad. If he was perfect it could not have happened. I replied that then he would not have been human and vulnerable. He said that he did not want to be mortal. 'I don't want to grow old and die.' I raised the idea of forgiving oneself for being mortal and not seeing it as a failure. He replied that he could start to imagine the possibility of that. 'But it scares me. I feel that if I isolate myself from others, I won't die. But then I feel lonely.'

And so Peter put his finger on our eternal dilemma. If one lives avoiding death, one cannot truly feel alive. Our knowledge of death cannot be completely denied and so 'we are all destined to suffer emotionally and experience a basic sadness' (Firestone, 1987). We have to be able to mourn this anticipated loss in order to experience fully the life that we have. This is a lesson that I needed to learn along with Peter.

References

Baumann, Z. (1992). *Mortality, immortality*. Palo Alto, CA: Stanford University Press.
Becker, E. (1973). *The denial of death*. New York: The Free Press.
Becker, E. (1975). *Escape from evil*. New York: The Free Press.
de Masi, F. (2004). *Making death thinkable*. London: Free Association Books.

Firestone, R. (1987). *The fantasy bond*. New York: Human Sciences Press.
Freud, S. (1915). Thoughts for the time on war and death. *SE, 14*: 275–300.
Freud, S. (1926). Inhibitions, symptoms and anxiety. *SE, 20*: 77–175.
Giraudoux, J. (1938). *Amphitryon 38*. (S. N. Behrman, Trans.) New York: Dramatists Play Service.
Goldman, D. (2003). The outrageous prince: Winnicott's uncure of Masud Khan. British Journal of Psychotherapy, *19*(4).
Heidel, A. (1946). *The Gilgamesh epic and Old Testament parallels*. Chicago, IL: Chicago University Press.
Hocart, A. M. (1954). *Social origins*. London: Watts.
Hoffman, I. (1998). *Ritual and spontaneity in the analytic process*. Hillsdale, NJ: The Analytic Press.
Joseph, B. (1982). Addiction to near-death. *International Journal of Psychoanalysis, 63*: 449–56.
Klein, M. (1948). A contribution to the theory of anxiety and guilt. *International Journal of Psycho-Analysis, 29*: 114–23.
Lacan, J. (1979) [1958]. *Ecrits: A selection*. London: Tavistock/Routledge.
Langs, R. (1997). *Death anxiety and clinical practice*. London: Karnac.
Lifton, R. J. (1979). *The broken connection*. New York: Simon & Schuster.
McDougall, J. (1989). *Theatres of the body*. London: Free Association Books.
Menaker, E. (1982). *Otto Rank: A rediscovered legacy*. New York: Columbia University Press.
Rank, O. (1972) [1936]. *Will therapy and truth and reality*. (J. Taft, Trans.) New York: Knopf.
Sandler, J. (1976). Countertransference and role-responsiveness. *International Journal of Psychoanalysis, 3*: 43–7.
Schneiderman, S. (1984). *Jacques Lacan: Death of an intellectual hero*. Cambridge, MA: Harvard University Press.
Schwartz, J. (2000). Commentary on David Black: Beyond the death drive detour – how can we deepen our understanding of cruelty, malice, hatred, envy and violence? British Journal of Psychotherapy, *18*(2).
Searles, H. F. (1961). Schizophrenia and the inevitability of death. *Psychiatric Quarterly, 35*: 361–5. In *Collected papers on schizophrenia and related subjects*. London: The Hogarth Press and the Institute of Psychoanalysis, 1965.
Sidoli, M. (2000). *When the body speaks*. London: Brunner-Routledge.
Slavin, M. O. and Kriegman, D. (1998). *Why the analyst needs to change*. Hillsdale, NJ: The Analytic Press.
Szasz, T. (1957). *Pain and pleasure*. New York: Basic Books.
Winnicott, D. (1949). Hate in the countertransference. *International Journal of Psycho-Analysis, 30*.
Yalom, I. (1980). *Existential psychotherapy*. New York: Basic Books.

8
RELATIONAL PSYCHOTHERAPY IN EUROPE
A view from across the Atlantic

Lewis Aron

It is a delight and a privilege for me to comment on the chapters written by (for the most part) European colleagues. It is also somewhat disorienting for me to hear a common language so familiar and yet spoken with a different accent, and so having the opportunity to regain my own orientation seems to me a good place to begin my comments.

My understanding of 'relational psychoanalysis', as I am accustomed to using the term, has been shaped by my personal experiences with the development of this form of psychoanalysis from its beginnings in New York in the 1980s. I described the history of this development in the first chapter of my book, *A meeting of minds* (1996). While I will not review this history in detail here there are several aspects of it that I will refer to and elaborate on in this context. But to start, it is worth noticing that the term I am familiar with is 'relational psychoanalysis' rather than 'relational psychotherapy'. There was never any question, within the circles in which I was associating, that this burgeoning of interest in relational theory and practice was a development within psychoanalysis rather than outside it. It was unquestionably of importance to the founders of this 'school', once it began to be thought of as a 'school', that is, that it was a school of psychoanalysis. It may be worth reviewing here that, when Greenberg and Mitchell, in what became an instant classic, *Object relations in psychoanalytic theory* (1983), used the term 'relational' they were referring to a group of theorists who themselves had neither self-defined as relational nor saw their own work as related to others or to any movement or trend that would later be regarded as relational. It was only Greenberg and Mitchell (1983), as historians and scholars of the development of psychoanalytic theory, who had categorized them retrospectively as belonging to the relational turn in psychoanalysis.

However, in the years immediately following the 1983 publication of their text, and certainly by 1988, the term relational was being used in a new way. Now it was being used explicitly and purposefully as a banner for a new school of psychoanalysis, a new movement that was being contrasted with classical theory and practice. This change in usage can be most easily seen in Mitchell's (1988) *Relational concepts in psychoanalysis*, which began to move in this direction. In his 1988 work, Mitchell extended his earlier collaborative work with Greenberg and moved beyond his position as a historian and scholar of psychoanalysis. Now he introduced two new innovations. First, he developed a framework, a structure to contain, or a plan for how to elaborate, a relational theory. Mitchell established a framework or a schema, a plan of action, that allowed a thinker to integrate relational concepts from a wide variety of different psychoanalytic theories and to formulate a unique relational integration. This framework includes three dimensions: a self pole, an object pole and an interactional pole. Mitchell demonstrated persuasively that relational theories could be divided among those that emphasized one or the other of the three poles. Having established this overall plan, Mitchell then began to develop his own particular integration of relational concepts into what he called relational-conflict theory. This second project depended on the first, but remained separate and independent of it (for a more thorough elaboration of this development, see Aron & Harris, 2005).

By 1988, a formal relational 'track' or 'orientation' was approved at New York University's Postdoctoral Program in Psychotherapy and Psychoanalysis. This helped establish the new movement as a formal alternative curriculum of study within a well-regarded psychoanalytic training program. In 1990, I introduced Mitchell to Paul Stepansky, Editor-in-Chief of the Analytic Press. This introduction was for the expressed purposes of beginning the first journal devoted to relational psychoanalysis, and, within one year, it led, quite astonishingly, to the creation of and publication of the first issue of *Psychoanalytic Dialogues: A Journal of Relational Perspectives*. By 1992 Mitchell had established the Relational Perspectives Book Series within the Analytic Press, and soon afterwards he asked me to join him as co-editor. By 1999, together with Mitchell, I edited what became the first collection of papers on *Relational psychoanalysis* (Mitchell & Aron, 1999) and the next year, just before his untimely death on 21 December 2000, he initiated activities to found the International Association for Relational Psychoanalysis and Psychotherapy (IARPP) of which I became the founding president. (Mitchell had originally asked me to be president, but I demurred, insisting that only he could be the first president of such an association. He had not wanted such a political and administrative position; it was never his interest, but he had reluctantly agreed to proceed if I would take on the vice-presidency and handle this aspect of the work. And then, tragically, life and death would dictate other arrangements.)

I am skipping over the details of the history but want to catch the reader up on the current status of relational psychoanalysis. *Psychoanalytic Dialogues* quickly became one of the leading journals in psychoanalysis as well as a model for promoting open and respectful exchanges of viewpoints. Having started out as the expression of a small group of like-minded analysts surrounding Mitchell in

New York City, it has truly become an international journal and now receives article submissions from around the world, as well as having an international readership. Similarly, IARPP, while originally put together by a small group of analysts largely from the United States, is now truly an international association with membership quickly growing around the world and an increasingly internationally representative board of directors and regular international conferences and activities. The Relational Perspectives Book Series (Routledge), now under the editorial supervision of Lewis Aron and Adrienne Harris with the assistance of associate editors Steven Kuchuck and Eyal Rozmarin, originated in 1990 under the editorial eye of Mitchell. I began working with Mitchell on the series after the very first book of the series was published and we now have more than 60 volumes with many more in various stages of production. Included in the Relational Perspectives Book Series are authors and works that come from within the relational tradition and extend and develop the tradition, as well as works that critique relational approaches or compare and contrast them with alternative points of view.

Given all this excitement and quick growth I am sure that you can understand my delight at being asked to review [what began as] a special journal issue concerning relational psychotherapy in Europe. Having reviewed the history of the 'relational psychoanalysis' with which I am familiar let me return to my thrill in reading the contributions to this special issue. Perhaps the first topic to take up is the broadening usage from relational psychoanalysis to relational psychotherapy. Now, of course, this is not new. The IARPP is explicitly an association for relational psychoanalysis and psychotherapy, and so clearly there is a tradition of thinking of relational contributions as involving more than just formal analysis. Furthermore, within relational circles, as compared with more traditional, mainstream or classical circles (each of these terms has its own problems), there has been a tendency to play down the sharp distinction between psychotherapy and psychoanalysis. At the New York University Postdoctoral Program in Psychotherapy & Psychoanalysis (where the first relational program was developed in 1988) we have a long history of eschewing the difference between psychotherapy and psychoanalysis.

I consider the question of the relationship between (analytically oriented) psychotherapy and (formal) psychoanalysis to be an important one to examine, and I believe that examining the distinctions from the point of view of contemporary relational theory will shed new light on this old problem. This is a topic that calls out for a comprehensive discussion, one that is well beyond what I can do here, but I want to make some brief points about it in this context. Psychoanalysis is clearly in crisis around the world with numbers of patients seeking analysis reported to be in decline and numbers of applicants to analytic training programs also in decline. Psychoanalysis is no longer the dominant paradigm in departments of psychiatry or clinical psychology, and it is on the defensive in regard to its scientific standing. There are important questions concerning whether its relatively new openness and pluralism is a blessing or a curse. Does our newfound pluralism represent a healthy openness and respect for divergence or does it represent a field in decline and fragmentation?

Psychoanalysts no longer agree on the essentials that traditionally defined an approach as specifically psychoanalysis. There was a time when analysts could agree on such fundamentals as: the free association method; transference and resistance; the use of the couch; the predominance of interpretation as the technical intervention of choice; neutrality, anonymity and abstinence as technical stances; a regressive transference neurosis as the *sine qua non* of analytic process; structural change as the analytic goal. I would argue that today every one of these fundamentals has been challenged. Analysts no longer agree across schools (and even within each school there is little consensus) on analytic goals, analytic technique or identifying an analytic process. Given this level of disagreement about the fundamentals defining psychoanalysis, it should come as no surprise that there is even less agreement on differentiating psychoanalysis from analytic psychotherapy. What is proper analysis to one analyst is now 'wild analysis' to another; similarly, what is psychoanalysis to one analyst is psychotherapy to another. Certainly all analysts would agree that they are interested in unconscious processes, but they can hardly agree about the nature of these processes or what constitutes 'the unconscious', and, furthermore, this is not helpful in distinguishing between psychotherapy and psychoanalysis because many psychotherapists who do not regard themselves as analysts also think about unconscious processes. Perhaps all that psychoanalysts now have in common is a commitment to seeing patients with some frequency over a long period of time, and even this definition is contested.

To go further, and of specific relevance to relational theory, many of the very factors that relationalists tend to champion in treatment (the relationship between patient and analyst, relational factors in change, relational dimensions of mind and of psychopathology) were viewed by traditionalists as the essential ingredients of psychotherapy and were not thought to be specific to psychoanalysis. In short, what relationalists tend to prize as the active ingredients of psychoanalysis were traditionally considered the stuff of psychotherapy. So, from a classical or traditional perspective (what used to be mainstream – although today perhaps it is the relationalists who are in the mainstream), what we are calling relational psychoanalysis was viewed as dynamic, supportive or relationship-based psychotherapy leading to transference cures and encouraging dependency on the relationship. By contrast, from a relational point of view, relational principles of conducting a treatment lead to what is better viewed as more comprehensive and better conducted psychoanalysis that uses the relationship to achieve deeper analytic aims.

I recognize that perhaps one reason that this theme caught my eye as I read these contributions is that much of what is called psychotherapy in the UK would in the USA be called psychoanalysis of one kind or another. Many of the training programs in the UK that go under the name psychotherapy would in the USA be calling themselves training programs in psychoanalysis. Many American psychoanalytic training programs teach students to do psychoanalysis on a three session per week basis, whereas a similar program in the UK would probably have to call itself a program in psychotherapy. My understanding is that this is because in the USA there are so many programs outside the umbrella of both the American Psychoanalytic Association (APsaA) and the International Psychoanalytic Association (IPA). In fact, it is quite relevant that neither the William Alanson White Institute nor the New York University Postdoctoral Program in Psychotherapy and Psychoanalysis is a member of the APsaA or the IPA. Perhaps this also explains one reason why it has been so important to relational theorists and clinicians in the USA, but also why it has been possible for them to insist on being identified as relational psychoanalysts. Relational psychoanalysis emerged and developed outside the national and internationally established psychoanalytic associations. It found a strong presence within the Division of Psychoanalysis (Division 39) of the American Psychological Association (APA), but it must be remembered that this is not an organization of psychoanalysts and it has no authority to determine who is, or is not, an analyst. It is precisely because it is not a regulating or accrediting agency that relational ideas were able to thrive in Division 39. Furthermore, because it was made up of psychologists, many of whom had been excluded from the dominant psychoanalytic organizations, the membership may have had a compelling interest in developing an alternative theory and clinical approach. Relational psychoanalysis in the USA has been a movement developed by and for outsiders, even as it has clearly had an enormous impact on the historically dominant groups.

The reason I am reviewing the history of this development in America at such length is that I think it may shed light on the different sensibility among therapists in the UK. Unlike in the USA, where the main theory we have had to emerge from has been American ego psychology, it seems to be that in the UK there has been a longer and stronger presence of object-relations theory in its various schools and manifestations that has affected not only the psychoanalysts *per se*, but all psychotherapists. It also seems to me that this common background in object-relations theory may well have lent itself to some increased readiness towards an integrative approach. In America, under the dominance of ego psychology, analysts were more likely to emphasize the differences between psychoanalysis and psychotherapy, rather than to highlight the similarities. Relational theory has shifted that ground in the USA and has encouraged much more acceptance of a variety of integrative approaches (see especially Frank, 1993; Wachtel, 1993). The sense of an acceptance of psychotherapy integration comes through clearly in this collection of papers and fits readily with a relational perspective.

I have been speaking of relational psychoanalysis as if it were one thing, a unified theoretical position or school, but that is a gross oversimplification. The version of relational theory that I am most familiar with emerged in New York in the 1980s. It was based on the tensions that existed in New York between the classical, American ego psychologists, on the one hand, and the interpersonalists, who had been a strong force on the East Coast since the time of Sullivan,

Fromm, Horney, Thompson and Fromm-Reichman. Relational theory, as Mitchell developed it here, emerged from decades of battles between these two camps. In the 1970s, with the emergence of British object-relations theory and home-grown American self-psychology, a new middle ground was opened. Relational theory emerged from within this opening. The term 'relational' itself was meant as a bridge to capture the interpersonal relations of the interpersonal school and the relational aspects of the object-relations school. From the beginning, relational was meant as a dialectical term, an attempt to mediate the tension between the more intrapsychic and the more interpersonal formulations.

But if the relational school is meant to be dialectical, then everywhere that relational theory develops it has to mediate between its own local tensions and conflicts. Relationalists who emerged in Chicago had to mediate between the clash that was so dominant there between self psychologists (of different stripes) and ego psychologists. On the West Coast where, since Bion's stay, Kleinians have been a forceful presence, relationalists have had to hold the tension between Kleinian, ego-psychological and interpersonal formulations. And so, in my view, it is only natural and legitimate that each local psychoanalytic culture would have to produce its own relational theory and forms of practice that mediate those tensions dominant within its own geographical sphere. Which brings us back to the collection of articles that were gathered in the issue of the *European Journal of Psychotherapy and Counselling*. One question on my mind as I read this collection of papers, mostly from British authors, is to wonder what are the particular tensions that these therapists are struggling with in their work and in their writing? Some of that will be apparent in my discussion to follow. Since there is much too much excellent material here for me to take each article up in detail, what I hope to achieve is to pick up on just a few key themes that run through the articles and to highlight some of what I view as common, centrally organizing relational considerations, themes that I think are viewed as central by relational therapists/ analysts on both sides of the Atlantic.

Orbach (Chapter 2) begins by pointing out that, in his published work, Mitchell had not recognized the influence of various radical social movements on relational theory. I agree with Orbach about this, although I have no doubt myself that she is correct in identifying these influences. I will speak briefly about some of the influences on Mitchell's work, because he certainly played the leading role in developing the version of relational theory that has most influenced me. But I want to make the point again here that there is no single relational theory or school, nor would Mitchell have wanted such a thing. There are many versions of relational theory. In fact, I would argue that relational psychoanalysis may well be the first school of psychoanalysis that did not develop around a single innovator. Freudian theory, Jungian, Kleinian, Kohutian, Sullivanian psychoanalysis, to take just a few examples, were largely developed by brilliant, creative individual leaders surrounded by their small groups. Relational theory is different precisely because it was the first psychoanalytic theory to emerge after psychoanalysis had become pluralistic and open to diverse theories. It was therefore not under

Mitchell's dominance – he never thought of himself as another Klein or Kohut. Just as simple examples, consider how different are the theories of Greenberg, Benjamin, Davies, Bromberg, Ogden, Stolorow, Renik, Hoffman – all of whose work Mitchell included under the term relational, and all of whom could rightfully claim to being leading innovators within a relational school. Again, to repeat my point, which I do not think has been made strongly or clearly enough in the literature, relational psychoanalysis is not a unified single school and to whatever degree it is considered a school at all, it is the first school of psychoanalysis not to be founded by a single towering leader who determined what (and who) is or is not a legitimate part of the school. For this reason, relational theory is itself much less unified, more diverse, and also sometimes more chaotic than previously established schools of psychoanalysis.

Now to return to Orbach's claim that Mitchell did not recognize some of the radical political origins of relational theory. Mitchell came from a left-wing politically minded family where politics were heatedly debated (see Rudnytsky, 2000). He told of one grandparent being a socialist, the other a communist and his father being a liberal-democrat, and of growing up with fights about politics. In college, after initially having read Freud in high school and then as a student being interested in Jung, Mitchell became bored with the academic psychology that was being taught and majored instead in political philosophy. I think that you can easily see the tremendous influence of his training in political philosophy on the structure of the argument of object relations in psychoanalytic theory where Greenberg and Mitchell put drive and relational models side to side with nineteenth-century political philosophy. The drive model was compared to political philosophies that emphasized the human being as an isolated individual, whereas relational theories were compared to models of the person as always part of a social community. (Of course, for my purposes here I am neglecting Greenberg's contribution to this classic work and focusing exclusively on Mitchell's background. This is in no way intended as a slight to Greenberg whose work has itself been, and continues to be, very important to me.) Not only was Mitchell academically focused on politics but he also became active in the anti-war movement, and the radical influences of the 1960s were all active influences, including the anti-war movement, feminism, the civil rights movement, the anti-psychiatry movement and the atmosphere of questioning authority that was epitomized in the bringing down of Richard Nixon's presidency. Mitchell was anti-authoritarian and had early on in his academic career been very influenced by Nietzsche. So I am in agreement with Orbach's main point here, but, in America, the relational analysts were writing within the confines of psychoanalytic journals and for psychoanalytic audiences and so perhaps these elements were played down, and this may bring us back to the specific emphasis on relational psychoanalysis versus psychotherapy.

The relational analysts writing in the USA were writing for a psychoanalytic audience rather than an audience of psychotherapists. It strikes me only now, as I am reading these British articles and comparing some of the tone to the literature with which I am familiar, that Orbach and others, because they were not part of the mainstream psychoanalytic institutions or because they were specifically addressing other audiences (women's groups, feminist therapists), may have from the start been writing for a broader audience that might have been more open to these less conventional influences. More importantly, again, the American relational scene developed out of the background of ego psychology with its focus on ego autonomy and the individual ego. In contrast, British psychoanalytic approaches and psychotherapeutic approaches have emerged against a background of object-relations theory, and so the two approaches understandably may have arrived at some destinations from different directions.

While Orbach here focuses mainly on British influences, I think that she highlights many of the same conceptual themes that I would in outlining the central clinical contributions of relational theory. I think that this is a good illustration of how relational theory varies from one place to another, struggling with different influences and tensions, but ends up with a certain common focus. For example, Orbach emphasizes a variety of manifestations of mutuality or reciprocity in the clinical situation. This is, in my view, one of the hallmarks of a relational approach. In *A meeting of minds* (1996), I differentiate mutuality from symmetry, and also try to explore a variety of different ways in which mutuality plays a role in analysis: mutual transferences, mutual resistances, mutual regression, mutual generation of data, mutual enactments, mutual regulation, mutual recognition and more. None of this implies a collapse into symmetry in that it is recognized that patient and analyst have different roles and responsibilities within a therapy.

Orbach also makes the very important point that a hallmark of relational psychoanalysis is that there is no single prescribed 'off the shelf' technique that will fit all analyses. Greenberg (2001) has very usefully pointed out that, while this is true in theory, in practice relationalists may have been guilty of encouraging a certain uniformity, an emphasis on being the 'good object', working along party lines. I think that Greenberg points to a legitimate concern and that this is one of the most significant issues for us to discuss today. We have come to see psychoanalysis as remarkably personal for each of the participants. Freud had tried his best to eliminate the analyst's subjectivity so as to keep psychoanalysis a science. There was no room for what Freud called 'the subjective factor' on the part of the analyst (letter by Freud to Ferenczi, 4 January 1928, cited in Grubrich-Simitis, 1986, p. 271).

Today we recognize the profound influence of the analyst's subjectivity, and so relational psychoanalysis must strive for a good fit between patient and analyst with no one prescribed technique. But how do we teach such a personal approach? We no longer have recourse to a specific manual of psychoanalytic technique. This is why it strikes so many of us as ludicrous to think that we could ever properly manualize a psychoanalytic treatment. But if it is so personal, so subjective, so much based on what the analyst feels in reaction to the patient, if each of the analyst's interventions is so uniquely determined by who they are as individuals and who they have become with specific patients, then we have to rethink not only how psychoanalysis is conducted, but also how psychoanalysis is taught. The teaching too must become more intersubjective and interpersonal. It is not that I do not think we have much to teach, quite to the contrary, I think that we have an enormous amount to teach, but it does not take the form of prescribed rules but rather we teach student analysts how to think reflexively about their clinical decision making with each specific patient based on the unique two-person situation that evolves in the analysis (for more on the uniqueness of each dyad and psychoanalytic education see Aron, 1999).

Nodelman's (Chapter 4) beautifully presented case perfectly illustrates so many of the fundamental assumptions of a relational approach and, in my view, her paper goes on to break new ground. Throughout the treatment we see the reciprocal processes of mutual influence and mutual regression, including the mutual regulation of regressive states. I am not fond of the word regression because it can too easily connote something backward or negative, but I am using it here as it is the traditional term for the many facets of altered states of consciousness within an analysis. I want to highlight regression as a critical concept that may shed additional light on the differences between American and British sensibilities. In an earlier article (Aron & Bushra, 1998), I discussed the idea of mutual regression, but also pointed to the striking differences between the American and British use of the term by a variety of theorists and schools. In America the emphasis had been on viewing regression as either an exaggerated defense induced in the patient by the analytic situation or as an aspect of the patient's psychopathology, not created by, but simply made more obvious in the analytic situation. In striking contrast British contributions focused on therapeutic regression as a facilitating process in its own right. By contrast with the American mainstream tradition, it is not trauma and frustration that are thought to induce regression, but rather indulgence, gratification, holding and a permissive, facilitating environment. (Later I will trace certain aspects of the relational approach back to Ferenczi, but I might say here too that Ferenczi's understanding of regression is critical to the discussion; see also, Aron & Harris, 1993.)

Nodelman's case, as she points out, highlights the relational unconscious and the ongoing place of enactment and interaction throughout an analysis. While interaction in my view is ubiquitous, that is you cannot talk about anything without in some way enacting what you are discussing, nevertheless, some enactments are particularly powerful. In this case, because of the patient's dramatic birth history, certain key issues cannot be put into words and must be enacted in order to be communicated. Nodelman acknowledges to us that she could not have moved forward with her patient if she had not also struggled with some of her own personal dynamic issues based on her own family history. It has become a hallmark of relational case reports that progress in analysis is based on both participants having to do personal work in reaction to each other. In traditional terms, transference and countertransference are interlocking processes that can be understood only in mutual dialectic relation. I think that Nodelman's paper raises very important questions about therapeutic regression, as well as the role of interpretation and verbal understanding, and forces us to examine when our need to verbalize and formulate meaning may actually interfere with significant analytic non-verbal work, work that takes place on the level of the body rather than only the verbal mind.

Cowan-Jenssen (Chapter 7) continues this focus on principles and controversies of the greatest importance to contemporary relational thinking. In my earlier remarks about Mitchell's background I commented on the influence of the trends of the 1960s. I should add that he was enormously influenced by existentialism and I believe that this aspect of his own relational theory has not been highlighted sufficiently. In describing the relational matrix (Mitchell, 1988), Mitchell focused on the self pole, the object pole and the interactional dimension, and these three were the major units of study, but Mitchell also acknowledged that there was a need to focus on the role of the individual's will. Sometimes, it seemed to me that Mitchell considered the will to be an aspect of the self pole, but at other times it seemed to be a dimension in its own right. My concern is that by including it under the self pole of the relational matrix it may not have received the attention it deserves. The notion of the will was one place where room could be made within relational theory for an existential focus. Certainly Hoffman's (1998) work makes clear that we tend to deny anxieties about death, but this idea has been most often associated with existential approaches, as in the work of Ernest Becker and Irving Yalom. Once the analytic situation is seen to evoke anxieties in both the patient and the analyst then, of course, anxiety over death is one of the central mutual fears that they both share and mutually deny.

Cowan-Jenssen's ideas also evoke Orbach's remarks about the necessary uniqueness of each analytic process. She challenges the idea that the psychoanalytic frame has fixed meaning. If psychoanalytic technique must be uniquely adapted to each patient and analyst pair then there is also nothing sacrosanct about a set length of session time. The frame is always negotiated in some ways between the patient and analyst and must meet both their needs. I think that she very successfully highlights the relationship between the frame and power in the analytic relationship. The idea that the analyst must protect the frame by standing firm sets the situation up with the analyst's inevitable assertion of power so as to protect the analysis. A relational approach assumes by contrast that the frame has no pre-fixed meaning and is therefore something to be negotiated between two individuals each with their own needs and conflicts. She also demonstrates yet again how the analyst can only understand and help a patient when the analyst him or herself struggles with their own issues, conflicts and anxieties evoked by the patient. In this case, anxieties about death, the body's fragility, and fears of both object loss and bodily decay need to be struggled with by and within the analyst and not only the patient.

Haberlin (Chapter 3), in one of the most beautifully told cases I can remember reading, continues to focus on the therapist's bodily vulnerability, relating one incident during her own pregnancy and the management of her patient's aggression during that vulnerable time. But, once again, this case raises many of the issues that we have been discussing and more. Here she brings in the contemporary relational focus on dissociation by illustrating mutual dissociations and the related enactments between her and her patient. The relational literature has been at the forefront of examining questions of gender, race and ethnicity in treatment dyads (see Aron & Harris, 2005; Aron & Putnam, 2007) and here Haberlin examines one way in which this interracial dyad re-enacts earlier racially complicated dramas. The case brings us back as well to very difficult questions about the analytic frame that we have already discussed in relation to Cowan-Jenssen and Orbach. Here, dilemmas involve the patient's sexuality, masturbating within the session and how the analyst deals with this 'acting in', as well as the previously mentioned matter of the patient's aggressive expressions during the analyst's pregnancy and, of course, the issue of the patient's wish to touch her stomach and her setting of limits on this touching. Importantly, there is a very natural use of self-disclosure (how could one not self-disclose a pregnancy?), but here Haberlin also discloses how she too will experience the interruption as a loss. Haberlin sets some limits firmly and naturally, but also expressed her own feelings of loss as earlier she had expressed her own desire not to be put into a position where she would feel like looking away from her patient. This is an important case example precisely because it does not just advocate self-disclosure or patient gratification, nor does it propose a simplistic set analytic frame to be maintained, but rather Haberlin presents us with a co-constructed analytic frame, a flexible and ever-evolving frame that needed to meet the needs of herself as well as her patient. Analytic structures are not abandoned or destroyed but neither are they rigidly pre-established or beyond negotiation. Her patient indeed found a woman who was a friend of her mind. I would add that I think it is not an accident that the case illustration centrally involves a time when she was pregnant. Having supervised a number of pregnant analysts I do think that there is something about the remarkable and inevitable 'self-disclosure', this literal change in the analytic boundaries, as well as in the changes in the psychology of the analyst, the intrusion of a quite literal 'analytic third' (see Aron, 2006), that highlights many of the relational issues and concerns about the frame that are being raised here.

Anderson's (Chapter 6) empirically-based contribution focuses on forgiveness. Here I believe that this collection of papers has highlighted central relational concepts. Relational theory has been traced back to the early dialogue and disagreements between Freud and Ferenczi (see Aron & Harris, 1993). In reading Ferenczi's clinical diary one gets a clear sense that he came to view a central aspect of the therapeutic action of psychoanalysis as entailed by a mutual forgiveness between patient and analyst, of a collaborative movement that 'leads the relationship away from a breach in the direction of reconciliation and understanding' (1988 [1932], p. 53). This focus has been extended in the contemporary literature by Beebe and Lachmann's (2002) work on disruption and repair as one principle of salience in the organization of the patient–analyst interaction, and by Safran and Muran (2000) in their work on relational ruptures and repairs. An excellent clinical illustration of the process of disruption and repair appears in the chapter by Cornell (Chapter 5), to which I will now turn.

In several ways many of the themes that we have been examining are pulled together in Cornell's paper. By presenting his very different clinical decisions with two different patients, Cornell brings to life the central principle stated by Orbach, namely that principles of technique, clinical choice points must be negotiated or co-constructed within each dyad – there is no off-the-shelf relational approach to technique. It is also critical, and I want to highlight this point, that Cornell's patient Ben does not just benefit from his therapist's openness and admission of vulnerability, but also from seeing that his therapist can withdraw defensively. This is critical for us to notice because of the warning issued to us by Greenberg (2001) that I discussed earlier. It is not just our good qualities or the aspects of us that make us 'good objects' that are seen as helpful by relational theory. It is all of our human qualities that may play a role in treatment; we must use all of ourselves, as Cornell does. And so his patient can benefit even from his defensive or withdrawn qualities, not only from his self-disclosures of his vulnerabilities and access to his own affects. It is too easy for relational theory to rationalize our natural tendency to want to be good objects to our patients, and Cornell demonstrates that all of our qualities can play a therapeutic role in analysis if only we can be open, authentic and non-defensive about processing these qualities for ourselves and together with our patients.

There is a good deal more to say about this terrific group of papers and about relational psychoanalysis today, but I should like to end by pointing to one more feature of Cornell's work that I appreciate very much and which I think is characteristic of a relational approach. Cornell tells us that he not only received permission from his patient to present this case but that in addition he showed the patient the case report and discussed it with him, bringing the reactions into the analytic work. There is a great deal to explore about this intervention into the treatment. Traditionally analysts were taught not to write about cases until they were concluded. Aside from the fact that this advice was first given when treatments were much shorter, it also does not seriously address the ambiguity in what it means for a case to be terminated or complete. In her recent book, *Writing about patients*, Kantrowitz (2006) studied analysts of diverse orientations and demonstrated that relational analysts were more likely to involve their patients in the write up and publication of case reports. While she judicially and even-handedly discusses the pros and cons of such involvement, I would argue for the overall benefits of such practice. It seems to me that in our internet age the likelihood that patients will read about themselves has increased exponentially. I think that there are strong ethical considerations involved here that support patients' rights to review material publicly presented about their treatments and lives. But, more importantly, it seems to me that a relational orientation leads one to expect that the patient will have important feedback on our view of their analysis, that our view as the analyst is not a privileged or superior view, but that their own perspective may have a great deal to teach us. Think of the benefit to psychoanalysis if each of our famous case histories had an addendum with the patient's view of their treatment. Might we have benefited if Breuer had asked Anna O to write her own narrative of their talking cure or if Freud had asked Dora to tell her own story of her analysis? Would we not have learned a great deal by having their reactions to the case history and even more importantly might they themselves have benefited from discussions with their analyst about how each viewed what was going on between them, if their analysts had been open to such discussion? Writing about patients is enormously complicated and, as Kantrowitz emphasizes, there are responsibilities, risks and ramifications that go with professional publication of case reports. I am not arguing that there is or should be one right way to proceed – that would be contrary to everything that relational theory has stood for. But I do want to advocate that we explore ways to involve our patients in our writing about them to see how best we can facilitate using this professional writing in the service of their analyses.

References

Aron, L. (1996). *A meeting of minds*. Hillsdale, NJ: The Analytic Press.
Aron, L. (1999). Clinical choices and the relational matrix. *Psychoanalytic Dialogues, 9*: 1–29 [Taylor & Francis Online].
Aron, L. (2006). Analytic impasse and the third. *International Journal of Psycho-Analysis, 87*: 349–368.
Aron, L. and Bushra, A. (1998). Mutual regression: Altered states in the psychoanalytic situation. *Journal of the American Psychoanalytic Association, 46*: 389–412.
Aron, L. and Harris, A. (1993). *The legacy of Sandor Ferenczi*. Hillsdale, NJ: The Analytic Press.
Aron, L. and Harris, A. (2005). Introduction. In *Relational psychoanalysis: Innovations and expansion*, Vol. 2, xiii–xxi. Hillsdale, NJ: The Analytic Press.
Aron, L. and Putnam, J. (2007). Commentary: Tapping the multiplicity of self–other relationships. In *Dialogues on difference* (J. C. Muran, Ed.). Washington, DC: American Psychological Association (pp. 64–72).
Beebe, B. and Lachmann, F. M. (2002). *Infant research and adult treatment*. Hillsdale, NJ: The Analytic Press.
Ferenczi, S. (1988) [1932]. *The clinical diary of Sandor Ferenczi* (J. Dupont, Ed.; M. Balint and N. Z. Jackson, Trans.). Cambridge, MA: Harvard University Press.
Frank, K. A. (1993). Action, insight, and working through outlines of an integrative approach. *Psychoanalytic Dialogues, 3*: 535–577.
Greenberg, J. (2001). The analyst's participation. *Journal of the American Psychoanalytic Association, 49*: 359–381.
Greenberg, J. R. and Mitchell, S. A. (1983). *Object relations in psychoanalytic theory*. Cambridge, MA: Harvard University Press.
Grubrich-Smitis, I. (1986). Six letters of Sigmund Freud and Sandór Ferenczi on the interrelationship of psychoanalytic theory and technique. *International Review of Psycho-Analysis, 13*: 259–277.
Hoffman, I. (1998). *Ritual and spontaneity in the psychoanalytic process*. Hillsdale, NJ: The Analytic Press.

Kantrowitz, J. L. (2006). *Writing about patients*. New York: The Other Press.

Mitchell, S. A. (1988). *Relational concepts in psychoanalysis*. Cambridge, MA: Harvard University Press.

Mitchell, S. A and Aron, L. (1999). *Relational psychoanalysis: The emergence of a tradition*. Hillsdale, NJ: The Analytic Press.

Rudnytsky, P. L. (2000). *Psychoanalytic conversations*. Hillsdale, NJ: The Analytic Press.

Safran, J. D. and Muran, J. C. (2000). *Negotiating the therapeutic alliance: A relational treatment guide*. New York: Guilford Press.

Wachtel, P. L. (1993). Active intervention, psychic structure, and the analysis of transference: Commentary on Frank's 'Action, insight, and working through'. *Psychoanalytic Dialogues, 3*: 589–603.

9

COMMENTARY ON RELATIONAL PSYCHOANALYSIS IN EUROPE

How is this dialogue different?

Chana Ullman

I am pleased to be given this opportunity to comment on six of the foregoing chapters which together illustrate how the relational perspective is changing psychoanalysis. My reading of these rich and often moving accounts of therapeutic interactions and impasses (as in the papers by Cornell, Cowan-Jenssen, Haberlin, Nodelman and Orbach) and of the theoretical as well as cultural contexts that inform them (as in Orbach's and Anderson's papers) induced my own movement as a reader between insider and outsider positions. I am an insider, for since I attended the first IARPP conference in New York City, I have embraced this perspective, seeking training analysis, supervision and professional affiliations that are consistent with this approach. I am now on the international board of the IARPP and a member of the Tel-Aviv Institute of Contemporary Psychoanalysis, which includes members from different schools in fruitful dialogue, but which Steven Mitchell helped to establish. Yet, I also read the papers with the interest and the judicious eye of an outsider, as I am less familiar with the relational perspective as practiced in Europe, more specifically the UK, where most of the chapters originate.

I shall begin with the perspective of the insider. Chapters 2–7 in this section of the book touch upon the most important controversies that contemporary psychoanalysis faces and indicate the points of tension between 'one-person' and 'two-person' models of psychotherapy and psychoanalysis. Taken together, the chapters chart a territory that can be described as uniquely relational. I have chosen to follow the threads that are explicit or implicit in order to map this territory. In so doing, I am taking the liberty of reading the chapters 'horizontally', by the issues raised, rather than 'vertically' one by one, hoping that dissecting them for my own purposes will not damage the authors' intent and the material's integrity. I am also aware that I may not be giving all the contributions equal space and equal explicit consideration, which does not in any way reflect my estimation of their value.

The issues brought up for me by these six contributions involve questions of technique (e.g. Cornell and Haberlin, on self-disclosure and frame), questions of analytic stance (e.g. regarding mutuality and neutrality as in Cowan-Jenssen, Nodelman and Orbach), questions regarding the salient content domains that therapists chose to attend to (e.g. Anderson's paper), and questions regarding the centrality and influence of the larger political and cultural context infiltrating the consulting room, as well as of the power relations within the analytic encounter (e.g. in Orbach's and Haberlin's papers).

Is the relational perspective a technique? Several of the authors touch upon questions of technique that have become sore points of controversy between the relational perspective and other schools of psychoanalysis. I am well aware that the term 'technique' may connote rigid rules that are contradictory to the spirit of the papers in this issue, which on the whole pronounce plasticity, uniqueness and authenticity as the ground rules of the relational therapeutic encounter. Differences in technique account for a small portion of the variability in research on outcomes of psychotherapy; it is the relationship that matters. It seems to me, however, that in its theoretical and clinical emphasis on the curative power of relationships, the relational perspective indeed helps us focus on what matters, namely, on the dialectics of the therapeutic relationship. In what follows, I will examine three of the chapters, aiming to clarify the recommendations that the relational perspective does offer, in my opinion, for conducting our interventions in dramatic moments as well as in the everyday ebb and flow of therapeutic interactions.

Cornell's paper on 'The intricate intimacies of psychotherapy and the question of self-disclosure' (Chapter 5) begins with a poignant clinical moment in which the traditional patient/therapist roles seem to be reversed. It is a moment in which it is the patient who expresses a need to protect the therapist, and it is the therapist who, as a result of the patient's intervention, experiences an insight into his own vulnerabilities. The patient tells his therapist that he 'does not have the right to keep hurting' him (by discussing his tormenting anxiety awaiting the results of cancer tests) and shares with his therapist the observation that every time he, the patient, used the word cancer 'it was like a shadow came over your face'. The therapist, stunned by this authentic unmasking of his own painful struggles with loss and fear of death, returns to the next session ready to validate the patient's perception and to follow the patient's lead in whether and how much to disclose about his own forays into the 'shameful' territory of fears, weakness and vulnerability. Cornell thoughtfully describes the different voices, his own and others, regarding the dilemma of self-disclosure. In this case Cornell chooses to disclose to the patient his own identification with the patient's children facing the threat of losing a parent, and his own history of losing his parents at an early age. The self-disclosure does not eradicate Cornell's therapeutic stance. This moving encounter results in moments of great intimacy, a meaningful 'meeting of minds'

(Aron, 1996) that is beneficial for the patient. The disciplined self-disclosure becomes another opportunity for a deeper understanding of the patient's own struggles. Allowing the patient access to his own subjectivity, the therapist enabled further transformation of the devalued and unacceptable parts of the patient's experience, into a source of meaningful and reparative engagement. Cornell fully recognizes the complexity and risks of self-disclosure, and cautions that self-disclosure would be unnecessary and even potentially harmful in other cases.

Disclosing aspects of the analyst's life indeed became a controversial marker of relational technique. It seems to me, however, that more crucial for the essence of relational technique is the recognition that explicit and implicit behavior of the analyst in the therapeutic encounter is itself already a 'disclosure', which has an impact on shaping the patient's transference, regardless of the therapist's conscious intent. It is this impact that becomes relevant for further dialogue whether or not that dialogue includes pieces from the therapist's own life. The hallmark of relational technique, it seems to me, is the ability to maintain the dialogue about the entanglement of the patient's subjectivity or transference (e.g. patient's need to protect his therapist), and the therapist's subjectivity or countertransference (e.g. therapist's sadness about his own losses and his identification with patient's children).

As Orbach points out, the disclosure already happens by the authenticity of the analyst's behavior. In Haberlin's paper (Chapter 3) it is the fact of the analyst's pregnancy that cannot be concealed. In Cornell's example, the therapy was furthered not by the specific knowledge gathered about the therapist's life, but by the patient's gaining access to the therapist's process of knowing and of struggling with conflict. Cornell's ability and willingness to experience, look at and negotiate authentically (Pizer, 1998) the drama in which both patient and therapist were actors, and to courageously and thoughtfully invite the patient to witness the unwrapping of Cornell's own participation in it, enabled progress. Embedded in Cornell's example are the crucial elements of good relational technique: recognizing our own countertransferential contributions to the treatment relationship, reflecting on the specific ways our own behavior is helping to form the reality that we share with our patients, maintaining the ability to forgo the privileged position of an outside authority on this reality, and engaging in this dialogue of the meeting of two subjectivities, while holding the patient's best interest in mind.

Similarly, in Haberlin's beautiful and poignant 'beloved' case, the principles of a two-person psychology are evident. The case demonstrates Haberlin's awareness and use of her subjectivity, her sensitivity to the racial and power imbalances in the dyad, her careful and deliberate self-disclosure, her co-construction of the analytic frame in a way that meets the patient's as well as her own needs. 'Beloved' reads like a suspense story that illustrates the relational conceptualization of a dissociated mind as a survival response to trauma, and of the pitfalls as well as healing powers of the efforts 'to draw out from the shadows the child who has been so abused'.

Two chapters, 'Mortality in the consulting room' by Cowan-Jenssen (Chapter 7) and 'The primal silence' by Nodelman (Chapter 4), illuminate additional questions that draw attention to unique aspects of relational technique. Both of them describe thorny impasses in the treatment of patients terrorized by living in an unreliable or handicapped body. Whereas the moment of connection in Cornell's paper originated in the patient's attempt to take care of his therapist in the context of an already close and compassionate connection, these two contributions describe a long period of stalemate in which both therapists experienced exasperation, helplessness and a sense of failure. In Cowan-Jenssen's paper the therapist unsuccessfully attempts to push away the patient's intrusive jokes and references to her body, age and children, whereas the patient continues to reject or ignore her interpretations of his hostility: 'At times it felt like we were two deaf people shouting at each other.' In Nodelman's account, the therapist comes to increasingly dread the sessions in which she continuously attempts to breathe life into the listless, detached, seemingly bored patient who proclaims her interpretations as useless. The impasse in both these cases seem to consist of a locked 'complementary relationship' in which therapist and patient are entangled in a 'doer–done to' seesaw (Benjamin, 2002), a life or death struggle, in which only one of the partners can survive, where the options are submission or resistance to the other's perspective (Ogden, 1994). How do we step out of these deadlocks, which we all recognize too well? Indeed, as Benjamin describes, and as Haberlin, Cornell and Nodelman come to realize and acknowledge, a complementary dyad often conceals an unconscious symmetry between therapist and patient. While the impasse may begin with the repetition or enactment of hated, feared or abandoned parts of the patient's self, it is the inevitable participation of symmetrical, though unique, fears and hidden vulnerabilities on the therapist's part that creates the deadlock. As long as the deadlock is experienced only as one-way resistance by the intrapsychic dynamics of the patient, the impasse continues. As both papers describe, the therapist experiences guilt, shame, rage and futility, and both parties continue in a sense of forced collaboration rather than genuine interest and connection.

The way out of these various impasses began with the therapists' private and specific recognition – forgoing their global self-blame and self-reproach – of their own specific resistance and contribution to the stalemate, and continued with their compassionate accommodation, surrendering albeit not submitting (see Ghent, 1990; Benjamin, 2002) to the patient's message. There are important differences in the clinical process presented as well as in the paths to resolution constructed by Cowan-Jenssen and Nodelman, which I will not elaborate here. But these chapters, together with Haberlin's powerful case description, can be taken to elucidate important principles of relational technique: first, the view of impasse or, to use Bromberg's term, of 'potholes on the royal road' (2000) not as analytic failures to be avoided or corrected by the analyst's return to a perfect attunement or empathic stance, or to her insistence on a neutral interpretive stance, but as inevitable opportunities for the most meaningful recognition of two imperfect subjects. Surviving the breakdown of communication and restoring a dialogue in which the other is not excluded becomes the crucial element of therapeutic action. Second, the clinical examples indicate that interpretations of the intrapsychic alone may fail until the intersubjective is recognized and becomes part of the dialogue and of the working through.

What does a relational analytic stance look like? The term 'analytic stance' refers to the position from which the analyst listens and speaks. It is a crossroad between theory and practice, providing the link between clinical practice and theoretical assumptions about the 'otherness' of analyst and patient, about the sources of analytic authority and about curative factors in the analytic encounter (Nebbiosi, 2006).

Orbach's chapter, 'Democraticizing psychoanalysis' (Chapter 2), passionately describes the differences between the classical analytic stance in and outside the consulting room (as in how to avoid encountering patients outside one's office) and the stance implied by relational psychoanalysis. In her description, which is probably influenced by her own close, expressive and direct style, as much as it is informed by the relational perspective, the stance of the relational analyst emerges as non-neutral, actively trusting and emotionally responsive, as creating a democratic climate in which mutuality is recognized and respected. As Orbach argues, this stance is grounded in the theoretical assumptions about the nature of attachment and the search for relationship as fundamental to human development. These assumptions are supported by the ambitious and rigorous research projects on early development reported by Beebe & Lachmann (1988), demonstrating mutual affective regulation in infant–mother dyads as important in constituting the self, and by Fonagy & Target (1997), who demonstrate the interdependence of attachment and mentalization, and attachment and reflectivity. As the young child influences and transforms the parent in the course of the normal adaptive developmental process, we are influenced and transformed by patients not merely in defensive projective maneuvers, as is indeed illustrated particularly in the cases presented by Haberlin, Cornell and Cowan-Jenssen.

The analytic stance embraced by Orbach is also one that insists on a democratic non-authoritarian, even subversive approach to the power differences in the consulting room. She reminds us of the covert use of psychoanalytic concepts central to the classical analytic stance, such as neutrality, anonymity and abstinence, to maintain hierarchical arrangements of power and privilege in the psychoanalytic domain. Renik (1995), for example, argued that adherence to the principle of anonymity is unconsciously motivated by the desire to maintain the idealization of analysts' superior knowledge. Gerson (1996) suggests that neutrality is embedded in male analysts' responses to female desire, guarding against their experience of the female patient as dangerously seductive. Orbach indeed reminds us of the roots of relationality in feminism, and in radical political movements of the sixties, a context in which she herself was active politically and professionally.

The relational analyst assumes mutuality, and this assumption already contributes to her listening and speaking from a less idealized, mysterious and hierarchical stance. It should be emphasized, however, that mutuality does not imply symmetry (Aron, 1996). As is also evident by the comparison with the parent–child dyad above, mutuality does not mean that both parties equally contribute to the relationship, nor does it imply equal responsibility. It is the patient who needs help and the analyst who is paid. The question then still remains: what is the authority by which we speak to our patients? It seems to me that this is a crucial question for those of us who attempt to understand, explore and minimize power relations within the clinic. This question remains open, but I wish to suggest one possible answer.

The classical analytic stance seems to locate the authority in the analyst's knowledge. As I write 'classical analytic stance', I am aware of oversimplifying the many differences among psychoanalytic schools and of the loose boundaries of this term – a point to which I shall return later. Still, traditionally, the analyst is the observer of a truth still hidden from the patient. Her knowledge is applied in the consulting room to uncover the truth which will set the patient free. It is assumed that analytic neutrality and anonymity are necessary to observe the clues for this unconscious truth.

The relational perspective, on the other hand, locates the authority in the dyad, assuming that the knowledge is not there to be applied, but to be constructed in the dialogue. The knowledge is not in the therapist and does not exist *a priori*, but is constructed in the dyadic process. The relational position is that the therapist is constantly subject to the patient's influence and can never know what is happening without having this very knowledge affected by this influence: 'The analyst position is always in flux and analytic knowledge is always fundamentally dialogical' (Seligman, 2006, p. 403). The ideal of the knowing analyst is replaced by the ideal of the analyst who can stand the uncertainty and the dialectical tension of 'standing in the spaces' (Bromberg, 1996), who is well aware that the truth constructed and recognized in his work with a particular patient is probably different from the truth that might be affirmed in this patient's work with another therapist. Following Priel (2006), I will add that this authority is always temporary and dependent on the patient's recognition of an authentic moment, as in an aesthetic experience. Analytic authority is also always paradoxical: while the treatment alliance is inevitably grounded in the patient's reliance on the analyst's training and benevolence, the therapeutic process itself aims at freeing her from this reliance.

Orbach persuasively shows how a neutral interpretative stance, in which the therapist needs to maintain her distance to be able to immaculately observe the unconscious, can translate into a constantly suspicious attitude towards the destructive internal world of the patient, and towards patients' longings and desires, defensively interpreted as 'unacceptable demands on the therapist'. Orbach's expressed dissatisfaction with common analytic terms such as countertransference and interpretation is therefore not a minor semantic point, but an ethical point, consistent with the relational stance. It is an effort to deconstruct the language that carries with it one-way hierarchies of knowledge. Her vivid examples portray the analytic stance of the relational analyst as one that liberates both patient and analyst from sacred tenets of the neutral, blank screen classical analytic stance.

I am returning now to my outsider position. While Orbach mentions in her introduction the many intellectual influences of 'classical psychoanalytic writers on the relational school', I believe that the contrasts evoked by her examples are mostly between a particular school of classical psychoanalysis, namely the Kleinian school, and the relational perspective. It is perhaps this contrast which is most salient in the current context of psychoanalysis in the UK. Analytic stance indeed has to do with context: the analytic community one belongs to, the training, as well as the theory. As an outsider to British psychoanalysis, I find Orbach's portrayal of classical analytic neutrality certainly recognizable but somewhat exaggerated. Amplifying the contrasts between the classical Freudians and Kleinians and the relational perspective is certainly necessary for the sake of clarity, but it brought up for me other contrasts, less explored by the contributions in this issue. For example, Kohut's ideas, hardly mentioned in this issue, are prevalent in the psychoanalysis practiced in the US as well as the Mediterranean (Italy, Israel). Kohut's self-psychology regards empathy and recognition rather than interpretation as the major curative factors in psychoanalysis. From this perspective the therapist's stance is not of suspicion and detached observation but of an empathic attunement. Longing and desires are acknowledged as deficits needing reparation rather than exaggerated demands. Indeed, many writers in the relational tradition view Kohut as an important precursor of relationality (Nebbiosi, 2006; Attwood & Stolorow, 1984). The epistemology of Kohut's theory is nevertheless fundamentally 'one-person': the understanding and empathy flow only in one direction, failures in empathy are to be corrected and the therapist has to strive to maintain the idealized position of perfect attunement.

What is unique about the relational therapeutic stance is not empathy and attunement, nor a permission to experience closeness to patients. In my training and in practice those aspects were abundant among Kohutian self-psychologists, object-relations oriented workers, even Kleinian analysts. It is rather the focusing of attention on two subjectivities, on the wishes and vicissitudes of connection and separation, rupture and repair, sameness and distinctiveness as enacted in the therapeutic dyad. In a similar vein, it seems to me that the humanistic tradition, as expressed for example by Rogers' client-centered psychotherapy and recognized in Britain as an important bridge to the relational perspective, or the primal scream therapy mentioned by Nodelman, are quite different and stand in sharp contrast to the relational position as they minimize the process of reflection on conflict, self-deception and unconscious dynamics influencing the here and now of the relationship.

I turn now to a discussion on content, context and reality in the relational perspective.

Cowan-Jenssen discusses universal fears of mortality and explores how the therapy hour may serve as a defense against this fear for both therapist and patient.

Two other papers in this issue use case material that centers on fears of mortality and disease (Nodelman, Cornell), one explores the idea of forgiveness as part of the therapeutic endeavor (Anderson), another explores the long-term consequences of horrific trauma (Haberlin), and yet another (Orbach) reviews the political underpinning of relational theory and starts its case presentation with the politics of the patient. There is a common ground to these choices regarding content. The authors draw our attention to universal existential concerns and to struggles that emanate from the reality of social life. These concerns have always been part and parcel of psychoanalysis' attempts to understand human suffering. In most psychoanalytic writings, however, they remained in the background, leaving the foreground to an unconscious internal world of fantasy and infantile urges. The relational perspective allows their movement closer to center stage. This is revealed by the many contributions of relational writers exploring the impact of race, gender, gender preference, economy and politics (to name but a few: Altman, 1995; Samuels, 1989; Layton, 1998) and the 'cultural unconscious' (Gerson, 2006) on therapeutic interactions.

The interest in existential, uniquely human strivings is also evident by the reframing of psychopathology in terms of universal struggles for contact, surrender or escape in relationships (as in Ghent's [1990] seminal paper on masochism as a distortion of the wish to surrender). It is also expressed and shaped by the role ascribed to real, not fantasy, past and present traumas, as profoundly affecting people's lives.

Consider in this context Nodelman's chapter 'The primal silence' (Chapter 4). She depicts the treatment of a man suffering from a mild form of cerebral palsy who came to therapy because he had never experienced falling in love. He recognizes in himself a 'certain disconnectedness and uneasiness in getting really close'. In her theoretical introduction, the author reminds us of the possible devastating effects of real complications at birth on both infant and parents. She describes early trauma as disrupting prematurely the symbiotic bond between infant and mother, endangering the very sense of self-continuity, as well as the role of secure attachments in repairing trauma. The chapter outlines the possible long-term consequences of the reality of early separation and loss of physical contact between infant and mother, of the threat of death or disability, of a prolonged state of crisis, all of which may result in the rupture of attachment and trust and in the use of dissociation and splitting by both parents and the developing child in order to survive the overwhelming affects created by trauma. The case presented indeed exemplifies some of the long-term consequences of early trauma: the profound attachment to the trauma, an inability to mourn losses (in this case the slight tremor the patient suffers from), a wish to magically undo the hurt (in this patient's fantasy of a 'big bang' return to the moment of birth), a detachment and inability to share affective responses. Nodelman describes listless, detached, dead sessions in which she unsuccessfully attempts to engage the patient and experiences her efforts as falling flat, as in attempts to 'jump start a car with a flat battery'. She increasingly comes to dread the sessions, her anxiety felt viscerally in her body, the anxiety of losing her patient. The impasse begins to dissipate when the therapist realizes her own participation and understands it as the enactment of a traumatized birth. The author uses her detailed and moving description of the treatment process to delineate important arguments about the uses of the body and about the curative function of silent regression in the presence of the other, in the process of mutual awakening and recognition.

I would like to speak to a different aspect of the successful outcome of this treatment. The turning point in the treatment occurred with the retrieval of hospital records which allowed both patient and therapist to encounter the reality of the patient's birth. Retrieving the records enabled both of them to recognize the actual suffering of the patient and his mother, and, in parallel, gave meaning to the suffering endured by his therapist in the course of their long stalemate. It also helped place the trauma experienced as dissociated and yet always present, as if in a bubble outside time and place, defying symbolization, in a moment delineated by time, place and records. Reviewing the records of the patient's traumatic birth allows, it seems to me, some closure and enables repair, bringing the dyad out of the deadlock. In contrast to classical psychoanalytic discourse which tends to downplay the effects of actual traumas and to elaborate the dynamics of the internal world of drives, fantasy and internalized objects, I wish to emphasize here the role of the actual in shaping development (see also Orbach's paper) and the function of the therapist as witness to real, catastrophic life events (Orange, 2003; Davis, 1996; Ullman 2006).

I believe similar issues are brought up by Anderson's paper on forgiveness (Chapter 6). This contribution reminds us of the larger cultural context in which psychotherapy takes place. It addresses the crossroad between current political discourse on reconciliation, traditional religious views and psychoanalytic conceptualizations of forgiveness. The paper examines forgiveness, traditionally relegated to the domain of the religious and spiritual, as a relational issue and as an aspect of therapeutic process.

Although I was less convinced by the author's qualitative research, the results of which remain sketchy, I found the chapter intriguing and thought provoking with respect to understanding unique contributions of the relational perspective. How does the relational perspective enlarge our view of forgiveness and its relevance to therapy?

Notwithstanding the work on forgiveness in couples relationships which Anderson cites, her review seems to indicate that psychoanalytic thinking relevant to forgiveness referred primarily to the study of the capacity to forgive. It is conceptualized then as a position or a quality of the individual. I concur with Anderson's suggestion that the research on attachment, mutual regulation and mentalization in parent–infant relationships may be relevant to understanding the capacity to forgive. Moreover, from a relational perspective, as Anderson indicates, one can conceptualize forgiveness primarily as a quality of a relationship. Clearly, forgiveness involves the person asking for forgiveness, or the doer of an offense, and the person who does or does not grant it. Both at the individual and at the group level it can be conceptualized then as an attempt to surrender doer–done to or victim–perpetrator positions.

Benjamin (2006) argues that parent–child interactions as well as therapist–patient interactions are fraught with inevitable ruptures, which cannot be repaired unless there is recognition of the violation. Psychotherapeutic work with victims of trauma indicates that a victim's grievance and rage cannot be surrendered until there is recognition and witnessing by another (i.e. the therapist) of the details of the story of trauma and of the evil, suffering or pain endured. This perspective may help clarify the important distinction Anderson raises between 'negative', namely grandiose or premature forgiveness and 'positive' forgiveness. How can the two be distinguished? From this relational viewpoint, one can argue that true forgiveness can occur between two subjects (individuals, groups or nations) in dialogue, it requires the acknowledgment and witnessing of an offense or harm done, either by the perpetrator or by a third party, an acceptance of 'otherness' and of asymmetry, and a hope of transformation of the relationship.

Anderson's paper brought up for me a meaningful personal experience. A while back, I participated in a workshop with German analysts from Heidelberg and Israeli-Jews from Tel-Aviv. The workshop consisted of a professional layer, which in this meeting remained the superficial layer, and a powerful personal meeting of two groups separated by the history of The Second World War. At the end of the second day of the workshop, having heard the emotional and moving testimonials of members of the two groups, having struggled with our own (Israeli) role as perpetrators of suffering, and having told the group the stories of my parents who are both survivors of the Holocaust, I told some German colleagues that I am going to visit my parents during the break. One of them said: 'Will you tell them about the workshop? Tell us what they said.' Visiting my parents later that evening, I told them about the workshop and about the German analyst's request. My parents were both visibly shaken. My father, now well in his eighties, fighting tears, said: 'Tell them we recognize that they want our forgiveness.' This experience clarified for me a question brought up by Anderson's work: what if there is no possibility of forgiveness? What if the evil endured is too monstrous? I believe Benjamin's concept of mutual recognition is crucial here: there can still be recognition of the need or desire for forgiveness. The merits of this perspective not only for work in the consulting room, but for action in the 'real' world are obvious.

These six chapters open a window to the ways in which relational thinking has revolutionized psychoanalysis. The contributions underscore the innovations of the relational school with respect to the practice of psychoanalysis and psychotherapy in not only allowing but in building on a different dialogue – a dialogue in which the analyst's participation, the recognition of mutual influence and multiple perspectives, and of the dialectics of relationships become building blocks for change. The papers also imply the theoretical innovations of the relational school, in particular with respect to the understanding of human development in the context of attachments and in the context of trauma, and with respect to the understanding of contextual influences (cultural, religious, political and economic) on the seemingly insulated analytic relationship. These innovations are not only invigorating but, indeed, essential if psychoanalysis is to remain as relevant and incisive in the twenty-first century as it was at the turn of the twentieth century.

While this material makes clear the break of relational psychoanalysis from the traditional 'one-person' models, I was aware, from my outsider position, of an underestimation of the continuity between the relational perspective and the contributions of classical analysts, including British innovators such as Winnicott and Fairbairn, giants on whose shoulders we stand. Perhaps the splits between the various schools of psychoanalysis on the one hand, and the affiliation of the relational perspective with the humanistic tradition on the other, are more pronounced in the UK than in other parts of Europe. While splits are sometimes inevitable and can be viewed as healthy in encouraging diversity, they tend to prevent an examination of what we stand to lose. I believe we should also examine what we stand to lose by these welcomed changes in our dialogue, namely, by shifting our gaze to the interpersonal rather than the intrapsychic, the actual rather than the unconscious, and by allowing interaction and self-disclosure in the analytic setting. As Mitchell (1988) argued, multiplicity of theoretical perspectives may not be a fault in need of correction, but a reflection of the diversity and complexities of human experience.

References

Altman, N. (1995). *The analyst in the inner city*. Hillsdale, NJ: The Analytic Press.

Aron, L. (1996). *A meeting of minds: Mutuality in psychoanalysis*. Hillsdale, NJ: The Analytic Press.

Atwood, C. and Stolorow, R. (1984). *Structures of subjectivity*. Hillsdale, NJ: The Analytic Press.

Beebe, B. and Lachmann, F. (1988). The contribution of mother–infant mutual influence to the origins of self and object representations. *Psychoanalytic Psychology, 5*(4): 305–337.

Benjamin, J. (2002). Terror and guilt. *Psychoanalytic Dialogues, 12*: 473–484.

Benjamin, J. (2006). Beyond doer–done to: An intersubjective view of thirdness. *Psychoanalytic Quarterly, 73*: 5–46.

Bromberg, P. (1996). Standing in the spaces: The multiplicity of self and the psychoanalytic relationship. *Contemporary Psychoanalysis, 32*: 509–535.

Bromberg, P. M. (2000). Potholes on the royal road. *Contemporary Psychoanalysis, 36*: 5–28.

Davis, J. M. (1996). Dissociation, repression and reality testing in the countertransference: The controversy over memory and false memory in the psychoanalytic treatment of adult survivors of childhood sexual abuse. *Psychoanalytic Dialogues, 6*: 189–218.

Fonagy, P. and Target, M. (1997). Attachment and reflective function: Their role in self organization. *Development and psychopathology, 9*: 679–700.

Gerson, S. (1996). Neutrality, resistance and self-disclosure in an intersubjective psychoanalysis. *Psychoanalytic Dialogues, 6*(5): 623–645.

Gerson, S. (2006). The elusiveness of the relational unconscious: Commentary on a paper by Juan Taubert-Oklander. *Psychoanalytic Dialogues, 16*(2): 217–225.

Ghent, E. (1990). Masochism, submission, surrender. *Contemporary Psychoanalysis, 26*: 108–136.

Layton, L. (1998). *Who's that girl? Who's that boy? Clinical practice meets postmodern gender theory*. Northvale, NJ: Aronson.

Mitchell, S. A. (1988). *Relational concepts in psychoanalysis.* Cambridge, MA: Harvard University Press.

Nebbiosi, G. (2006). The semicircle and the bow: Attachment sexuality and analytic stance in contemporary psychoanalysis. Paper given at the annual conference of TAICP, Tel-Aviv, Israel, December.

Ogden, T. (1994). *Subjects of Analysis*. Northvale, NJ: Aronson.

Orange, D. M. (2003). The post-cartesian witness and the psychoanalytic profession. Unpublished manuscript.

Pizer, S. A. (1998). *Building bridges: The negotiation of paradox in psychoanalysis.* Hillsdale, NJ: The Analytic Press.

Priel, B. (2006). Authority as paradox: Transformations of Don Quixote. *International Journal of Psychoanalysis, 87*: 1675–1689.

Renik, O. (1995). The ideal of the anonymous analyst and the problem of self-disclosure. *Psychoanalytic Quarterly, 64*: 466–495.

Samuels, A. (1989). *The plural psyche: Personality, morality and the father*. London and New York: Routledge

Seligman, S. (2006). The analyst's theoretical persuasion and the construction of a conscientious analysis. *Psychoanalytic Dialogues, 16*(4): 397–405.

Ullman, C. (2006). Bearing witness: Across the barriers in society and in the clinic. *Psychoanalytic Dialogues, 16*(2): 181–198

Part II

MAINLY CRITIQUES

10

THE RELATIONAL TURN IN PSYCHOANALYSIS

Revolution or regression?[1]

Zvi Carmeli and Rachel Blass

In this chapter, the authors discuss the Relational turn in psychoanalysis that has supposedly taken place in the course of the past 25 years. They spell out the foundational claims of the Relational group and its view that it has revolutionized psychoanalysis by bringing its relational potential to fruition. After clarifying these Relational views, the authors explain why they think that the change introduced is misguided and not as revolutionary as it appears. The authors argue that counter to its self-perception, the relational group in fact reverts to a pre-analytic conception of the person and to an authoritarian stance in relation to the patient. While presenting himself as liberal, unassuming and non-authoritarian in contrast to the traditional analyst, in his belief in his power to know what the patient is missing and to give it to him, the Relational psychoanalyst, in effect, adopts a benevolent paternalistic dogmatism. It is here that the regressive move that actually lies at the heart of what has been referred to by some as the relational revolution in psychoanalysis is best exemplified.

Introduction

In this chapter, we will discuss the Relational turn in psychoanalysis, the revolution toward a relational perspective in psychoanalysis that has supposedly taken place in the course of the past 25 years. While there are local variants, the primary force behind the notion of this being a real turn is the American Relational School or perhaps group (as it is a bit too broad to be considered a school). The group's basic claim is that psychoanalysis in some very limited sense may have always included relational elements, but its true relational potential had not until recently been fully recognized and actualized. Indeed, the group maintains, seeds of relational thinking and clinical practice may be found in some of Freud's work, however, the true father of the Relational approach is Sandor Ferenczi and his relational legacy may be seen to run through the teachings of Fairbairn, Balint and Winnicott, ultimately coming to fruition in American Relational psychoanalysis. This legacy is thought to be supported empirically by the findings of Attachment theory and infant research such as that of Daniel Stern and to be philosophically grounded in post-modern thinking. This powerful combination of sensitivity to relatedness, hard-nosed science, and contemporary philosophy also seems to allow one to perceive and embrace the relational contribution deeply embedded in other theories. Hence the warm feelings at times toward Kleinian thinking – feelings that quite clearly go unreciprocated.

We will briefly spell out the foundational claims of the Relational group; what this relational potential is that is only in recent years coming to fruition and in what sense it is considered to be revolutionary relative to traditional psychoanalysis. After clarifying these Relational views, we will then explain why we think that the change it introduces is misguided and, moreover, not really revolutionary; that counter to its self-perception, the Relational group in fact reverts to a pre-analytic conception of the person and to an authoritarian stance in relation to the patient.

What is relational about relational psychoanalysis?

So what is Relational psychoanalysis? Of course, in a sense, all psychoanalysis is relational. From Freud's earliest writings it was clear that it was not insight or understanding *per se* that brings about change, but insight within the analytic relationship. Transference, which is a form of relationship, is explicitly the cornerstone of analytic practice. It involves reliving one's inner world with the analyst and the analyst using his or her experiences, what the patient arouses, to gain understanding and to convey it back to the patient sensitively. And even on the purely theoretical level, at the centre of all analytic thinking on motivation and pathology are Oedipal dynamics and pre-Oedipal dynamics which are about relationships, fears, love, greed, need, in dyadic and triadic contexts. Relational psychoanalysis does not deny any of this.

What then does Relational psychoanalysis add? Well, there are a wide range of propositions and technical innovations that come under the heading of Relational psychoanalysis, but we would like to focus now on two positions that are foundational and which seem to unite the Relational camp (beyond the specifics and differences):

1 Relational analysts claim that man is inherently relational: that is, Relational analysts hold that the individual cannot be understood except as part of the system of human relations in which he lives and develops. Indeed, Freud and his followers, what we may refer to as a traditional camp, have posited that the individual is shaped by relationships and relationships of certain therapeutic kinds are needed for change in later life. But this implies that there is an individual, a person independent of those relationships, who is shaped and changed by them. This is often referred to as a Cartesian

worldview, a view of man as ontologically isolated. For Relational analysts, in contrast, the person *is* his or her relationships. There is no standing beyond them. This will also have implications for how motivation and experience are conceived. Relational analysts will regard the traditional approach to these as a reflection of the isolated view of the individual. Recognizing Freud's awareness of the role of relationship in bringing about emotional experiences (e.g. the connection between the Rat Man's anxiety and his relationship with his parental objects), Relational analysts will stress that Freud's fundamental understanding of these experiences is ultimately in terms of energetic processes aroused by the relationships. And regarding the works of other traditional analysts they will point to the fact that such experiences are ultimately described as being derived from inner object relations, not actual ones. In these descriptions of experience (albeit relational), the individual is viewed as an organism standing on his own. Similarly, various forms of self-serving drives are considered (according to Relationalists) to be what underlies the individual's search for relationship in traditional analysis. In contrast, in Relational psychoanalysis what motivates is the quest for relationship itself and emotion is derived from the relational context and understood in terms of that context. But even if one accepts the notion of there being emotional states and motives that are internal, there is the question of how they acquire their meaning. Here too the Relationalists would see a contrast between the traditional view and their own. From their perspective, traditional psychoanalysis sees the meaning of the drives as given, innate like the drive itself, inherent to the drive. This is very different from the Relational perspective, which would consider the meanings associated with experiences and drives as acquired only within the cultural context in which they exist. In this sense, the individual and even his basic motivations are meaningless when separated from the cultural–relational system in which he develops and, as such, he cannot be understood apart from that system. As Stephen Mitchell explains, 'Desire is experienced always in the context of relatedness, and it is that context which defines its meaning' (1988: 3).

2   The relational view of the mind and truth: This second position is tied to the previous one, but has a more specific emphasis. Here it is argued that not only can we not view the individual as standing on his own, that relationships are inherent to who he is (his experiences and motivations), but that the idea that his mind has an objective existence, there to be discovered, is an illusion. This is a misguided view, based on the isolationist conception of the individual, characteristic of traditional psychoanalysis (grounded on a positivist approach of nineteenth-century science). In line with this, the traditional analyst would be concerned with the contents of the mind and its structures, as though these were truths there to be described, interpreted, discovered, independent of the context (the relationships) in which they are realized and expressed.

And once again, in contrast, the Relationalists would hold that in their view the mind is an interactive phenomenon whose contents are not present within it but are rather created within the interactive context in which it is realized.

> Meanings are constructed anew in each interaction: . . . they are always contextualized, contested, contingent, situated, decentered, etc., and . . . none can be construed to be objective and unvarying givens from either inside or outside.
> (Wallerstein, 1998: 1022)

In line with this, for example, there could be no such thing as a difficult patient, for there is no patient *per se* independent of his analytic relationship (as Brandchaft and Stolorow [1994] argue). This has far-reaching consequences for analytic treatment. From this view, the therapeutic process cannot be seen as a process of discovery, of coming to know one's inner truth, to be integrated with it. Rather, in the absence of any given contents the process becomes one of change, a process in which the configuration of the mind fluctuates in consequence of the influence of the new relationships that are formed between analyst and patient.

Many of the more specific, technical modifications that one finds in the Relational literature are derived from this. From this perspective, we no longer have an analyst helping a patient find himself, but rather an analyst who is a partner to a new relationship. The analyst may not be an equal partner, in the sense that he knows that it is the patient who is coming to him with his needs and not vice versa; it is the analyst who has responsibilities toward the patient. But he is equally a participant in a new relationship and he ascribes to himself no special expertise in understanding the patient's psychic reality, for there is no given reality waiting to be understood. This is associated with a non-authoritarian stance that is required of the Relational analyst (in contrast to the analyst as potential knower), a stance of humility and doubt. Moreover, since it is the reality of the patient–analyst relationship that is transformative, who the analyst really is, what he gives in reality – not in terms of how the analyst's reality is construed by the patient – becomes central to the analytic process. In line with this, the Relational analyst will consider it important to form a good and, in a sense, corrective relationship with the patient, offering a relationship different than the harmful ones of the past. This may entail some self-disclosure in which the analyst shares from his own experience, explains what he really meant, or apologizes for errors and misunderstandings. For what is important is not how the patient interprets reality (he has no fixed internal way of doing so that would be meaningful to discover) but the new reality itself. Stephen Mitchell describes a patient who repeatedly attacked him and finally asked him how he would have treated her if the relationship between them were not therapeutic. He writes:

> I ended up saying something like, 'If this were not an analytic relationship, if this were out on the street . . . and I weren't your analyst, I probably

would say 'FUCK YOU!' But I am your analyst.' She laughed, and I laughed, and the tension was broken.

(Mitchell, 2000: 142)

What we are pointing to here is that in this Relational turn in psychoanalysis, underlying the talk of relationship and the technical innovations, what is actually the bone of contention is a certain view of the human being. The Relational analysts claim that in contrast to the isolated view of man of traditional psychoanalysis, which considers his mind as a container of objective truths there to be discovered, their view is one of inherent relatedness. The individual's experiences, motivations, and meanings do not reside in him, so to speak, but are formed anew, time and again, in the various relational contexts in which the individual finds himself – one significant such context being the analytic relationship. Relational psychoanalysts have often referred to the development of this difference between their conception and that of traditional psychoanalysis as a shift from a one-person psychology to a two-person psychology. And this shift in the conception of the person is, in their view, revolutionary. Again we may turn to Mitchell. He writes:

> Psychoanalytic theories of the past several decades have undergone what Kuhn . . . calls a paradigm shift. The very boundaries around the subject matter of psychoanalysis have been redrawn, and that broad reframing has had profound implications for both theory and practice.
>
> (1988: 17)

Why the relational view is not revolutionary

In discussing why the Relational view is not revolutionary, we will stress two points: First, that the shift described entails a misrepresentation of both traditional and Relational psychoanalysis; differences are emphasized that are not really there. Second, that the changes that have been introduced entail a step back, a regression from the radical view of the person that traditional psychoanalysis has offered – and continues to do so. It leads back to a pre-analytic view of therapy founded on an authoritarian and suggestive relational process rather than the liberating one that is inherent to the Freudian revolution.

Let us begin with the misrepresentations: It may be seen that traditional analysis is not as un-relational as the Relationalists would have it. The individual in Freudian theory is perceived as deeply influenced by his environment and shaped to his very core by the relationships in which he developed. He not only has relationships as a reflection of some deeper inner processes, but the drive indeed is seeking an object and is shaped by objects. (There is an object involved just as much in the need for a relationship as there is an individual self who is needing.) Similarly, Klein's thinking is based on an inner world of phantasies, but these too are shaped by experiences of relationship. The good and bad breasts are tied to experiences of satisfaction and frustration with the mother's breast. Indeed, these experiences are shaped by need and phantasy; the picture is complex, but in this complexity the relationship is never left out. Also in the description of the traditional analyst as a positivistic scientist coming to authoritatively discover underlying truths, uninfluenced by the flow of the relational context, it may be seen that quite a bit of distortion is taking place. While there may be some analysts who acted or still act like this, it is not possible to see this as an inherent component of traditional psychoanalysis. Traditional analysts will normally use the experience of the relationship, their feelings and sensitivities, to struggle to understand what is going on, and on the basis of this offer interpretations, not as God-given truths but rather as attempts to formulate what can be seen at the moment, recognizing that the interpretation may be influenced by relational factors that may help and/ or hinder getting a better grasp of the truth of the matter.

It seems that one way in which Relational psychoanalysis deals with the blatantly relational aspects of traditional psychoanalysis is by regarding them as infiltrations of Relational thinking into traditional psychoanalysis. Thus Greenberg and Mitchell (1983) take note that in some of Freud's writings (e.g. in *On Narcissism*, *Mourning and Melancholia*, and *The Ego and the Id*) one may see a relational paradigm finding expression, but they refer to it as secondary to Freud's intrapsychic drive paradigm (which is his primary one) and in opposition to it. This, of course, is to beg the question; to not allow for the possibility that Freud held a dialectical position which included both drive and relationship. That is, rather than acknowledging that traditional psychoanalysis is relational, its non-relationality is pre-supposed and thus the presence of relationality is interpreted as the infiltration of a Relational perspective (which was only later to be discovered).

Not only is traditional analysis more relational, but Relational psychoanalysis is much more traditional than Relational psychoanalysis would have it. It may be seen that despite the talk of inherent relationality, Relational psychoanalysis actually continues to maintain a view of the individual as a discrete entity – indeed an entity in relationship, like the traditionalists understand it – but still a discrete entity. Relational psychoanalysis may sharpen our recognition of the diverse and complex ways in which interpersonal interaction affects the patient's experiences, and contribute in some ways to an understanding of the multi-layered ramifications of that influence, but it does not express any essential change in the way in which the patient's experience and mind is perceived in and of itself. That is, Relational analysis continues to posit the existence of a mental world that is internal and private and responsible for the way in which experience is constructed and given meaning. New terms are used to describe this internal, private world. Relational analysts will speak of organizing principles rather than representations or internal objects (Stolorow & Atwood, 1992) of unformulated experience rather than unconscious contents (Stern, 1997), of an interactive process of construction of a limited range of possible realities rather than the interpretation of psychic reality (Hoffman, 1991), but many of the same ideas are retained.

Moreover, when one critically examines the clinical material described by Relational analysts, one can see that contrary to their claims regarding the new conception of the individual as inherently relational, what we are presented with is a process aimed at 'creating' an autonomous and free subject who is attuned to his environment but not created by it. As in the case of traditional analysts, for example, the specific features of the environment in which the patient was raised – his community, nationality, or country – are usually not mentioned in case descriptions because they are not seen as part of the subject's inner core and indeed there is an inner core, which, in effect, is regarded as standing beyond any such chance environmental features.

Similarly, contrary to the inherent motivation for relatedness of which Relational analysts speak, one may see that in their case illustrations the relationships are described, understood and valued in terms of their various self-serving needs, in terms of what they offer the individual qua individual. For example, a relational commitment that leaves the individual within his or her familiar framework may be referred to (by Relationalists) as pathological for not opening the individual to new relational possibilities (this is how Mitchell [1988] understands Penelope's loyalty to Odysseus in Homer's Odyssey).

So we hope here to have shown that traditional analysis is more relational and Relational analysis more traditional than they are portrayed by Relational psychoanalysis. It is for this reason that it is difficult to conceive of Relational analysis as revolutionary. Contrary to their declarations, the Relationalists simply did not bring about a paradigmatic change in the conception of the individual. Relational analysis has remained what in relational terms would be referred to as 'a one-person psychology'.

But now we would like to turn to our claim regarding the regressive rather than revolutionary nature of Relational psychoanalysis. While Relational psychoanalysis has exaggerated the idea of its having introduced a paradigmatic change, it has nevertheless introduced clinical and technical changes and we may wonder about their nature; how they stand relative to traditional psychoanalysis. Here what we argue is that they constitute a step backwards, rather than an advance. In a nutshell, the focus on the real interaction that Relational psychoanalysis recommends, the focus on what is really going on between the patient and analyst – not the interpretation of these in terms of the patient's psychic reality, and their inner unconscious meaning – involves a retreat to a pre-analytic stance. This is a stance in which one helps the other through encouragement, suggestion and offering a more benevolent environment. In essence, it is an educational, corrective position well-known from social work and religious contexts (such as the Salvation Army). Indeed, it studies the details of the patterns of the relationship, listens with care to the emerging dynamics, but then corrects, directs.

Hoffman tells of how he chatted with his patient about a video tape of a TV show that the patient had given him to watch and that some of what was said was not 'of any special interest analytically'. He adds: 'Incidentally, that ostensibly "inconsequential" part from the point of view of the analytic work was actually a very important part of the experience because it was spontaneous and informal and not explicitly analyzed' (Hoffman, 1996: 128). The video included an exchange between father and son that takes place following a suggestion by the son's therapist. Hoffman refers to this:

> We talked about the analyst's specific suggestion with regard to the father, and together we mulled over the question of whether there was any way the patient could approach his father that might create the opportunity for a breakthrough in their relationship. The patient did not think so, and I felt he was right. He said he was moved when the son and the father hugged at the end. I said I had been moved, too, but that I understood that his feelings had special poignancy in light of the seemingly impenetrable barriers between himself and his own father.
>
> (ibid.: 129)

What was radical about the introduction of what one may today regard as traditional psychoanalysis is that it offered the individual a path to finding and becoming himself by the analyst resisting the temptation of being benevolent and curing through suggestion and kindness. By the analyst interpreting the transference rather than becoming the good transferential object the patient could come to know who he is, own himself (his meanings, his constructions), act from within, and see the world as it is, rather than only in light of projections. What Relational analysis offers instead is the reality of a relationship, and a phantasied one at that, one coloured by the patient's projections from his inner world which in essence go unacknowledged as such. While presenting himself as liberal and unassuming in contrast to the authoritarian analyst of old, in his belief in his power to know what the patient is missing and to give it to him, the Relational psychoanalyst, in effect, adopts a benevolent paternalistic dogmatism. It is here that we find the regressive move that actually lies at the heart of what has been referred to by some as the relational revolution in psychoanalysis.

Note

1 This paper was presented as a lecture at the conference 'The relational: Cutting edge or cliché in psychotherapy and counselling?' at the University of Roehampton, November 2009.

References

Brandchaft, B. and Stolorow, R. D. (1994). The difficult patient. In *The intersubjective perspective* (R. D. Stolorow, G. E. Atwood and B. Brandchaft, Eds.). Northvale, NJ and London: Jason Aronson (pp. 93–112).

Greenberg, J. and Mitchell, S. M. (1983). *Object relations in psychoanalytic theory*. Cambridge, MA: Harvard University Press.

Hoffman, I. Z. (1991). Discussion: Toward a social-constructivist view of the psychoanalytic situation. *Psychoanalytic Dialogues, 1:* 74–105.

Hoffman, I. Z. (1996). The intimate and ironic authority of the psychoanalyst's presence. *Psychoanalytic Quarterly, 65:* 102–136.

Mitchell, S. A. (1988). *Relational concepts in psychoanalysis: An integration.* Cambridge, MA and London: Harvard University Press.

Mitchell, S. A. (2000). *Relationality: From attachment to intersubjectivity.* Hillsdale, NJ and London: The Analytic Press.

Stern, D. B. (1997). *Unformulated experience: From dissociation to imagination in psychoanalysis.* Hillsdale, NJ: The Analytic Press.

Stolorow, R. D and Atwood, G. E. (1992). *Contexts of being: The intersubjectivist foundation of psychological life.* Hillsdale, NJ: Analytic Press.

Wallerstein, R. S. (1998). The new American psychoanalysis: A commentary. *Journal of The American Psychoanalytic Association, 46:* 1021–1043.

11

IT'S THE STUPID RELATIONSHIP

Ian Parker

Relational psychoanalysis promises to connect the personal and the political, and so poses a particularly painful challenge to 'Left Lacanians'. It seems to force a choice between the 'Left' and 'Lacanian' sides of our practice. It rubs at a sore point in Lacanian work, at a point of uneasy alliance between radical politics on the one hand and, on the other, the one-to-one frame of abstracted, individualised and limited horizons of change in the consulting room. I take up some of the questions that the relational turn poses for us on the Left, which I think is where much of the appeal of this turn is now, and for us Lacanians who are sometimes on the Left as well.

Introduction

There have been a number of attempts to manage the connection between the clinic and activism in the English-speaking world, and we can sketch out three attempts here. A first option is to maintain a strict separation of different domains of practice, and so an influential strand of conceptual work clustered around the Frankfurt School has been radical, even Marxist in some variants, but has been chary of extrapolating from cultural analysis to what goes on in the clinic (e.g. Fromm, 1932/1978; Marcuse, 1974). This position entailed the following conclusions, sometimes linked, even embodied in the same individual or text: that a good psychoanalytic training regardless of its political orientation is a prerequisite to progressive interventions; that we should abandon psychoanalytic practice if we are to engage in politics; that we need to subordinate political analysis to categories derived from conservative psychoanalysis (e.g. Kovel, 1988; Orbach, 2003; Wolfenstein, 1993).

A second option is to use clinical work as an instrument to politicise subjectivity, and this option turns psychoanalysis into something instrumental to social change, into an instrument of a particular kind, precisely because it turns against psychoanalysis as much of the time being a practice that is intent on putting people in their place and leading them to cynicism or stoicism. This course of action also leads to an embrace of an ethics of the good in which some romantic image of natural forces replicates, only ostensibly in reverse, psychiatric prescriptions, or an ethics of the redistribution and balancing out of individual needs which conforms to a kind of psychology, or an ethics of duty, to conform to the rule of enjoyment and a flourishing of pleasure that continues the line of psychotherapeutic exploration (Parker, 2010). Reich (1972) serves as an all too convenient warning here and his career pertains in different ways to each of these ethical pursuits. In addition, his adventures seem to indicate that politicised psychoanalysis would itself eventually adapt itself to some quite bizarre anti-psychoanalytic ideas (Chasseguet-Smirgel & Grunberger, 1986; Kovel, 1986).

But then there is a third option born of innovations in clinical practice that were just as problematic as the instrumental radicalisation of individuals or the attempt by social theorists to steer clear of the consulting room. One could say that Ferenczi's (1994) attempt to equalise the encounter between analyst and analysand involved boundary-breaking – 'active therapy', 'mutual analysis' and then sexual partnerships – that was taking seriously the relational aspect of psychoanalysis at the very same moment as it blurred the boundaries between fantasy and reality. There was a connection between a new understanding of relationships in childhood and relationships in analysis. On the one hand there was a turn back from analytic attention to sexual fantasies to what really happened to the child, a turn back from Freud's shift of attention to fantasy which inaugurated psychoanalysis as such, an idea which surfaced again later in the concern with observable 'object relations'. On the other hand there was a turn back from abstinence on the part of the analyst to being present to the analysand, providing reassurance and disclosing what they made of reality or what the analyst made of an internal reality that would give deeper insight into the analytic relationship. Then the clinical interventions of Sullivan (1997), who as a gay man had a different stake in challenging mainstream psychoanalytic pathologisation of sexual relationships in the name of what was known about their fantasy sub-structure, combined an emphasis on social context with the seduction of patients, clinical interventions now read as a precursor to what it might mean to queer psychoanalysis (Hegarty, 2004; Wake, 2008). The third option, then, is to introduce into the consulting room a relational sensitivity that would mirror conceptual work on the importance of relationships in child development and in processes of political change. Even if Sullivan was not a psychoanalytic gay rights activist he did prefigure what it might mean to connect how we might aim for social revolution – how we might aim for it rather than simply positing it as an ideal – and how we might aim for personal change in analysis.

Inside psychoanalysis a trajectory from the interpersonal to the intersubjective to the relational is thereby set in train that will eventually connect with a renewal of feminist arguments inside the socialist movement, arguments that the personal is political and that the way we struggle for social change will prefigure what the outcome of that struggle will be (Benjamin, 1988; Orbach, 2007). Relational psychoanalysis then draws together these two strands, though it has tended to be the journey through American object relations to relational concepts and the subjectivity of the analyst in the work of Mitchell (1997) that has been emphasised in recent clinical debates (cf. Aron, 2007).

The question of countertransference, of what should be made of it as a resource for thinking about what is going on for the analyst and what should be disclosed of it in order to connect with and bring about mutative effects for the analysand, has taken centre stage (Heimann, 1950). However, in the background there are assumptions about actual relations that inform the development of object relations, which then bear fruit in a particular notion of 'transference' and what is to be done about it.

Signifiers of transference

So, we turn to a key defining characteristic of Lacanian psychoanalysis, which is the attention we give to signifiers. In the clinic, we can see the importance of this attention to signifiers with respect to transference. I want to emphasise this by delineating three traditions of work on transference in psychoanalysis. There is, first, a tradition of work that views psychoanalysis as always having been concerned with some form of attachment between infant and mother, and then by implication between adult human beings, including those in psychoanalysis. This model of transference sees it as a special kind of glue holding people together (e.g. Fonagy et al., 2004; Stern, 1985). The second tradition has come to value what is intersubjective in the psychoanalytic relationship, and focuses on what intuitive responses on the part of the analyst may tell the analyst, and potentially also the analysand, about what is going on between them. The guiding motif of this approach is that the relational dimension of human activity also operates as a kind of conduit for feelings that can be accessed by partners in the relationship (e.g. Fairfield, Layton, & Stack, 2002; Samuels, 1993).

The first tradition focuses on language, and in this Lacanian tradition transference is defined by the repetition of signifiers, those that will be of specific value to the analysand and which appear in their speech as they produce a representation of themselves to the analyst. They are signifiers that recur in the language of the analysis, and include the signifiers introduced into the analysis by the analyst as well as the analysand. The Lacanian analyst tries to avoid appeal to a domain of feelings hidden beneath the signifiers, feelings perhaps thought of inside the analyst in a separate domain of countertransference, and avoids recourse to a 'meta-language' that would provide a point of escape from the effects of signifiers to a place from which the transference could be interpreted to the poor analysand who remains trapped within it.

Relational psychoanalysts seem to borrow from and oscillate between the first and second traditions of work on transference I have outlined here, and here is a key difference between those traditions and the Lacanian attention to signifiers as such.

We could say in Lacanese that the first overall covering explanation of transference, which treats it as a particular subset of the attachment of the subject to their objects, operates somewhere between the imaginary – complementary relationships which we all experience with our others – and the real. However, this 'real' is an imaginarised version of the real rather than that which is resistant to representation and impossible to access – the Lacanian real; this real is conceived as something that can be observed or reconstructed by the analyst.

The second tradition provides an overall covering account for transference that operates somewhere along a dimension running between the imaginary and the symbolic. Here, however, this symbolic is not a structured system of signifying processes that operates independently of the subject – the Lacanian symbolic – but is, instead, a realm of communicational material in which each subject is embedded and through which they might discover their shared humanity. This is the symbolic as the domain of common sense, which gives to this account of transference and countertransference as a form of 'empathy' a particular appeal.

The third tradition, the Lacanian tradition, articulates the symbolic to touch the real. This real has at its core the impossible-to-symbolise traumatic discovery of sex for the subject, and Lacan argues that the mark of this real is nowhere more evident than in the repetitious failure to write the sexual relationship for the subject as something complementary or harmonious. Sex and a sexual encounter is not, therefore, 'relational' but is conceptualised as impossible, as a non-relation (Lacan, 1998).

Relations and empty signifiers

There are four conceptual elements that it may be useful to bear in mind here in the shift to 'relations' in order to emphasise that what we call a 'non-relation' is embedded in a kind of 'relational' model of human subjectivity. My concern is not with whether we have a relational conception or not – although, yes, that should be our starting point – but with how our use of this term comes to be filled with ideological contents. The conceptual element is Marx's (1845) characterisation of the human being as 'an ensemble of social relations', a characterisation that is given different inflection in relational psychoanalytic attention to attachment and in Lacanian accounts of the necessity for the child to process inchoate bodily states through the mediating externalised form of the 'Other' (Verhaeghe, 2004). The second element which is also present in Marxism, and which owes something to a working through of its conceptual debt to Hegel, is 'negativity', and this force which powers dialectical logic expresses itself in psychoanalytic theory in accounts of the vicissitudes of the drive, sometimes conceived of as death drive and 'aggression' or the less biologically loaded term, 'aggressivity'. These first two elements themselves operate dialectically, in an opposition of social relations and negativity that complicate how we think about social relations as such. A third conceptual element that we need to introduce here, and which has been named as such in relational psychoanalysis more than in Lacanian psychoanalysis, is power, the reproduction of power relations inside the clinic (Ullman, 2007). It is only if we take power seriously that it makes sense to think through the possibilities of the fourth conceptual element, which is that there are 'pre-figurative' aspects of analysis. However, if power is taken seriously this also has limiting effects on what pre-figurative work is possible inside the clinic.

In Lacanian terms we might think of pre-figurative work as involving a shift from the register of the imaginary, that realm of idealised communication in which we think we understand each other, to the register of the symbolic, in which we forge the kinds of social bond through which something like that understanding is enacted in practice. Power operates against this progressive political shift through a reduction, condensation, crystallising of given symbolic forms into how we conceptualise how we stand in relation to others, from a reduction of the register of the symbolic to the imaginary. Negativity disrupts the easy flow of communication at each level and between them, operating as the 'real' which is resistant to symbolisation and which frustrates understanding. This invites us to think of the ensemble of social relations as the linking of those three registers of symbolic, imaginary and real, a linking that Lacan describes using the curious figure of the Borromean knot in which each ring intersects with the other two and holds them in place. My claim here is that the linking of the three realms by way of the fourth is not given substance by Lacanians in one particular signifier which would then have ideological weight, nor should it be (Thurston, 1998).

Now I want to bring in something of the Left of Lacanian theory, and do this briefly by noting Ernesto Laclau's argument that the political field includes peculiar kinds of signifiers he calls 'empty signifiers', which are sites of ideological struggle. The unachievable 'fullness and universality of society', as Laclau (1996, p. 53) puts it, is worried away at in his work, and empty signifiers like 'emancipation', 'liberation' or 'revolution' are seen as manifestations of an ideological struggle over what would count as fullness or universality. This is not necessarily to say that these are bad ideals or that the struggle to fill these empty signifiers with content is mistaken, even if Laclau and his followers and many Lacanian analysts have come to be morbidly suspicious of them. It seems to me that relational psychoanalysis is inspired by exactly that kind of utopian impulse to invest empty signifiers with content, something that I see as a positive thing, something that puts democratisation back on the agenda again in politics at least, if not immediately in the clinic.

My argument is that the signifier 'relation' in the relational psychoanalytic turn is what might be more accurately termed an 'empty signifier'. So we now find a terrain inside psychoanalysis where there is just such a yearning for 'fullness and universality', and the hope that it may be expressed in 'relation'. As an empty signifier, 'relation' seems to connote at least the following: (i) a relation between analysand and analyst, (ii) a relation between infant and caregiver, (iii) a relation between self and other, (iv) a relation between individual and collective, (v) a relation between the personal and the political and (vi) a relation between the clinic and the world. I want to try and disentangle the way these six different binary oppositions are woven into each other, and so work out how 'relation' is functioning.

Ensembles of power

Let us begin with what we hope for, what we might be aiming for in psychoanalysis. The relational turn in psychoanalysis raises a question about the end of analysis, and the extent to which it is possible to go beyond Freud's (1937) rather pessimistic formulations about the interminable nature of it, the impossibility of circumventing the rock of castration or the 'repudiation of femininity'. Shifting attention to the process itself rather than aiming for an idealised endpoint at which the analysand believes themselves to be completely free is something that is hinted at in Freud's work and taken further in different ways in relational psychoanalysis and in Lacanian psychoanalysis.

The problem is that just as Freud's formulations set limits on what can be achieved in analysis, so do those of relational psychoanalysis (and I am not at all claiming that Lacanians do not also set such limits). If the relationship between analysand and analyst is modelled on and rooted in the relationship between infant and caregiver, then there is already imported into the clinic a particular conception of power and an ideological understanding of what the first most important ensemble of social relations is into which a human being takes form as a sentient being. The signifier 'attachment' is potent here, which is why I needed to draw attention to that first tradition of work around transference that is concerned with attachment. The danger is that this 'attachment' links those two first kinds of relation – (i) analysand and analyst, (ii) infant and caregiver – but then makes it difficult to prefigure another form of relating outside the frame of what attachment is understood to be.

For Lacanians, the end of analysis can be conceptualised as entailing a shift in relation to knowledge, knowledge that is incomplete, evanescent, lost again soon after it appears in analysis as the truth of the subject. It is a kind of knowledge the relation to which repeats the subject's relation to their objects as always already lost. The connection between the first two relations – analysand and analyst, infant and caregiver – therefore offers a kind of knowledge that Lacanian psychoanalysis aims to de-complete. The analysand gives up the pretence that there is any fullness or universality to this knowledge about themselves as individuals.

Dialectics of authority

Let us shift a bit further to the Left in the argument. There are two significant intertwined aspects of the concern with 'relations' in the clinic in relational psychoanalysis, with one aspect calling on the other in order to forge an alliance between this form of psychoanalysis and radical politics. One aspect is the attempt to connect the kinds of relations that are built in the clinic with those outside, and the other is the more ambitious hope that the kinds of relation we would aim for outside the clinic provide the best kind of context for therapeutic change; the way in which therapeutic change takes place would thereby anticipate and enable the kinds of relations we are aiming for in the outside world. The connection now is between (iii) self and other and (iv) individual and collective, the third and fourth of the relations evoked in relational psychoanalysis. The hope for connection of this kind has been captured in the claim that the relational turn is 'democratizing psychoanalysis' (Orbach, 2007), and there is some resonance here with the claim within the broad Lacanian tradition that democracy is the only context in which psychoanalysis is able to thrive (e.g. Roudinesco, 2006; Stavrakakis, 2007).

Lacanians in the clinic do not go all the way with the democratising impulse that would dissolve the authority of the analyst. One reason for this is precisely that challenge to authority, the hysterical questioning of the master of whatever sex by analysand of whatever sex, is also designed to anticipate and subvert the formation of the analysand as another little master, master in their own house (Samuels, 2009). One of the lessons of transference is that power can only be tackled in psychoanalysis if it is taken seriously in the first place.

Actually, here I think relational psychoanalysts might agree with me, but the point I want to emphasise which flows from this argument is that the outcome of the dialectical relationship between analyst and analysand is not democratic synthesis of shared perspectives on the world nor is it triumphal emergence of the analysand as the one who knows. Instead, we could say that the analysand learns something about the relational aspect of subjectivity – they are who they are only by virtue of their difference with others – without actually enacting that relation as an ideal. That is, identity as such is dropped as an ideal, and so a 'relation' as such as an ideal is also dropped.

Here is an instance where relational psychoanalysis does helpfully pose questions to us Lacanians, about what is said about 'desire' among our followers in political theory. We sometimes hear, for example, that Lacan (1992, p. 319) insists that the subject should not give up on their desire, and his quote is wheeled out that 'the only thing of which one can be guilty is of having given ground relative to one's desire'. This can be read to make it seem as if the desire of the subject as sovereign self is pitted against others and as if this is equivalent to the domain of the individual as set against what the collective might desire of it. Lacan, however, locates 'one's desire' as 'desire of the Other', and so the relation between self and other is deconstructed; this deconstruction of the relation between self and other thereby also reconfigures the relation between individual and collective such that the way one becomes a subject with an unconscious – an unconscious which is itself the 'discourse of the Other' – is by way of collective relational processes. If anything, the enactment of desire as something only individual is a betrayal of what that desire actually is. We are thereby able to unpack some ideological specifications of the 'individual' self as that which is pitted against the other as something 'collective'. So, the connection between the third and fourth relations – (iii) self and other, (iv) individual and collective – is, in Lacanian psychoanalysis at least, dismantled.

Politics of the personal

The way we think about the fifth relation, between the personal and the political, also needs to be disconnected from the sixth relation, between the clinic and the world, disconnected from and then rearticulated with it. Here we need to take account of the ideological effects of psychoanalytic discourse which feeds the therapeutisation of subjectivity and politics in contemporary capitalism (Parker, 2009). This therapeutic ethos feeds into the clinic in two ways. First, there is the well-meaning attempt to democratise psychoanalysis that takes place inside the clinic, to make it something that is itself more immediately therapeutic and compatible with the amelioration of heterosexism and racism, for example, in the outside world. Second, there is an ideological rendering of the space of the clinic as the proper space of personal change, and so the infusion of the clinic with a particular moral–political agenda ends up reducing the political to the personal.

The personal is already political, but the clinic can only operate as a place to unravel contemporary subjectivity as an ideological formation if we insist on a radical disjunction between this site and the world. It is precisely because psychoanalysis breaks from everyday conversational procedures – because it refuses the 'relational' dimension of interaction and the attempt to forge an intersubjective space between speakers – that the analyst is able to provoke a questioning of what power is for the subject. What is at stake here is whether we should or should not map the fifth relation, personal and political, onto the sixth, concerned with the clinic and the world (Parker, 2010).

Conclusions

There is a world of difference between the attempt to fill empty signifiers with content in order that we might define and achieve the 'fullness and universality of society' and to attend, instead, to how those signifiers are sites of conflict, division, and political struggle. According to this argument, which accords with Lacan's argument, the desire of the analyst is to obtain 'absolute difference'. Lacan here sets psychoanalysis as a practice of the symbolic and the real against an ideal of harmonious accord between different viewpoints which reduces the symbolic and the real to the imaginary. One might say that at stake is a choice between common sense and psychoanalysis. It is the stupid relationships that comprise contemporary common sense and the stupid appeal to relationships that Lacanian psychoanalysis throws into question. Relational psychoanalysis does risk falling into common sense, and it would do so if it did indeed configure those six 'relations' I described in such a way as to map analysand, infant, self, individual, personal and clinic onto each other in opposition to an assemblage of analyst, caregiver, other, collective, political and the world outside the clinic.

At the same time, relational psychoanalysis poses a series of questions about what a 'relation' is that is not simply reduced to insisting that 'it's the relationship, stupid'. These questions may enable us Left Lacanians to think again about the relation between the Left and Lacanian sides of our work so that what we would prefer to see as this 'non-relation' does at least include an articulation of those two sides of the equation, then even a re-articulation of debates with broader domains of psychoanalysis and politics.

References

Aron, L. (2007). Relational psychotherapy in Europe: A view from across the Atlantic. *European Journal of Psychotherapy and Counselling*, 9(1): 91–03.

Benjamin, J. (1988). *The bonds of love: Psychoanalysis, feminism and the problems of domination*. New York: Pantheon.

Chasseguet-Smirgel, J. and Grunberger, B. (1986). *Freud or Reich? Psychoanalysis and illusion*. London: Free Association Books.

Fairfield, S., Layton, L. and Stack, C. (Eds). (2002). *Bringing the plague: Toward a postmodern psychoanalysis*. New York: Other Press

Ferenczi, S. (1994). *Further contributions to the theory and technique of psychoanalysis*. London: Karnac.

Fonagy, P., Gergely, G., Jurist, E. L. and Target, M. (2004). *Affect regulation, mentalization, and the development of self*. London: Karnac.

Freud, S. (1937). Analysis terminable and interminable. The Hogarth Press and the Institute of Psycho-Analysis, vol. XXIII. In S. Freud (Ed., 1966–1974) *The Standard Edition of the complete psychological works of Sigmund Freud* (J. Strachey, Trans.). London: Vintage.

Fromm, E. (1932/1978). The method and function of an analytic social psychology: Notes on psychoanalysis and historical materialism. In *The essential Frankfurt School Reader* (A. Arato and E. Gebhardt, Eds.). Oxford: Blackwell.

Hegarty, P. (2004). Was he queer ... or just Irish? Reading ethnicity and sexuality in the biography of Harry Stack Sullivan. *Lesbian and Gay Psychology Review*, 5: 103–108.

Heimann, P. (1950). On countertransference. *International Journal of Psycho-Analysis*, 31: 81–84 [Web of Science®].

Kovel, J. (1986). Why Freud or Reich? *Free Associations*, 4: 80–99.

Kovel, J. (1988). *The radical spirit: Essays on psychoanalysis and society*. London: Free Association Books.

Lacan, J. (1992). *The ethics of psychoanalysis 1959–1960: The seminar of Jacques Lacan Book VII* (Original work published 1986; D. Porter, Trans.). London and New York: Routledge.

Lacan, J. (1998). *On feminine sexuality, the limits of love and knowledge, 1972–1973: Encore, the seminar of Jacques Lacan, Book XX* (Original work published 1975; B. Fink, Trans.). New York: Norton.

Laclau, E. (1996). *Emancipation(s)*. London: Verso.

Marcuse, H. (1974). *Eros and civilization: A philosophical inquiry into Freud*. Boston: Beacon Press.

Marx, K. (1845). *Theses on Feuerbach*. Retrieved from www.marxists.org/archive/marx/works/1845/theses/theses.htm

Mitchell, S. (1997). *Influence and autonomy in psychoanalysis*. Hillsdale, NJ: The Analytic Press.

Orbach, S. (2003). Therapy from the left: Interview with Susie Orbach. *European Journal of Psychotherapy and Counselling*, *6*(1): 75–85.

Orbach, S. (2007). Democratizing psychoanalysis. *European Journal of Psychotherapy and Counselling*, *9*(1): 7–21.

Parker, I. (2009). *Psychoanalytic mythologies*. London: Anthem Press.

Parker, I. (2010). *Lacanian psychoanalysis: Revolutions in subjectivity*. London: Routledge.

Reich, W. (1972). *Sex-poll: Essays, 1929–1934* (B. Ollman, Ed.). New York: Random House.

Roudinesco, E. (2006). The psychotherapist and the state. *European Journal of Psychotherapy and Counselling*, *8*(4): 369–374.

Samuels, A. (1993). *The political psyche*. London and New York: Routledge

Samuels, A. (2009). Carnal critiques: Promiscuity, politics, imagination, spirituality and hypocrisy. *Psychotherapy and Politics International*, *7*(1): 4–17.

Stavrakakis, Y. (2007). *The Lacanian Left: Psychoanalysis, theory, politics*. Edinburgh: Edinburgh University Press.

Stern, D. N. (1985). *The interpersonal world of the infant: A view from psychoanalysis and developmental psychology*. New York: Basic Books.

Sullivan, H. S. (1997). *The interpersonal theory of psychiatry*. New York: Norton.

Thurston, L. (1998). Ineluctable nodalities: On the Borromean knot. In *Key concepts in psychoanalysis* (D. Nobus, Ed.). London: Rebus Press.

Wake, N. (2008). Sexuality, intimacy and subjectivity in social psychoanalytic thought of the 1920s and 1930s. *Journal of Community and Applied Social Psychology*, *18*: 119–130.

Wolfenstein, E. V. (1993). *Psychoanalytic-Marxism: Groundwork*. London: Free Association Books.

Ullman, C. (2007). Commentary on special issue on 'Relational psychoanalysis in Europe': How is this dialogue different?, *European Journal of Psychotherapy and Counselling*, *9*(1): 105–116.

Verhaeghe, P. (2004). *On being normal and other disorders: A manual for clinical psychodiagnostics*. New York: Other Press.

12

RELATIONAL ETHICS

From existentialism to post-existentialism

Del Loewenthal

It is argued here that commenting on relational ethics is best done from a post-existential rather than existential perspective, which has perhaps more in common, albeit with important differences, than existentialism with developments in relational psychoanalysis, psychotherapy and counselling. There is some recognition of both contradiction in a relational approach based on knowledge and our search for meaning. The chapter outlines a practice-based approach termed 'post-existentialism' where the problematics of such a search for meaning might be helped by considering some implications of the ethics of Levinas, which are taken as being more post-existential than the existential ethics of Buber.

Introduction

My own interests, which overlap with questioning 'relational' psychological therapies, include exploring such questions as: what helps or hinders an exploration of the most effective expressions of our and other psychological therapists' (and their teachers') desire to help? Is it possible to have both justice and action? Are, for example, our theories mainly perpetuating unintentional violence? Has traditional thoughtfulness been replaced by theories with fields of knowledge, territories, and ownership of subject disciplines policed by economic licensing arrangements, which, in turn, attempt to control language and thought, appropriating difference sometimes in the name of difference? Alternatively, in examining the issue of psychological therapy as a practice of ethics in terms of ideas of truth, justice, and responsibility, are there ethical post-existential considerations from which we can assist in an embodied way so that we can help others not do violence to others? Indeed, is it possible for us as psychological therapists not to interrupt our own and others' continuity, not to play roles in which we no longer recognize ourselves and whereby we betray not only our commitments but our own substance?

This chapter takes as its starting point recent trends in relational psychoanalysis and argues that a primacy should be given to practice rather than theory. Furthermore, if we wish to consider ethical practice then existentialism with its inherent narcissism is less helpful than Levinasian ethics, which can be seen as having important implications for what is termed here 'post-existentialism'. Rozmarin says:

> Thinking relationally, psychoanalysis cannot avoid revisiting its most basic premises: a thought constructed of, and deliberating a *relation* cannot ultimately entertain absolute notions. In a relation there is no one location, no one knowledge, no one self and no one truth. Thinking relationally, psychoanalysis is beginning to contemplate its very nature as a discourse, its status as a 'theory' (Aron & Harris, 2005), and the notion of truth itself (Ghent, 1992).
>
> (Rozmarin, 2007: 333)

Rozmarin goes on to show, drawing on the French philosopher Emanuel Levinas, contradictions in a relational approach based on knowledge. In this chapter, I am suggesting a practice-based approach where what emerges in the therapeutic relationship might be called 'post-existential' (if not 'post-phenomenological') as we are looking at psychoanalysis, psychotherapy and counselling after post-modernism.

From Frie and Orange's (2009) *Beyond Post-modernism*, it would appear that the so called relational school of psychoanalysis seems to have some similarities with post-existentialism. Here Orange writes, 'we are all – like it or not – post-modern existentialists searching for connections and meanings, trying to find our way'.

Orange concludes that a middle ground is possible for psychoanalysis 'drawing on the undervalued traditions of dialogue and ethical phenomenology'. She calls for a moderated post-modernism focusing on lived experience, suspending our interest in categories and in the facts studied by the natural sciences, and viewing relatedness as our primary human situation. Interestingly, in the last half page of Frie and Orange's book, Orange references Levinas and ethical relations. However, the middle ground for relational psychoanalysis may be different to what I am terming here 'post-existentialism' which I will now briefly introduce.

Within the post-existential an attempt is made to offer a space where we might still be able to think about how alienated we are through valuing existential notions such as experience and meaning, whilst questioning other aspects such as existentialism's inferred narcissism and the place it has come to take up with regard to such aspects as psychoanalysis and the political. The post-existential would also include the post-phenomenological and, vitally, the notion of the relational. For example, Merleau-Ponty's notion of being open to what emerges in the between (Merleau-Ponty, 1962), as well as his notion of embodiment, would be given primacy over Husserlian notions of intentionality. As a result, questions such as those of mystery, an unknown and an unconscious, and the non-intentional can be re-examined.

A third element is the extent to which we might consider more recent ideas – for example, those of Saussure, Levinas, Derrida, Foucault, Lacan, and Wittgenstein (as explored, for example, in Loewenthal & Snell 2003) – without becoming too caught up in them. Because of the limitations of space, there is only scope for an introduction to Levinas here. It is hoped that by having a possible space to explore what some would now call our 'well-being', theoretically through post-existentialism, and methodologically through post-phenomenology, that this can provide a loose base, without concerns of any further generalization, for a greater possibility of accepting, rather than escaping, who we are.

However, what needs to be stressed is that if we are really to start with practice and see that this is what Freud and others discovered first, and only later attempted to put theories to, then all theory, whether it be that of Levinas, Freud or anyone else, will always only have implications and not applications – something which perhaps various relational schools amongst others find difficult to stay with. What follows is within what might be termed post-modern ideas of us being 'subject to', whether it be an unconscious (Freud, Jung), writing (Derrida), language (Saussure, Lacan), ethics (Levinas) etc. Thus with post-existentialism both psychotherapist and client would be 'subject to' rather than subjects (with the danger they would see others as objects) and both would hopefully be potentially changed by what emerges in the relationship, which neither will be able to completely control, but rather each may find themselves in places that have taken them beyond their experience.

It is perhaps also important to note that whilst a Levinasian influence on practice would not seek reciprocity, rather than being considered a one-person psychology approach it might be considered beyond a two-person psychology approach, as there is an attempt to go outwards – for the ethical to precede the ontological – for the other rather than a return to me. I shall now attempt to explain this in more detail.

I wish to start by considering whether ethics is separate from practice. If ethics is defined, for example, as putting the other first (Levinas, 1961), then should we all be striving towards this? An argument here is that ethics is not extraneous to transformative practice. Is separating ethics from practice perhaps fundamentally unethical? If this is the case, then this has profound implications for the development of practitioners whether the relational context is therapeutic, educational, or managerial.

An implication of ethics as a basis of practice is that there is an implied transformation where the well-being of others comes before well-being for myself, including my apparent vested interest group. If I now take the terms 'psychological therapist' and 'client' as naming those potentially in relation in all therapies, then an important question could be: 'What does it mean for the person who is the psychological therapist to put the person who is the client first?' A corresponding question might be: 'What does it mean for the client to appropriately put the psychological therapist first?' This form of post-existential human relations is very different to that used in our pervading managerialism of consumer relations, for we may, in putting the other first, have to consider ourselves to be responsible for the others' responsibility.

I think it is useful to explore what it means 'to put the other first'. It seems very different to giving one's life for others and hopefully helpful in clarifying consumerist confusion about the terms 'client-centred' and 'choice' which are currently being used in the UK and other European public services, where I, for example, have been working on an EU project on ethics and the relational as a basis for managing patient-centred care for older people (Loewenthal, 2005). Can we all have well-being and the goods? How can we be involved in what we do for the good (Loewenthal, 2002)? 'Involvement' can mean being entangled, twisted, and confused, perhaps enabling us to not have to see the consequences of our actions through facing the face? Is it possible for us to also learn through our relationships and be moved by something other than the thought of hatred that seems too often to accompany the fundamentalism of a 'Bin Laden' or a 'Bush'? And can we be moved by something other than the increasingly dominant market ideology with, as has been suggested (Barber, 2000), the attempted privatization of all things public and the commercialization of all things private affecting our relationships including what is meant by the notion of public service and how we attempt to educate.

I would like to explore the ethics of the relational, first by comparing aspects of the philosophies of Buber (who is taken to be existential) and Levinas (who I now consider to be post-existential and opposed to the post-modern as he holds open the possibility of being 'just in the moment' with another). I then wish to give an example of the values which, to quote the educationalist Michael Polanyi, if not taught and learned, then might be imparted and acquired through our relationships whether these be of the client and the psychological therapist, or indeed the learner and the teacher, the managed and the manager, or the researched and the researcher.

Why Levinas?

It has been suggested that:

> In the twentieth century, continental philosophers developed a new type of foundation for ethics ... A relatively new line of thought made a distinctive *relation to other people* the central feature of ethics ... Martin Buber ... and Emmanuel Levinas are considered the most prominent members of this tradition [own emphasis].
> (Becker & Becker, 1992: 528–529)

Thus the inter-subjective, existential and post-existential theories of the ethics of Buber and Levinas are the main focus here, as opposed to other notions of ethics which do not make a distinctive relation to other people the central feature. But why Levinas rather than Buber?

Again drawing on Becker and Becker (1992: 528–529), Buber's (1922) two fundamental relations of 'I–It' and 'I–Thou' can be seen to exist between psychological therapist and client. In the 'I–It' relation, the psychological therapist offers herself only partially, using the client as a means to some predefined end, grasping the client as a type and experiencing her own self as a psychological therapist as a detached, isolated, separate subject. In being in an 'I–Thou' relation, the psychological therapist offers herself wholly, participates with the other in an event that takes its own course, grasps the concrete particularity of the client, and emerges as a person in terms of reciprocity. For Buber, only in the 'I–Thou' relation does the psychological therapist achieve genuine presence. 'I–It' relations remain locked in the past. The 'I' of the 'I–Thou' is fundamentally different from the 'I' of the 'I–It'. It is the relation that constitutes the selves of psychological therapist and client. Buber would, however, have acknowledged that, in practice, psychological therapist and client live in continuous dialectics between these two poles. Furthermore, the 'I–Thou' relation does not really unite psychological therapist and client; instead, they achieve a reciprocity that acknowledges their distinctness.

Although, for Buber, the 'I–Thou' relationship cannot become a goal, it is to be preferred. The person as psychological therapist should risk and offer himself fully and be genuinely addressed by the other, and therefore become genuine. A psychological therapist who did not experience the 'I–Thou' would be greatly impoverished and so hence would be the client. An example of this is to be found in the Henry James short story *The Real Thing*, where a commercially successful photographer earns his money selling photographs of what appear to be royalty, but are in fact photographs of actors (the constructed image, perhaps similar to the attempted construction of known competency-based outcomes in, for example, emotional learning). However, one day, some actual royalty, down on their luck, offer to pose for him. What happens is that soon there is a tension brought about in the taking of the photographs by a photographer telling 'real' royalty how to look and the photographer re-engages the actors. The 'royalty', after further unsuccessful employment as the photographer's domestics, are fired. Now would they have been better photographs if the photographer had photographed the tension with the real royalty (more 'I–Thou' rather than 'I–It')?

Buber is existential and modern, with the 'I' in the centre, and this 'I' is returned to, such that 'Thou' is seen in relation to the 'I', so that even a claim for distinctness is a difference in relation to the 'I'. Thus, the client is only seen as being different in comparison to something of the psychological therapist. There is always a return to the psychological therapist; perhaps if both attempt to be subjects and not really be subject to, the client cannot really be other.

Some implications of post-modernism for psychological therapeutic relationships

So far, this account might be seen as phenomenological, with both psychological therapist and client being changed by what emerges between them. But what of phenomenology in the contemporary world? What happened to Buber and phenomenology in the post-modern era? While the term 'post-modernism' is often under suspicion (for example, Eagleton, 1996) and is already being used historically, I have been involved in arguing that it can still have important implications on how relationships are examined (Loewenthal & Snell, 2003). I am now arguing that Levinas is post-existential, in that though we are subject to, for Levinas (subject to putting the other first), the sharing of meanings can sometimes be possible. The relation of the psychological therapist to the client would define the ethical, but the other would remain wholly alien and inassimilable. The client's proximity is prior to the psychological therapist's 'presence' and makes it possible; no totality (a whole that assimilates its parts) can integrate psychological therapist and client. The relation to the client is like a relation to infinity: perpetually beyond experience, making the organizing structures of experience possible. It precedes and conditions experience.

For Levinas, unlike Buber, the client's absolute transcendence prevents symmetry and reciprocity. From a Levinasian reading, the client becomes manifest through the face. It is the face of the client that both commands the psychological therapist not to harm, and solicits the psychological therapist's aid. For the psychological therapist to acknowledge the client's face is for the psychological therapist to have responsibility to the client and for the client. Thus the ethics of psychological therapeutic practices would not be about ethical codes, for to start with them would be unethical, and would concern primarily the relation to the other. Levinas challenges the ego-centric, narcissistic representation of the person by arguing that we are subject to putting the other first, with the consequence that we are responsible for the other's responsibility. Does this lead to a very different type of existentialism?

Emmanuel Levinas was born in Lithuania, in 1905, of Jewish parents. His family moved to the Ukraine, where he was during the Revolution of 1917, before he settled in France as a young man. He spent most of the rest of his life there, surviving a prisoner-of-war camp, and died in 1995. During 1928–1929, he was in Freiburg, where he attended the lectures of Husserl and encountered the writings of Husserl's student, Heidegger. Husserl, like Freud, was born in Czechoslovakia and both were to write seminal works appearing in 1900 (Freud on *The Interpretation of Dreams* and Husserl on *Cartesian Meditations*), both after having attended lectures on descriptive psychology by Brentano in Vienna. Husserl, thanks to the interventions of Wilhelm Wundt, now recognized as a founding father of psychology, developed the notion of phenomenology. Levinas, in turn, is now credited with bringing phenomenology to France and greatly influencing Sartre, de Beauvoir, Merleau-Ponty, and such post-modern thinkers as

Lyotard and Derrida. The development of phenomenology can be further considered as 'post-phenomenology' (see Loewenthal, 2006), with implications for such practices as psychological therapy through such authors as Derrida and Roudinesco.

'To be or not to be?' is the wrong question

If we start with questions of well-being, what seems to happen is that we slip into questions where transformations have to revolve around my being, such that should we then ever look at another's being, we do so only by taking ourselves as the measure. Levinas argues that ethics (putting the other first) must always precede ontology (the study of being). Yet, for Hamlet, as for Heidegger and most of Western thought, the question has been, 'to be or not to be'. Primacy is thereby given to the ontological, with perhaps devastating consequences. This has formed the unquestioned basis of many practices, with their emphasis on autonomy, egocentricity, and notions of a bounded, unitary self (Loewenthal, 1996).

Levinas was very interested in Hamlet (Levinas, 1985: 22); he challenged the ontological by suggesting that ethical questions must always come before those of being, and this, it will be argued, is a phenomenological, rather than a moral, necessity. For Levinas, as perhaps for Shakespeare, Hamlet is asking the wrong question, the result being that those he is closest to are killed off. This is because he puts himself first rather than the other first. By asking the question, 'to be or not to be?', Hamlet shows himself to be concerned with himself before he is concerned with anyone else.

For Levinas, there was also a related important reading, in that by asking this question, it was as if Hamlet could be in charge of his own death. 'Hamlet is precisely a lengthy testimony to this impossibility of assuming death' (Levinas, 1989: 42). The tragedy of Hamlet is that he tries to stay on top of that which he cannot. Do most therapists, educationalists, managers, photographers, and so on, encourage a similar fate for themselves and their clients?

Greek versus Hebraic: Autonomy versus heteronomy

It might be argued that it is not only photography that is more about pictorial rather than written representation (the 'look' rather than the 'book'), more caught up with the Greek rather than the Hebraic, rather like those management theories where all chief executives, even vice-chancellors, are encouraged to have visions rather than being locked away for mentioning them. Yet it is the notion of heteronomy that may be useful in order to consider whether Levinasian ethics might form the basis of well-being. Levinas points out that 'every philosophy seeks truth. Sciences too can be defined by this search' (cited in Peperzak, 1992: 47). None of the professions mentioned are an exception in claiming that they seek the truth. Yet Western culture can be seen to contain two major philosophical traditions, the Greek and the Hebraic, each with its own underlying assumptions about the ways that truth, in terms of relationships, can be thought about and experienced. Furthermore, it is the Greek notion of autonomy that has more often than not assumed cultural dominance over the notion of heteronomy.

So we encourage the 'me first' rather than the 'other first'

I will first quote Levinas on heteronomy at length, before going through his text in more detail. The same will then be done for what he has to say on autonomy. Levinas describes the idea of truth in terms of heteronomy in the following way:

> Truth implies experience. In the truth, a thinker maintains a relationship with a reality distinct from him, other than him, 'absolutely other' . . . for experience deserves its name only if it transports us beyond what constitutes our nature. Genuine experience must even lead us beyond the Nature that surrounds us, which is not jealous of the marvellous secrets it harbours and, in complicity with men, submits to their reason and inventions; in it, men also feel themselves to be at home. Truth would thus designate the outcome of a movement that leaves a world that is intimate and familiar, even if we have not yet explored it completely, and goes towards another region, towards a beyond. Philosophy would be concerned with the absolutely other; it would be heteronomy itself . . . Truth, the daughter of experience, has very lofty pretentions; it opens upon the very dimension of the ideal. In this way, philosophy means metaphysics and metaphysics inquires about the divine.
>
> (cited in Peperzak, 1992: 47)

Levinas's notion of heteronomy raises questions regarding notions of truth. He seems to be saying that truth is not something outside experience (and yet, although this may seem contradictory, it is beyond our nature). But this does not mean that one's experiences are the yardstick for truth. We cannot claim to have 'the truth' because it is our experience ('I've experienced it, so you can't take it away from me').

Experience is that which gets us in touch with what is other than that which we are. It is not 'what we are', and it takes us beyond what we have been. So what we feel 'at home' with may stop us genuinely experiencing. We can conceive of and experience our environment as something complicit with us and submissive to our preconceptions, but genuine experience in the Levinasian sense is a reaching towards a beyond, away from what familiarity surrounds us. Can it therefore be only in a relationship where the other is put first, in dwelling with the absolutely other, that truth is to be found? We will not arrive at truth if we see the beyond as something to be colonized and incorporated, which academics are often so good at. The truth will always be beyond.

This has enormous implications, including for ethics and the training of such practices as the psychological therapies, education, and management. We cannot appropriate truth to our experience: it is outside us. We have always, as psychological therapists, to be prepared to go beyond our 'gut reactions'. Only then do we have a chance, momentarily, to reach a truth with another. We tend, as Lyotard points out, to delude ourselves as to what is 'truth' by forgetting that it is subject to our theories, to the place we are in, and the position we take up, which we can then start to think of as 'natural', as our nature (Lyotard 1984). Truth becomes dependent on, for example, what school of psychological therapy we are in, and the danger is that this 'truth' must be upheld as the particular theory shores up our position as psychological therapists and the universities and psychological therapy organizations that legitimize us. Shouldn't truth be beyond that? Yet we jealously guard our position, in a way that can lead to perversion and injustice.

Levinas perhaps helps us to raise crucial questions about ethics and vested interests. Our theoretical orientation, or club membership, can therefore never come before truth and justice. If one feels 'at home', then may one be perpetrating violence? Truth is leaving well-being 'at home'. One cannot be 'at home' with the truth; sometimes feeling things are 'right' is wrong. For Levinas, if we are 'at home', it is always about 'me first', my place in the sun, in which case philosophy is needed to legitimize the corruption – to make us feel 'at home'.

In contrast to heteronomy, Levinas describes the Greek notion of autonomy as follows:

> But truth also means the free adherence to a proposition, the outcome of a free research. The freedom of the investigator, the thinker on whom no constraint weighs, is expressed in truth. What else is this freedom but the thinking being's refusal to be alienated in the adherence, the preserving of his nature, his identity, the feat of remaining the same despite the unknown lands into which thought seems to lead?
>
> (cited in Peperzak, 1992: 47–48)

Now we may all strive to be autonomous and in doing so not wish to consider that we reduce Others to the Same: to be only within our vision. If we do have doubts about autonomy, then we seek a philosophy, or school of therapy, to reassure us. In autonomy, one can be subject to nothing; it is as if we were the subject. A problem for psychological therapists is that autonomy is attractive and can be sold to our clients. Heteronomy is always in danger of being incorporated into the philosophy of autonomy. Thus certain notions of autonomy go unquestioned in our culture. However, it is not being suggested that autonomy should be dismissed, but that heteronomy should come first. For example, in education, the heteronomous learner might be considered more important than the autonomous learner. It is argued, therefore, that Hamlet, and most psychological therapeutic practices, have wrongly chosen autonomy over heteronomy, encompassing every Other in the Same. The Other becomes a bit-player with, at best, a walk-on part on our stage. Thus, the client is a bit-player on the psychological therapist's stage (perhaps we, at best, train people to look good rather than be good).

The psychological therapies as ethical practices

For Levinas, 'The face is exposed, menaced as if inviting us to an act of violence. At the same time, the face is what forbids us to kill' (Levinas, 1985: 86). As psychological therapists, academics, and managers, what then are our values? I am assuming that we will always be subjective: our values determining how we hear and what we say. That is, in so far as we are able to say what our values are. So it is vital for our practice that we attempt to consider what we regard as essentially human: under what circumstances is the world an alive and meaningful place for us as people who are psychological therapists? Is it when we can assertively go after that which appears important to us (autonomy), or does it begin with putting the other first (heteronomy) in a way that recognizes the Otherness of the Other (their alterity)? In this way, our values and ethics are linked. Levinasian ethics are not therefore about my right to exist, it isn't even just about the Other's right to exist, but can be seen as my responsibility for the Other's responsibility to others.

Let us take Freud's three impossible professions: psychoanalysis, education, and management. Freud suggested the reasons why they are impossible is that one can be sure beforehand of achieving unsatisfying results. Yet surely, by inevitably being subject to that which we will never have full agency over, is to be educated for life rather than through the technical application of government-inspired competencies. This can produce unthoughtful psychologisms in the hope of autonomy, at best Oakeshott's (1991) 'minds with no atmosphere'. Being subject to, regardless of whether we see this as being – to an unconscious, to language or, in the case of Levinas, to ethics – opens up the potential of being educated for not knowing, and above all, for well-being in terms of justice.

There are of course important criticisms of Levinas in terms of, for example, issues of gender and that he might unwittingly be caught up in a worldwide increasingly Christian conspiracy created by those who can't take the rawness of life and have instead come up with an aesthetic called 'ethics' initially based on a confused story of Abraham telling half-truths to his son Isaac. However, if Levinasian ethics can be considered in terms of their implications, and not become a new technical mantra, then one implication is that if we put our concerns first, rather than those of the Other, then we are at best privileging a notion of well-being that is to do with giving a primacy to autonomy at the expense of others, and our society in general. Thus, a heteronomy that is putting the Other first may be what is most appropriate in enabling well-being. Not only is it the case that without such relational learning our lives will be impoverished, but if we hope therapeutic education can be primarily directly taught without some face-to-face, then this is more to do with the violence of late modernism with its associated apparent success in removing the radical in the development of these cultural practices (Loewenthal, 2006; Lyotard, 1984; Parker, 1997). For, as Heaton (1993) argues, if we think practice can become subordinate to theory (including Levinasian theory) and the knowledge generated, with all the advantages for technicians to be trained, this can also take away from a thoughtfulness that can lead to well-being, whereby, through a relationship, individuals can, for example, also clarify their own and others' desire to help. Thus ethics cannot be a basis for practice, though it can usefully have important implications.

Furthermore, therapeutic education without giving a primacy to actual practice will further move away from Plato's entreaty to see therapeia as the wisdom of regarding scientific and technical thinking as important but secondary to the resources of the human soul (Cushman 2001). Seen thus, the psychological therapies for one are in grave danger of losing their way (Loewenthal 2004); interest in relational psychological therapies has the potential to return us to starting with practice but with the danger that we will still not be able to let go of our theories and our ego-centricisms. Perhaps if we are able to face the Other as one human being meeting another, we will be more able, as Levinas suggests, to not do theoretical violence to this other. Well-being is not training people to appear to be concerned about the other person: is this really acknowledging the other? Instead of being primarily concerned with systems of power and knowledge, perhaps we should all be more concerned with justice on a case-by-case basis, for, as Levinas writes, real justice in well-being cannot be appropriated or territorialized, but requires us, from and through our relationships, to be just in the moment with another.

References

Aron, L. and Harris, A. (2005). *Relational psychoanalysis v.2: Innovation and expansion*. Hillsdale, NJ: The Analytic Press.
Barber, B. (2000). Ballots versus bullets. *Financial Times*, 20 October, p. 1.
Becker, C. and Becker, L. (Eds.) (1992). *A history of western ethics*. New York: Garland.
Buber, M. (1922). *I and thou*. New York: Scribner.
Cushman, R. (2001). *Therapeia: Plato's conception of philosophy* (new edition). Piscataway, NJ: Transaction.
Eagleton, T. (1996). *The illusions of post-modernism*. Oxford: Blackwell.
Frie, R. and Orange, D. (Eds.) (2009). *Beyond postmodernism: New dimensions in clinical theory and practice*. New York and London: Routledge.
Ghent, E. (1992). Foreword. In *Relational perspectives in psychoanalysis* (N. Skolnik and S. Warshaw, Eds.). Hillsdale, NJ: The Analytic Press (pp. xiii–xxii).
Heaton, J. M. (1993). The sceptical tradition in psychotherapy. In *From the words of my mouth: Tradition in psychotherapy* (L. Spurling, Ed.). London: Routledge.
Levinas, E. (1961). *Totality and infinity: An essay on exteriority* (A. Lingis, Trans.). Pittsburgh, PA: Duquesne University Press.
Levinas, E. (1985). *Ethics and infinity: Conversations with Philippe Nemo* (R. Cohen, Trans.). Pittsburgh, PA: Duquesne University Press.
Levinas, E. (1989). Time and the other. In *The Levinas Reader* (S. Hand, Ed.). Oxford: Blackwell.
Loewenthal, D. (1996). The postmodern counsellor: Some implications for practice, theory, research and professionalism. *Counselling Psychology Quarterly*, 9(4): 373–381.

Loewenthal, D. (2002). Involvement and emotional labour. *Soundings, 20:* 151–162.

Loewenthal, D. (2004). Should either psychology or psychiatry be the basis of psychotherapy? *International Journal of Critical Psychology, 4*(4): 214–222.

Loewenthal, D. (2005). Case studies in relational person centred care. In *Managing integrated care for older persons in Europe* (P. Vaarama and R. Piper, Eds.). Helsinki: European Healthcare Management Association (pp. 153–179).

Loewenthal, D. (2006). Psychotherapy, ethics and the relational. In *Culture, psychotherapy and counseling: Critical and integrative perspectives* (L. Hoshmand, Ed.). Thousand Oaks, CA: Sage (pp. 205–226).

Loewenthal, D. and Snell, R. (2003). *Post-modernism for psychotherapists.* London: Routledge.

Lyotard, J.-F. (1984). *The post-modern condition: A report on knowledge.* Manchester: Manchester University Press.

Merleau-Ponty, M. (1962). *The phenomenology of perception* (C. Smith, Trans.). London: Routledge Kegan-Paul.

Oakeshott, M. (1991). *Rationalism in politics and other essays.* Indianapolis, IN: Liberty Fund.

Parker, I. (1997). *Psychoanalytic culture: Psychoanalytic discourse in western society.* London: Sage.

Peperzak, A. (1992). *To the other: An introduction to the philosophy of Emmanuel Levinas.* Indiana, IN: Purdoe University Press.

Rozmarin, E. (2007). An other in psychoanalysis: Levinas's critique of knowledge and analytic self. *Contemporary Psychoanalysis, 44*(3): 333.

13

ORDINARY STORIES OF INTERMINGLING OF WORLDS AND DOING WHAT IS RIGHT

A person-centred view

Pete Sanders

Anecdotes from psychotherapy literature and personal experience are presented in support of the thesis that relational therapies are the evidenced, philosophical, ethical and moral rebuttal of mechanical psychotechnological therapies.

Introduction

This chapter is a short series of questions and stories or vignettes assembled in response to the invitation to speak on behalf of the relationship in relational psychotherapy at the Universities Psychotherapy and Counselling Association Conference at Roehampton University in November 2009. I decided not to begin by defining relational psychotherapy since as a person-centred therapist I take it as both axiomatic and almost over-defined in the person-centred literature (Cooper et al., 2007; Rogers, 1951, 1959; Tudor & Worrall, 2006). Indeed, for many years it did not occur to me that psychotherapy could be anything other than an activity rooted in, or inseparable from, relationship. Similarly, I wondered what all the fuss was about when the fanfares for relational psychotherapy began. It had not occurred to me that psychotherapy could be anything other than a self-with-otherself activity, I–thou, rather than observer–observed, doctor–patient, psychotechnician–human–computer, or even therapist–client.

A further problem for the person-centred relational therapist is that understandings of person-centred theory and practice have, alongside all other psychotherapy approaches, continued to be elaborated over the 35 or more years of my career and I am no better at hitting moving targets after 35 years' experience. As Art Bohart (Bohart, 1995) wrote when asked for a definition, 'Will the real person-centered therapy please stand up?' I am persuaded that definitions with the duration of a flashbulb don't matter. I leave it to others to debate what is meant by such terms as 'the real person-centred therapy' or 'relational therapy'. So in my remaining words I'll tell a few stories in order that readers may work out in what ways, if any, they help explore understanding of relational therapy.

I will start by declaring a few of my assumptions:

1 One's model of personhood determines one's position regarding relational work.
2 The relational nature of human being is described by primate attachment and elaborated by the various versions of attachment theory (e.g. Bowlby, 1997a, 1997b, 1998; Fonagy et al., 2004).
3 The 'psyche' in the term 'psychotherapy' determines that it is the type of therapy that a human self has with another human self. Furthermore, the human self is a construct that is predicated upon the existence of other human selves. As John Shlien explained: 'The mind emerges through a process of communication. This involves social interaction on the basis of what Mead calls 'significant symbols' (usually words). A significant symbol is one that is 'reflexive', that is, when it is used it presupposes another person ... Acknowledging the other is essential to the existence of mind, from beginning to end' (Shlien, 2003a, p. 39; original emphasis).
4 Relationality is a human capability so fundamental and essential that I do not wish to waste time debating whether it is innate. It is not difficult to achieve. It happens. All humans recognise that there is a serious breach of functioning when relationality is absent or fails. The problem is how to use it wisely and well in the service of flourishing, love and peaceful co-existence.

This chapter will be dismissive of non-relational approaches to change, in particular, medicalised, reductionistic, dose-oriented, mechanistic psychotechnologies. This is a statement regarding the offerings of therapists, not a statement regarding the change processes experienced by clients. By this I mean that unlike the formulations of non-relational approaches, the kind of change I aim for in relational psychotherapy is not the repair of some faulty mental machinery, the un-learning of a maladaptive recipe for living, the reprogramming of a neuro-computer, nor is it, as Jurgen Kriz put it, like 'beating the dents out of a tin can' (Kriz, 2008, p. 7). In person-centred relational therapy, the client develops or grows through and with their present moment of experiencing to a new, different one, embracing a host of other healing events and experiences, unique to the trajectory of the individual client's life along the way. It is an organismic growth model (Tudor & Worrall, 2006). Human beings do not learn to overcome, live with or otherwise deal with distress. They are not mended, cured, spiritually reconnected or made whole. Furthermore, that each human being is unique is not a slogan, since – confusingly for those with a taxonomic compulsion – they might experience their growth as all and none of the above things: relational psychology sets the client free to construct, experience and understand their process of change in any way they can. So, as far as the client is concerned, they might indeed be being cured, healed, repaired, re-programmed or even be having the dents knocked out of them. The therapist enters the therapeutic relationship with no pre-conceptions or agenda, other than facilitating growth.

Are relationships effective?

If we survey a wide range of research, we see that the vast majority indicates that the therapeutic relationship is associated with good outcome. Parenthetically, I do not intend to be distracted by discussions about what 'good outcome' means (and remember neither have I defined 'relationship'). I direct readers to Duncan, Miller and Sparks' (2004) entertaining accounts of psychotherapy research, and the information from the hand-outs section of Miller's (2010) website (www.scottdmiller.com/?q=node/4).

Some of the most telling recent research was reported by the cognitive behavioural clinical psychologist Richard Bentall (Bentall, 2009a) in which he describes the trajectory of the SoCRATES project. The study, a large, three-centre randomised controlled trial, looked at the outcome of using Cognitive Realignment Therapy with over 300 people with robust diagnoses of first- or second-episode schizophrenia.

Preliminary analysis showed that both CBT and person-centred therapy were better than medication alone, but results also pointed to a large and unexpected central difference. One of the battery of measures asked patients to rate the therapeutic alliance after the third and ninth treatment sessions. Conventional statistical analysis showed that the patients' ratings of the therapeutic alliance predicted improvements in symptoms up to 18 months following treatment. Good news for relational therapists, except, and I quote Bentall: 'on its own, this observation does not establish that the therapeutic alliance is causal' (2009a, p. 259). The holy grail for relational therapists would be to be able to demonstrate a causal relationship between the therapeutic alliance and outcome in a diagnosis of severe and enduring psychological distress. Bentall continues:

> Fortunately, [using] new statistical methods developed by Graham Dunne [Professor of Biomedical Statistics] at Manchester University . . . we found that the differences between the treatment groups and the differences [between the treatment centres] could be entirely accounted for by the therapeutic alliance rated by the patients at the end of the third session (a result, incidentally, completely in accord with Miller's observations).
>
> (ibid., p. 260)

Bentall goes on: 'The extent to which the therapists could relate effectively with the patients, rather than specific psychotherapeutic techniques, seemed to completely explain the positive effects of treatment' (ibid.).

So a prominent cognitive behavioural researcher not only comes out in favour of the Dodo bird hypothesis (Rosensweig, 1936), but enthusiastically declares, at the conclusion of his recent presentations, that 'good relationships are a universal therapeutic good' (Bentall, 2009b).

What minimal conditions must be met so that relational therapy is possible?

In the 1990s, the burgeoning World Wide Web stimulated many innovations in computer-mediated relationships. In workplace settings, the new area of computer-supported co-operative work blossomed, with its concepts of 'social presence' and 'psychological distance'. The degree to which relationships might be built and maintained by computer-mediated communication was explored further by Lea and Spears (1995) in their essay 'Love at first byte? Building personal relationships over computer networks'. The world of psychotherapy followed quickly; for example, in 1998, Murphy and Mitchell (1998), in their account of email therapy, reported a case where a client wrote a note of thanks to a counsellor (a real note from a real client). Here is an extract:

> In just our brief exchange of messages you have left me with a sense that you are a caring, creative, helpful, hopeful soul. This is hard to achieve in person, let alone in the imperfect world of electronic communication. Your warmth and humanity shine through the pixels on my screen, and come at a time when I need them most. For this I thank you and congratulate you. The irony is not lost on me that I find a true person in the virtual void at the same time as a doctor in my home county has given me short shrift.

It is clear that a meaningful therapeutic relationship was experienced by the client in question, even though, as Lea and Giordano (1997) note, there are severe constraints on computer representations of the complex, chaotic, a-temporal and a-rational – elements which psychotherapy theorists obsessively dissect. Digital new media demand from psychotherapists serious reflection on the nature of the necessary conditions for therapeutic relationships and how these may be communicated.

Years before personal computers were invented I was challenged by Harold, a first-year undergraduate. He had been referred to me because he had attempted suicide. I introduced myself:

> Hello, I'm Pete, you must be Harold. I know that Dr X asked you to come and see me because you took an overdose a couple of weeks ago. I don't know if I can help but I will listen to anything you might want to talk about.

Harold had already agreed with the receptionist that the session would be tape-recorded to play to my supervisor.

We sat in silence for maybe 30–45 seconds. I reiterated my opening gambit, saying something like, 'I am happy to listen to anything you would like to talk about.' We sat in silence for further a minute or so, after which I would probably have said something like, 'It can sometimes be difficult to know where to start. I will wait until you are ready.' Harold and I sat in silence for a few more minutes and I had soon exhausted my repertoire of possible responses to silence. We sat for the remainder of the session in silence until I said, 'It is time to finish now. I will be here next week at the same time if you want to come.'

Harold did indeed come to the session on time the following week, during which he said nothing. This pattern was repeated for a further six sessions. My practice supervisor would listen sagely to my introductions and endings, and even a portion of the silence in between and advise me to 'hang on in there'. I hung on in there and hung on every flicker of the eyes (Harold would look at the wall), every slight movement of his hand, arm, foot, chest, every breath. Every moment was pregnant with the possibility of his first utterance. He was at the centre of my attention and I concentrated on his every move. Then, midway through session eight, Harold spoke. He said, 'Please don't stare at me.'

Clearly, sufficient human transactions occurred in those silences for Harold to deem it worth his while to return, punctually, every week for eight weeks before speaking.

What is the active ingredient in relational work?

Some find it rewarding to examine the fleeting moments of connection in therapy. Occasionally, such a moment seems to carry more than its fair share of responsibility for healing. Here is a story told by Shlien:

> He heard his thoughts coming out of the television set. His mind was transparent; he was the object of an experiment by the FBI; he raged, wept, begged, denied, was sly, and was life-threatening. Often during interviews, guards were stationed outside my office door by the hospital director. Mike and I went through hell together – he in his own hell, I in mine with my own fears, and both hells intermingled. Eventually there came a time when he understood that much more about his life and had so much more control that he was given a grounds pass, and we could meet on the lawn, alone and safe.
>
> At some point during the last of these meetings, he began to cry softly, saying, 'They talk about love and affection. I know what that means. The only good thing I ever had [his engagement to a girl] was taken away from me, broken up.' He blew his nose, dropped his handkerchief, and as he picked it up, glanced at me. He saw tears in my eyes. He offered me the handkerchief, then drew it back because he knew he had just wiped his nose on it and could feel the wetness on his hand. We both knew this, and each knew the other knew it; we both understood the feel and the meaning

of the handkerchief, the stickiness and texture, the sympathy of the offering and the embarrassment of the withdrawal, and we acknowledged each other and the interplay of each one's significance to the other. It is not the tears, but the exquisite awareness of dual experience that restores consciousness of self (and not a word was spoken during this episode).

(Shlien, 2003b, p. 186)

When Shlien later reflects upon this moment he says: 'There is something full of grace in his gesture with the snotty handkerchief and something ungainly, not "graceful," about it at all. It has the ambivalence that characterizes most of life' (ibid.).

This was interpersonal confirmation, and self-affirmation. Through this relational moment Mike discovered that he can know. He discovered that he does know, and he can be known, understood, and can reciprocate in kind. Through this knowing there is a confirmation of being, the recognition of another's humanity and confirmation of one's own. This knowing requires some degree of self-with-other encounter.

Why are relational approaches apparently politically unpopular?

In 1957, Martin Buber, in response to Carl Rogers asking him why he had never become a therapist, said:

> It was just a certain inclination to meet people. And, as far as possible, to just change if possible something in the other but also let me be changed by him. I already then as a young man – I felt I had not the right to change another if I am not open to be changed by him, as far as it is legitimate . . . I cannot be, so to say, above him, and say 'No! I'm out of the play. You are mad.'
>
> (Buber, cited in Anderson & Cissna, 1997, p. 21)

Shlien's words describing his work with Mike echo Buber's position: 'Mike and I went through hell together – he in his own hell, I in mine with my own fears, and both hells intermingled.' Buber and Shlien draw attention to an aspect of relational therapy familiar to its practitioners: a particular form of necessary and inevitable involvement, reciprocity and co-creation.

Early in my career I had a client who was a deeply religious person – a woman who had been a nun from her teenage years to her late twenties. On leaving the convent she met a man, they courted and they planned to marry. Before their marriage, however, she was extremely nervous about sex because she had been kept in ignorance about it by her family and the church. She had the foresight to ask a priest for guidance. When they met, as part of her 'preparation' for marriage, he subjected her to sexual abuse. As she fled in extreme distress he admonished her and told her that her immortal soul would go to hell for eternity if she told anyone and furthermore she was responsible, since she, by her very existence, had tempted him.

Although I am an atheist, being with her, encountering her, as she told her story of assault on her body and, even more despicably in her world, on something ultimately precious, her very immortal soul, changed me. John Shlien's words never seemed so full of meaning; we went through hell together – she in her own hell, I in mine with my own fears, and both hells intermingled.

A couple of years ago I watched an item on the local television news. The reporter interviewed a single mother with a small toddler. They had a one-bedroom high-rise flat with condensation and mould on the walls. The child had a chronic chest infection and the mother was at her wits' end. Viewers were taken into each of the few, cramped rooms with stained floors and tissues blocking up holes in the window. The item did finish, however, on what was intended to be a positive note – at least I could detect no irony when the reporter announced that the young mum was suffering from depression and had been prescribed anti-depressants.

I railed at the television. I was furious, not least with myself and my overwhelming feeling of impotence. What have we become, I thought? I wove this story into writing about social iatrogenesis, the medicalisation of life, the evils of diagnosis and the medical model. I felt better, for the moment. But my anger had not completely dissipated. I later imagined what it would be like to practise a manualised psychotechnological therapy and meet such a client. I imagined the practitioner teaching the client to think positively about life. I railed against psychotechnology and I felt better, for the moment.

Now I think about that young mum and her baby, and imagine what would happen if she came into my GP-practice consulting room, where I work as a counsellor. True to form, as I had with my deeply religious client, and just like Martin Buber and John, I would encounter her, risk being changed by her. I then realised the two main benefits of psychotechnological psychotherapies.

First, what a relief it would be as a therapist to not become engaged. To not have our lives intermingle. Just some symptom-taking and then out with the manual. A few thought exercises, homework for the client, tick some boxes for number of suicidal thoughts per day and off to my warm dry home for my tea. And the second benefit? What a relief for a government. No wonder mechanical, medicalised, dose-oriented psychotechnologies are the approved treatments for depression. What government would approve a treatment where tens of thousands of therapists actually engaged with the lives of their clients? Could they risk those therapists realising that the only way to save their own sanity was to become politicised themselves and act in concert with their clients to change the world we live in?

Conclusion

Relationality is not difficult to achieve. It happens. In fact, you have to actively prevent it from happening by putting things between the two selves involved.

Techniques, instruments, obsessive measuring: psychotherapy in the twenty-first century has become a parade of psychotechnologies. Evidence based, of course. Psychotechnologies that serve to protect the therapist. And though there may be evidence to suggest that they work, there is also evidence that good relationships cause positive change. The problem is, it takes two to relate. If we dispense with the smoke and mirrors there is no elephant in the room, just the client and therapist. Given the choice, do you treat your client like a faulty machine, a crashed computer, a dented tin can or a human being? Relational therapy is not only about doing only what works; it is also about doing what is right.

References

Anderson, R. and Cissna, K. N. (1997). *The Martin Buber – Carl Rogers dialogue: A new transcript with commentary*. Albany, NY: State University of New York Press.

Bentall, R. P. (2009a). *Doctoring the mind: Why psychiatric treatments fail*. London: Allen Lane/Penguin.

Bentall, R. P. (2009b). The therapeutic relationship in CBT for psychosis. Presentation at the 16th International Symposium for the Psychological Treatment of the Schizophrenias and Other Psychoses. Copenhagen, 15–19 June.

Bohart, A. C. (1995). The person-centered psychotherapies. In *Theory and practice*, (A. Gurman and S. Messer, Eds.), 85–127. New York: Essential psychotherapies, The Guilford Press.

Bowlby, J. (1997a). *Attachment and loss. Vol 1: Attachment* (2nd edition). London: Pimlico.

Bowlby, J. (1997b). *Attachment and loss: Vol 3: Loss* (new edition). London: Pimlico.

Bowlby, J. (1998). *Attachment and loss. Vol 2: Separation* (new edition). London: Pimlico.

Cooper, M., O'Hara, M., Schmid, P. F. and Wyatt, G. (2007). *The handbook of person-centred psychotherapy and counselling*. Basingstoke: Palgrave.

Duncan, B. L., Miller, S. D. and Sparks, J. A. (2004). *The heroic client: A revolutionary way to improve effectiveness through client-directed, outcome-informed therapy*. San Francisco, CA: Jossey-Bass.

Fonagy, P., Gyorgy, G., Jurist, E. L. and Target, M. (2004). *Affect regulation, mentalization, and the development of the self*. London: Karnac.

Kriz, J. (2008). *Self-actualization*. Ross-on-Wye, UK: PCCS Books.

Lea, M. and Giordano, R. (1997). Representations of the group processes in CSCW research: A case of premature closure? In *Social science research, technical systems and cooperative work*, 5–25 (G. Bowker, L. Glasser, S. L. Star and W. Turner, Eds.). Mahwah, NJ: Erlbaum.

Lea, M. and Spears, R. (1995). Love at first byte? Building personal relationships over computer networks. In *Under-studied relationships: Off the beaten track*, 283–301 (J. T. Wood and S. Duck, Eds.). Thousand Oaks, CA: Sage.

Miller, S. C. (2010). *Scholarly publications, handouts, vitae*. Retrieved from www.scottdmiller.com/?q=node/4

Murphy, L. J. and Mitchell, D. L. (1998). When writing helps to heal: Email as therapy. *British Journal of Guidance and Counselling, 26*: 21–32.

Rogers, C. R. (1951). *Client-centered therapy: Its current practice, implications and theory*. Boston: Houghton Mifflin.

Rogers, C. R. (1959). A theory of therapy, personality and interpersonal relationships as developed in the client-centred framework. In *Psychology: A study of a science*, 184–256 (S. Koch, Ed.). New York: McGraw-Hill.

Rosensweig, S. (1936). Some implicit common factors in diverse methods of psychotherapy: At last the Dodo bird said 'Everybody has won and all must have prizes'. *American Journal of Orthopsychiatry, 6*: 412–415.

Shlien, J. M. (2003a). A client-centered approach to schizophrenia: First approximation. In J. M. Shlien, *To live an honorable life: Invitations to think about client-centered therapy and the person-centered approach* (P. Sanders, Ed.). Ross-on-Wye, UK: PCCS Books (pp. 30–59). Originally published in 1961 in *Psychotherapy of the psychoses* (A. Burton, Ed.). New York: Basic Books (pp. 285–317).

Shlien, J. M. (2003b). Empathy in psychotherapy: Vital mechanism? Yes, Therapist's conceit? All too often. By itself enough? No. In J. M. Shlien, *To live an honorable life: Invitations to think about client-centered therapy and the person-centered approach* (P. Sanders, Ed.). Ross-on-Wye, UK: PCCS Books (pp. 172–190). Originally published in 1997 in *Empathy reconsidered* (A. Bohart and L. S. Greenberg, Eds.). Washington, DC: American Psychological Association (pp. 63–80).

Tudor, K. and Worrall, M. (2006). *Person-centred therapy: A clinical philosophy*. Hove: Routledge.

14

STAYING IN DIALOGUE WITH CBT

Tom Strong

Holding that a conversational object (CBT) is an unfinalizable conversational project, as evidenced by House and Lowenthals's (2008) Against and for CBT, *this article considers CBT as a dialogic practice consistent with Mikhail Bakhtin's writings on dialogue. This dialogic approach to CBT is described as involving a delicate negotiation of words and ways of talking, in contrast to approaches where therapists hold clients and themselves to a CBT manual or protocol. Instead, the kind of negotiated dialogue described invites reflections on clients' ineffective meanings, followed by collaborative efforts to overcome the 'linguistic poverty' of those meanings. CBT is thus recast as Wittgenstein's conversational challenge of finding ways to go on together.*

Introduction

Conversational object (CBT) is a fascinating conversational work-in-progress. A polyphony of administrative, scientific, clinical, and lay voices shows lots of talking about, critiquing, and efforts to revise a loosely defined conversational object. On full display are what the dialogue theorist Bakhtin (1981, 1984, 1986) called centripetal and centrifugal tendencies as different constituencies vie for the next articulations of this conversational object. Centripetally, many have advocated for a scientifically defined CBT of replicable (i.e. manualized) practices; centrifugally, one finds creative new hybrids of practice (e.g. mindfulness-based stress reduction). Outside of therapist discourse, one finds a considerable cultural uptake of CBT, enough for governments (Prime Minister's Office, 2008) and economists (Layard, 2005) to join as cultural partners in CBT's polyphony. But CBT as a conversational project has also been a source of concern for some therapists, something quite evident in a rather unique book – *Against and for CBT* by House and Loewenthal (2008).

What sentiments were House and Loewenthal tapping into when readers were snapping up their popular book? Surely, a therapeutic approach which had been proven effective in addressing suffering, that was easy to understand, and that could prompt the UK government to add funds to mental health services didn't need a book that was 'against' it. CBT, thanks in part to Lord Layard (2005), had finally broken through years of cultural derision to become a proven therapy for alleviating depression and anxiety, and it also offered ways of shoring up the economy. So, why did this hard-won legitimacy for CBT prompt a book with 'against' as the first word of its title?

Some of the antipathy seems related to a particular approach to CBT that had risen to dominance through emulating biomedicine's evidence-based approach to practice. That CBT, a straw man for the 'for' authors (e.g. Mansell, 2008), had served up sufficient scientific warrant for the UK government to get behind Layard's cultural and economic prescription. I came to a greater appreciation of Layard's cultural prescription when hearing from his psychologist colleague, Ian Clark, at the European Congress of Psychology in Oslo in July 2009. Taking people's suffering seriously, through calculating the social and financial costs of that suffering, was no small undertaking, and helped to get therapy on the UK national radar as an economic as well as quality of life issue. Where my appreciation plummets is when Layard seizes on the 'evidence' base that seems to warrant the exclusive use of CBT – largely because there has been little other convincing science to suggest that therapeutic approaches other than CBT can be helpful. While the science behind this approach to CBT has largely gone unquestioned (see Strong, Busch & Couture, 2008), a mixed blessing for therapy arrived at therapy's doorstep.

We now have 'proof' that therapy makes personal and economic differences but the 'proven' CBT derives from a biomedical discourse and orientation to practice that irks many therapists. This approach to CBT whereby psychiatric symptoms are diagnosed then treated with scientifically supported manualized treatments was THE approach of concern for most of the 'against' writers in *Against and for CBT*. The 'for' authors had written of a CBT open to new developments, a CBT that was apparently addressing the 'againsters' concerns. Still, I couldn't help but feel that the 'for' authors had advocated for a CBT quite different from and incompatible with the scientific CBT that had won over Layard. My concern through all of this is with the conversational practice of therapy. It is that concern which prompts the comments which follow, and which hopefully adds to CBT's journey as a conversational work-in-progress.

CBT's diverging conversations

Two diverging conversations seem to characterize CBT's development: a scientific one that, frankly, appears like a prescribed monologue; and a more dialogic approach that will serve as the focus of the comments which follow. Many sort-of CBT againsters like me (Strong, Lysack & Sutherland, 2008) were concerned about an expected adherence to CBT's scientifically supported manuals and reliance on diagnostic procedures that seemed overly mechanistic. Good therapy, from a dialogic perspective, is a delicate negotiation with clients, not a well-administered conversational script. But, this view stands in stark contrast to that advocated by David Barlow in his keynote address to the Canadian

Psychological Association convention in June 2009. There, Barlow spoke of a psychological science that would soon eliminate the need for schools of therapy, and that therapy would be reduced to a few well-adhered-to manuals for addressing diagnosed conditions. That was the approach to therapy that had concerned me. Assigning clients bit roles in therapist-prescribed conversations that follow from a reduction of clients' concerns to a symptom discourse seemed a gross simplification of therapy. Barlow's keynote reminded me of concerns I encountered in the 1980s when at another conference I heard the cybernetician Heinz von Foerster describe an enduring preoccupation of psychologists and psychiatrists to reduce clients to 'trivial machines'. The founder of ethnomethodology, Harold Garfinkel (1967), had similarly railed against this tendency of social scientists to make 'cultural dopes' out of people studied. Drawing heavily from the ideas of Bakhtin (1981, 1984, 1986), my dialogic approach to CBT has focused on relational encounters where words come alive in new meanings and implications in the immediacies of talking and listening. A CBT approach of diagnoses and corresponding lab-developed manuals seemed to trivialize therapeutic dialogue, reducing it to a therapist-led monologue into which clients were inducted and directed. Regardless, the common element of both approaches is that when CBT is successful, something helpful transpires from how therapist and client talk and listen to each other.

The genre of CBT that has come to dominate the field is easy to understand, easy to evaluate, easy to use, because it is well-scripted, and it was the first therapy to emulate evidence-based medicine. The 'treatment' of depression and anxiety, backed by evidence, seemed like yet another medical triumph. Small wonder that CBT (the scripted version) came to corner the mental health marketplace. What therapist wants to claim that her or his 'alternative' approach to practice lacks evidential support? But, taking this genre of CBT to task – its manuals, the strict lab conditions and controls required for CBT to be properly administered and evaluated, even the odd-sounding notion of 'doses' of CBT – its use of medical metaphors seems wonky when one considers therapy as a conversational practice.

Bakhtin (e.g. 1981, 1984, 1986) offered instructive ideas and life experience from which to consider CBT on dialogic terms. Entering academic life in the heady initial days of the Marxist revolution, Bakhtin wrote of the creative and indeterminable potentials that can arise from people as they make their words come alive in the immediacies of dialogue. The differences between speakers, the implications of their words for themselves and each other, the sense of trying to get beyond the limitations of what was already understood, are but a few of the elements of what makes dialogue and the words used in it alive. It is in therapists' and clients' responsiveness to each other that they invite and work out the kinds of differences I'll be describing as central to a dialogic view of practice. But, for Bakhtin, that responsiveness and range of creative potentials both waxes and wanes. When dialogue wanes or gets ideologized, speakers default to restrictive language games or genres. CBT has seen both centripetal and centrifugal approaches to therapeutic dialogue. Bakhtin's centrifugal dialogic ideas did not fare well in Stalin's cultural monologue: they cost him 40 years in the Gulag (Clark & Holquist, 1984).

While the CBT 'for' authors in House and Lowenthal's (2008) book advocate for an evolving CBT, things can get controversial (or rapidly centripetal) if one asks: how does one correctly practice CBT? The right/wrong framing of this question raises the hackles of postmoderns but can be important to those who research the practice of CBT, administer mental health funding, sit on professional practice review boards, or make legal decisions. How far can CBT therapists stray from evidence-based manuals and still practice the kind of CBT they are institutionally funded and authorized to use with clients? Given that certain manualized approaches to CBT have found empirical support, what are therapists to make of the recurring and overwhelming evidence (e.g. Hubble, Duncan, & Miller, 1999) that therapeutic effectiveness owes more to the quality of the therapeutic alliance than correctly administered 'doses' of therapies such as CBT? Questions like these follow from what amounts to considering therapy's yin and yang: its instrumental and responsive sides. It also speaks to another familiar dichotomy: counselling is an art and a science; not one or the other.

CBT as dialogue?

A dialogic approach to practice offers humble answers to questions like those above, and for proponents of 'modern' approaches to CBT such an approach no doubt offers less than what a 'treatment' should deliver. A very different orientation to problems, clients, communications, and 'efficacy' is called for in dialogic practice than from those approaches to CBT focused on diagnostic and manualized conversations. Perhaps the key difference comes with seeing the therapeutic dialogue as a delicate negotiation: of orientations, of meanings, of ways of talking, of actions, and of evaluations. Traditionally, many of these features of therapy have been seen as therapist's prerogatives. The warrant for these prerogatives has been their professional and scientific knowledge that is seen to be brought to the therapeutic conversation. The conversational work of therapy was something they were to manage – for clients. There can be something familiarly reassuring about this stance when equated with the medical encounter, with the doctor who accurately tells us what our problem is and what can treat 'it'; this is the most commonly emulated metaphor for what we do. A dialogic therapy where problems and therapeutic processes are negotiated with clients can sound daft or an abrogation of professional responsibility.

It is perhaps the 'co' thing implied by the word dialogue, or in 'co-constructing' therapeutic realities (e.g. Friedman, 1993), that can make some therapists feel uneasy, particularly for the different conversational involvement it implies. For the most part, therapy has been portrayed as a process whereby clients present their concerns or goals and therapists manage the process from there. The communications that occur are seen to largely inform the therapist-managed process, with such communications typically seen as transmissions and receptions of information to map on to the therapist's discourse, judgements, and prescriptions. By this account therapy proceeds according to assumed conversational pathways, where what gets said or heard similarly owes something to roles and contributions expected at familiar junctures in such conversational pathways. In Wittgenstein's (1953) language, there is a presumed 'grammar' (the 'rules' of what he called 'language games': who says and does what, when) to such communications and familiar conversational order can be the result. But, such conversational order can be part of what is up for negotiation and fits a conversational heuristic that Anderson (e.g. 1997) asks therapists to consider: how can therapeutic dialogue be different from the conversations clients have been having with themselves and others?

Some might take Anderson's suggestion in a different direction than intended: therapy, thanks to the media, clients' prior experiences, and its equation with medicine, offers a very familiar 'grammar' – so one should not assume that CBT offers clients a novel conversation. But, a novel conversation is not something for the therapist to engineer alone, despite the literature on therapist involvement in therapy's conversational work understandably being focused on the therapist's communication. In the 1970s and 1980s, our field witnessed and to varied extents benefited from close examinations of the practice of prominent figures such as Carl Rogers, Virginia Satir, and Milton Erickson. Their approaches to practice were micro-analysed and translated to particular conversational practices that could then be learned and used by therapists and students of therapy (e.g. Bandler & Grinder, 1975, 1976; Carkhuff, 1969). This extended to therapist questions, the directives given to clients, even to stories told. Clients' involvement in such conversations has received less of a focus – and, dialogically speaking, this is like the sound of one hand clapping. What Goffman (1967) described as dialogue's 'facework' – how speakers negotiate or conversationally work out their process and content – seems downplayed when it comes to client involvement in discussions with us. A dialogic approach to CBT must recognize and contend with clients' efforts to negotiate therapy's content and process, regardless of the linguistic prowess of master therapists.

Delicate content negotiations?

On the content side, there would be words and meanings up for negotiation. It would be wrong, however, to see such negotiations as not already occurring or available to clients in their conversations elsewhere. To paraphrase Bakhtin (1984), our words have 'other claims on them', a stance quite unlike that of Humpty Dumpty in Lewis Caroll's *Through the Looking-Glass, and What Alice Found There*, who claimed he was Master of 'his' words, making them mean whatever he wanted. Humpty's claim, undeniably a fiction, translates in practice to imposing on or negating others' meanings. People clearly cannot make any meaning fly culturally, or relationally. What makes it possible to say things and generally be understood is that people use words in similar ways. To use them dissimilarly is to invite conflict, misunderstanding, or even involuntary committal in psychiatric facilities. So, the notion that we can re-story our lives, reframe our meanings, and adopt our own discourses – irrespective of how these will be received by others – is understandably suspect. The discourse analyst Tannen (1998) described this as a key element of why we increasingly have an 'argument culture'. That said, we are not shackled to the meanings we share with others either. Still, as changes in meaning or action are proposed by people in relationship – meanings or actions that affect their relations – there typically is some conversational work to do, as people generally do not foist their meanings and actions on each other, nor do they accept them as such.

Like the earlier presentation of CBT as a conversational project having different meanings and practices, it can help to see any 'cognition', word, story, or discourse clients labour under as a product of a stuck negotiation. To the eighteenth-century philologist Vico (2001), such negotiations stall when there is 'linguistic poverty', calling for 'poetic wisdom'. Die-hard realists typically see such meanings as given; while some critical discourse analysts see such meanings or cognitions as culturally imposed. How meanings get so fixed ('fossilized or fetishized' in the language of Newman & Holzman, 1996), of course, is at odds with the notion of developing adaptive or effective cognitions advocated by Beck (1979) through his Socratic dialogues with clients. The practice of CBT – its focus on maladaptive 'cognitions' – can derive from well-established traditions of dialogue where reflection upon and modification of client meanings occurs. I should first, however, account for my recurring use of scare quotes around the word cognition as this use is central to why I see CBT as a dialogic practice.

There is a tendency in portrayals of the conversational work of therapy to look past the words clients use in talking with therapists. One premise behind this dismissal of client words is that the brain runs on different information (i.e. language) than that which people use (and generally get by on) in everyday discourse. Wittgenstein (1953; Harre & Tissaw, 2005) saw this as an odd process of double description whereby people somehow use different languages externally than they do internally. Discourse and dialogue theorists tend to see the languages people use in everyday dialogue as articulating and animating the same realities or thoughts they live by. Thus, clients' words show evidence of those realities and need to be engaged with as such. But, a not uncommon conversational move comes with the therapist offering whatever 'official articulation' of clients' spoken reality fits with their discourse. As a move in a negotiation towards what Bakhtin (1984) described as 'inwardly persuasive' discourse (i.e. the client's) this is unproblematic as a dialogic practice, but taken as a pronouncement of how things are or should be it becomes a therapist's ideological imposition. I was relieved to read the 'for' authors in House and Loewenthal's (2008) book distancing themselves from CBT practices where therapists were to adjudicate and prescribe correct meanings based on the words clients use.

For Bakhtin (1984) and his colleagues (e.g. Volosinov, 1987), there is a need for individuals to make language their own, to 'people' it with their intentions and understandings; otherwise, they become mere ventriloquators and enactors of others' words and discourses. Gestalt therapists (e.g. Perls, Hefferline, Goodman) related to such words or discourses as 'introjects' needing the conversational equivalent of proper digestion, a discursive chewing over of what may have gone uncritically swallowed. That kind of conversational digestion is a central feature in CBT and many other therapies: critical reflections on the effectiveness of the words and metaphors clients 'live by' (Lakoff & Johnson, 1980). Critical reflection in this manner is thus guided by client judgements and evaluations, without a need for spoon-feeding by therapists. This seems, however, to be one of those places where therapists struggle over how much they should defer to the client 'as expert' (Anderson, 2005; Anderson & Goolishian, 1992).

Negotiating therapy's process turn by conversational turn

Clients and therapists bring their different interpretive histories to their dialogues and this extends to how they make meaning in and from their dialogues. Added to that, they respond from differences over other aspects of how they might 'go on together' to use a pithy phrase from Wittgenstein (1953). Conversation analysts see 'going on together' as a turn-by-conversational-turn negotiation (Linell, 2005; Roy-Chowdhury, 2006), as speakers respond in ways shaped by their prior conversation while also talking so as to shape their future conversation (Heritage, 1984). In everyday conversation, there are plenty of examples as people conversationally work up shared understandings while still proposing to each other differences of opinion, activities to be jointly enacted, and so on. In the language of 1980s hypnotherapy instruction (Zeig, 1980): pace, pace, pace (i.e. staying with the present context) then lead (proposing new initiatives hopefully welcomed by clients). Dialogically, 'going on together' is a mix of what our field calls rapport and intervention, a mix of the yin and yang of receptive and instrumental communicative interactions. However, the word intervention needs closer examination as does the notion that clients take up some interventions that fit their interpretive histories, while declining others.

One element in the social constructionist therapies can be initially hard to grasp: dialogue is as much a coordinated performance of meaning as a semantic exchange of information (Strong & Tomm, 2007). Questions, accordingly, can be seen as interventions (Tomm, 1988); or, to use the language of the narrative therapist Jenkins (1990), they can be understood as invitations to talk from particular discursive positions. Thus, solution-focused therapists (e.g. De Shazer, 1994) who ask what clients are doing when problems are not happening are inviting discussion of client resourcefulness where none had seemed apparent or significant. Seen as a rhetorical move in negotiating how therapist and client might 'go on together' such questions invite a particular discussion focus, while also passing over others – such as more discussion about problems. One could argue that more than an invitation occurs when a client is asked to talk about success over failure, that the therapist exerts institutional and cultural forms of power expectedly so clients have no choice but to defer to the therapist. It concerns me how therapists construct what Sampson (1993) called a serviceable other (i.e. a helpless client needing their help) when positioning clients as participants in therapy.

It can help to see another process element as negotiable in therapy: the language game (Wittgenstein, 1953), discourse (Pare, 1995), or speech genre (Bakhtin, 1986). These are the systematized and patterned ways of communicating and thinking people use to understand and be influential. Wittgenstein went so far as to refer to these ways of communicating and thinking as 'forms of life'. A spiritual language game of bereavement is clearly different from a biomedical one focused on depression, yet these two dialogues could clearly be about the same phenomenon. Part of my earlier reference to Vico's (2001) 'poetic wisdom' becomes relevant here in seeing dialogue as served by many discourses, language games, or speech genres, and a challenge is to avoid becoming ensnared in one. Similarly, one relational challenge can be to get beyond conflicting or uncoordinated speech genres, discourses or language games to find ways of talking and listening that are generative and collaborative. Lyotard (1988) articulated this concern in *The Differend: Phrases in Dispute*. Relationally it can be difficult, or impossible, for people to 'go on together' when they lack a common language game with its shared meanings and ways of talking. In that overused metaphor of dance, failures to share or coordinate discourses or language games are tantamount to conversationally stepping on each other's toes.

Seldom is therapy considered conversational work. While there is talk in the literature about interventions, about good therapeutic alliances, and about things a therapist is supposed to say, for the most part our conversational work is portrayed as if there was no client responding to it, or us to them. If talk is referred to it is in the broad sense – therapist A said X to client B – or it is an account of what was talked about, not the actual talking and listening itself. As phenomenologists might tell us, such third-party accounts are quite different from the lived experience of being face-to-face in dialogue (Zahavi, 2007).

To 'co-construct' therapeutic dialogue is for therapist and client to treat differences over how their conversation should develop as legitimate aspects of conversational work. Therapeutic dialogue is 'for' clients and is typically conversationally managed as such. Conversational management sounds like a crass depiction of what therapists who practice CBT do. The crisp prose used to depict such dialogues in therapy textbooks and articles seems to idealize what transpires in actual dialogues. Any close-up examination of therapeutic dialogue shows a much less tidy back and forth of talk occurring, much of it without words as in this quote from Goffman:

> It is not the shout of responsive action that talk mostly needs and seeks to get but murmurings – the clucks and tsks and aspirated breaths, the goshes and gollies and wows – which testify that the listener has been stirred.
>
> (1974: 541)

Goffman reminds us of a mundane level of communication that precedes words, or perhaps undergirds them. It is a level of communication that is conspicuous when improperly coordinated, yet good conversation is usually forgiving and rife with instances where speakers momentarily fall out of sync with each over meanings, body language, even cadence. That said, clients still selectively listen to us as much as we do to them, make their own evaluations (typically in silence) of what transpires as the dialogue unfolds, interpret what we say in ways we cannot control and, as Rennie's (e.g. 1994) research highlighted, do a lot of deferring to us. What to do about that deference has been a longstanding source of debate among therapists in CBT and elsewhere. As Latour (2000) would say, what makes human science (or by extension the practices of scientist-practitioners) 'objectively human' is that humans can object to how they are engaged with or described. This extends to how or whether they participate in the therapist's view of how the professional dialogues of counselling should occur. Taking up an assigned speaking part in someone else's restrictive language game or conversational protocol is clearly different from participating in a dialogue where one's participation shapes the process and its outcomes.

Conversational resources and resourcefulness for CBT dialogues

There are, of course, many resources and ways to be resourceful when participating in therapeutic dialogue. Surely, the proliferation of so many therapies, each offering clients some ways of being helpful, is evidence of this. The notion that replicable methods are what make possible scientifically warranted practice has been a central tenet in the development of that approach to CBT championed by Layard. In such an approach, it is the manualized method that is seen as the curative agent to stick with, according to the medicalized discourse that spawned such an approach. The converse can seem like conversational anarchy. What is a therapist without some established procedures and methods to guide practice?

Conversational resources and resourcefulness are different ways of thinking about the dialogic potentials of CBT. They speak of what can be used or catalysed in the course of therapeutic dialogue. If the heart of ethically practiced CBT is critical reflections on, and modifications of, the words and ways of talking one uses to 'go on' in the face of previously ineffective words and ways of talking, then there can be many resources and resourceful ways of talking (Strong & Turner, 2008), some of which involve improvising the dialogues of therapy (Newman, 2003; Strong, 2007). Both hermeneutic scholar Gadamer (1988) and Wittgenstein wrote of problems that come with conflating 'truth and method', yet methods in therapy are often seen as more than therapeutic resources; they are the means by which therapy must be done. Milton Erickson spoke of his therapies as having an n of 1, meaning that he customized his dialogues with clients depending on the resources and understandings clients brought to therapy.

It helps to see dialogue as helpful in bringing forth client resources and resourcefulness, much like Bakhtin's view that words can be similarly brought to life in the back and forth of dialogue. The assumption that clients bring to therapy unrecognized resources that can be talked into significance and effective use has become a cornerstone of the constructionist approaches to therapy (Madsen, 1999). This involves more than a therapist pointing out to clients what they overlook that they can use; what matters is how such resource-focused language games and their by-products are negotiated and 'peopled' by clients. Flexible and resourceful language use is a considerable resource that therapists bring to their dialogues with clients (Strong, 2002). This extends to how intentions are articulated (Anderson, 1997) as well as to how problems are co-authored so as to be solvable (O'Hanlon & Weiner-Davis, 1989; White & Epston, 1990). For Heidegger (1962), language has the potential to disclose 'new worlds' – in this case beyond the world in which a person is ensconced in a problem. Whether therapists orient to untapped client resources or resourcefulness, or use language resourcefully in negotiating solvable problems with clients, a key departure from traditional 'diagnose and treat CBT' is a focus on resourcefulness. That clients might change by recognizing and mobilizing what they don't have to be taught or that a problem 'dis-solves' as clients put new language to 'it' (Anderson, 1997) points to very different ways of conceptualizing how dialogue helps clients get beyond ineffective 'cognitions'. Helpful therapeutic dialogue engages clients and therapists in a process that neither determines on their own; it is the negotiation of their differences, in ways clients find helpful in 'going on'.

Considerations of rigour in dialogic CBT?

What might it mean to practice CBT dialogically, and with rigour? It was reassuring to read the 'for CBT' authors as saying that good CBT practice involves more than holding therapist–client dialogue to what is laid out in manuals. Rigour in a dialogic sense speaks to a careful relational coordination, something Hoffman (1998) once described as 'always staying within an inch of the client's experience'. It can also relate to what Michael White described as the 'rigorous application of preferred ideas' (personal communication, 1990). The tension between what Hoffman reported (in describing White's practice) and White's endorsement of rigorously applying ideas points to how client and therapist talk as a careful negotiation of what enables the client to effectively go on where this was not previously possible. Social constructionist or dialogically oriented therapists (e.g. Seikkula & Arnkil, 2006) see a fluid language of problems and solutions as focal to engaging clients in therapeutic dialogue. Engaging clients' language (i.e. their cognitions) in a language seen as negotiable involves 'wordsmithing' (Strong, 2007) the therapeutic dialogue at important conversational junctures.

Therapists are not performing conversational surgery; they are working with clients' investments in what has been 'inwardly persuasive' language. It is easy, given the cultural and institutional power differentials afforded to therapists, for them to drive these client investments and preferences conversationally underground, as was pointed out by CBT 'againsters' Guilfoyle (2008) and

Proctor (2008). So, in response, ways to welcome and invite client resistance to therapist discourse are needed, acknowledging and enabling their editor-in-chief role with respect to any language proposed for going on together – a role they exercise beyond therapy anyway. Most challenging perhaps in what I am raising is therapist involvement in negotiating and coordinating of judgements as they feature in guiding the therapeutic dialogue. Orienting to conversational protocols can seem a whole lot easier than being responsive to what might seem like client whims over words and ways of talking. But, that would overlook the considerable extent to which such protocols in therapy (e.g. Peräkylä et al., 2008) still have some element of what Garfinkel (1967) referred to as 'ad-hockery' in how therapist and client conversationally work out the use of such protocols. Ultimately, for a dialogic approach to CBT to be effective, an inwardly persuasive and effective language (taken up and enacted by the client) emerges from such conversational work or negotiations.

Some might ask: where is the rigour in a therapeutic dialogue if its course can be altered by clients' input? Might therapeutic dialogue become excessively client-directed and should not therapists manage the dialogue for both parties? Such questions underscore a recognition that not just any dialogue is therapeutic; clients typically come to therapy because, on their own and from their everyday conversations, they have not gotten what is needed. This is where earlier mention of a dialogic approach to CBT as being 'humble' resurfaces. While some in the CBT literature approach diagnosis and intervention as if these were procedures that are logarithmically determinable and prescribeable (e.g. Rush, 2001), a dialogic approach to therapy has no such predetermined structure. What matters is how therapist and client collaboratively talk beyond ineffective understandings to understandings clients deem effective and inwardly persuasive.

Shotter (1984, 1993; Shotter & Katz, 1999) has, for years, raised themes like these in his writing. Drawing from thinkers such as Bakhtin, Harold Garfinkel, Wittgenstein, Vygotsky, and Merleau-Ponty, Shotter has fashioned a rather unique view of the 'conversational realities' that develop between speakers in the face-to-face immediacies of their dialogues. Counselling textbooks and articles fail to do justice to these immediacies and they tend to be lumped together in that somewhat mystical term, rapport. Among Shotter's concerns is how people who are unfamiliar with each other develop a shared sense of what is appropriate and negotiable between them; what he calls a conversational reality. Such a conversational reality owes much to how speakers, like clients and therapists, keep the content and process of their dialogues acceptably familiar. Departures from what is familiar or accepted are matters to be negotiated between them. Such negotiations and coordinations cannot be pre-scripted or imposed on one's conversational partner. The dialogues Bakhtin described, those Shotter was highlighting the contours of, find their aliveness precisely in how therapist and client fall into and out of coordinated conversation, how they deal with each other's differences of meaning or conversational performance in the moment. The rigour of a dialogically practiced CBT comes with how this occurs as client and therapist collaboratively ferret out ineffective words and ways of talking for critical reflection and replacement with more effective language for going on.

Staying in dialogue with CBT

Everything I have been raising can be similarly considered in how CBT as a conversational project goes forward. The approach to CBT I raised my concerns about ('diagnose and treat CBT') has a science incapable of ending dialogue about how CBT might go on. To return to Bakhtin, the word of any dialogue is unfinalizable. Indeed, a theme common among those 'for' CBT in House and Loewenthal's (2008) book is that CBT has seen developments that are already moving CBT beyond static protocols. In this respect, CBT is no different than the myriad of developments that occurred in psychodynamic therapy after Freud and his disciples established early standards for practice. Some of this also plays out in larger cultural conversations where the varying concerns of people in different eras and contexts have given rise to therapeutic methods particular to those eras and contexts (Cushman, 1995; Hacking, 1999).

Given the centripetal and centrifugal tendencies of dialogue, it should not be surprising that CBT would have seen its own phases in which convergence on purportedly correct methods seems in focus. A behavioural era in psychotherapy was followed in the 1960s by the wide-open era of humanistic and growth-oriented therapies (think primal screaming and RD Laing). Where EE Sampson could call cognitive behavioural therapy an ideology over a generation ago, we now have forms of CBT that include meditation, psychodynamic principles, and even suggestions like that which I have been making here: that CBT go dialogic.

The dialogic approach to CBT I have been describing will already be familiar to therapists who see people's articulations of experience as socially constructed. But to construct a socially shareable experience means to negotiate (i.e. co-construct) effective versions of it, in words and ways of talking, with those intended to share it. The antipathy that House and Loewenthal (2008) gave voice to in their edited book speaks to a needed phase in a problematic dialogue in CBT's development. With the imprimatur of a particular science, the endorsement of Lord Layard, and a government thinking it had found a cultural prescription to address a health and economic issue, one approach to CBT temporarily seemed to preclude other approaches to therapy, and that riled more than a few therapists. So, in dialogic fashion, the CBT dialogue continues to develop in generative ways from responses like those in House and Lowenthal. I've sidestepped the science issues here (for a partial treatment of these issues see Strong et al., 2008), but even if one tried to equate CBT with medical treatments, one need look no further than treatments purportedly capable of eradicating diseases like tuberculosis or smallpoxes: superbugs untreatable by these treatments are developing as a (dialogic?) response. Bakhtin once wrote that there is no final resting place for the word. There are only negotiated responses and where they next take us. As a conversational project, the evolving ideas and practices of CBT can only benefit from the kinds of critical reflection and generative discussion evident in House and Loewenthal's (2008) *Against and for CBT*.

Acknowledgement

The author conveys special thanks to The Social Sciences and Humanities Research Council of Canada, John Shotter, Andy Lock, and Ken Gergen.

References

Anderson, H. (1997). *Conversation, language and possibilities*. New York: Basic Books.

Anderson, H. (2005). The myth of not-knowing. *Family Process, 44*: 497–504.

Anderson, H. and Goolishian, H. (1992). The client is the expert: A not-knowing approach to therapy. In *Constructing therapy: Social construction and the therapeutic process* (S. McNamee and K. J. Gergen, Eds.). London: Sage Publications (pp. 25–39).

Bakhtin, M. (1981). *The dialogical imagination* (M. Holquist, Ed.; C. Emerson and M. Holquist, Trans.). Austin: University of Texas Press.

Bakhtin, M. (1984). *Problems of Dostoevsky's poetics*. Minneapolis, MN: University of Minnesota Press.

Bakhtin, M. (1986). *Speech genres and other late essays*. Austin, TX: University of Texas Press.

Bandler, R. and Grinder, J. (1975). *The structure of magic*. Palo Alto, CA: Science and Behavior Books.

Bandler, R. and Grinder, J. (1976). *The structure of magic II*. Palo Alto, CA: Science and Behavior Books.

Barlow, D. (2009). Towards a unified transdiagnostic treatment for emotional disorders. Keynote Presentation at the Canadian Psychological Association Convention. Montreal, Canada, 12 June.

Beck, A. T. (1979). *Cognitive therapy and the emotional disorders*. New York: International Universities Press.

Carkhuff, R. (1969). *The art of helping, Vol. 1*. New York: Holt, Rinehart, Winston.

Clark, K. and Holquist, M. (1984). *Mikhail Bakhtin*. Cambridge, MA: Harvard University Press.

Cushman, P. (1995). *Constructing the self, constructing America: A cultural history of psychotherapy*. Cambridge, MA: Perseus.

De Shazer, S. (1994). *Words were originally magic*. New York: Norton.

Friedman, S. (Ed.) (1993). *The new language of change*. New York: Guilford

Gadamer, H.-G. (1988). *Truth and method* (2nd revised edition) (J. Weinsheimer and D. G. Marshall, Trans.). New York: Continuum.

Garfinkel, H. (1967). *Studies in ethnomethodology*. Englewood Cliffs, NJ: Prentice Hall.

Goffman, E. (1967). *The interaction ritual: Essays on face-to-face behavior*. New York: Pantheon Books.

Goffman, E. (1974). *Frame analysis: An essay on the organization of experience*. New York: Harper & Row.

Guilfoyle, M. (2008). CBT's integration into societal networks of power. In *Against and for CBT* (R. House and D. Loewenthal, Eds.). London: PCCS Books (pp. 233–240).

Hacking, I. (1999). *The social construction of what?* New York: Harvard.

Harre, R. and Tissaw, M. (2005). *Wittgenstein and psychology: A practical guide.* Aldershot, UK: Ashgate.

Heidegger, M. (1962). *Being and time* (J. Macquarrie and E. Robinson, Trans.). New York: Harper & Collins (Original published in German, 1927).

Heritage, J. (1984). *Garfinkel and ethnomethodology.* Oxford: Blackwell.

Hoffman, L. (1998). Setting aside the model in family therapy. *Family Process, 24,* 145–156.

House, R. and Loewenthal, D. (Eds.) (2008). *Against and for CBT: Towards a constructive dialogue?* Ross-on-Wye: PCCS Books.

Hubble, M., Duncan, B. and Miller, S. (Eds.) (1999). *The heart and soul of change.* Washington, DC: American Psychological Association.

Jenkins, A. (1990). *Invitations to responsibility: The therapeutic engagement of men who are violent and abusive.* Adelaide, AU: Dulwich Centre Publications.

Lakoff, G. and Johnson, M. (1980). *Metaphors we live by.* Chicago, IL: University of Chicago Press.

Latour, B. (2000). When things strike back: a possible contribution of 'science studies' to the social sciences. *British Journal of Sociology, 51*(1): 107–123.

Layard, R. (2005). *Happiness: Lessons from a new science.* London: Penguin.

Linell, P. (2005). *Approaching dialogue.* Amsterdam: John Benjamins Publishing Company.

Lyotard, J.-F. (1988). *The differend: Phrases in dispute* (G. van Abbeele, Trans.). Minneapolis, MN: University of Minnesota Press.

Madsen, W. (1999). *Collaborative therapy with multi-stressed families.* New York: Guilford.

Mansell, W. (2008). What is CBT really and how can we enhance the impact of effective psychotherapies such as CBT? In *Against and For CBT: Towards a constructive dialogue?* (R. House and D. Loewenthal, Eds.) Ross-on-Wye, UK: PCCS Books (pp. 19–32).

Newman, F. (2003). Undecidable emotions (What is social therapy? And how is it revolutionary?). *Journal of Psychology, 16,* 215–232.

Newman, F. and Holzman, L. (1996). *The end of knowing.* New York: Routledge.

O'Hanlon, W. and Weiner-Davis, M. (1989). *In search of solutions.* New York: W. W. Norton.

Pare, D. (1995). Of families and other cultures: The shifting paradigm of family therapy. *Family Process, 34*(1), 1–20.

Peräkylä, A., Antaki, C., Vehviläinen, S. and Leudar, I. (Eds.) (2008). *Conversation analysis and psychotherapy.* New York: Cambridge University Press.

Prime Minister's Office. (2008). *Clarifying statement to the Government's Response to the Psychotherapy E-Petition.* Government of the United Kingdom, 7 May. Retrieved from www.number10.gov.uk/Page15454

Proctor, G. (2008). CBT: The obscuring of power in the name of science. In *Against and for CBT* (R. House and D. Loewenthal, Eds.). London: PCCS Books (pp. 241–254).

Rennie, D. (1994). Clients' deference in therapy. *Journal of Counseling Psychology, 41,* 427–437.

Roy-Chowdhury, S. (2006). How is the therapeutic relationship talked into being? *Journal of Family Therapy, 28,* 153–174. doi: 10.1111/j.1467-6427.2006.00344.x

Rush, A. J. (2001). Practice guidelines and algorithms. In *Treatment of depression: Bridging the 21st century* (M. M. Weissman, Ed.). Washington, DC: American Psychiatric Press (pp. 213–242).

Sampson, E. E. (1993). Identity politics: Challenges to psychology's understanding. *American Psychologist, 48*, 1219–1230.

Seikkula, J. and Arnkil, T. (2006). *Dialogic meetings in social networks*. London, UK: Karnac.

Shotter, J. (1984). *Social accountability and selfhood*. Oxford, UK: Blackwell.

Shotter, J. (1993). *Conversational realities*. Newbury Park, CA: Sage.

Shotter, J. and Katz, A. (1999) 'Living moments' in dialogic exchanges. *Human Systems, 9*, 81–93.

Strong, T. (2002). Collaborative 'expertise' after the discursive turn. *The Journal of Psychotherapy Integration, 12*, 218–232.

Strong, T. (2007). Practitioner dialogues in counselling psychology. *Australian Journal of Counselling Psychology, 8*(3), 3–7.

Strong, T. and Tomm, K. (2007). Family therapy as re-coordinating and moving on together. *Journal of Systemic Therapies, 26*(2): 42–54.

Strong, T. and Turner, K. (2008). Resourceful dialogues: Eliciting and mobilizing client competencies and resources. *Journal of Contemporary Psychotherapy, 38*, 185–195.

Strong, T., Busch, R. S. and Couture, S. (2008). Conversational evidence in therapeutic dialogue. *Journal of Marital and Family Therapy, 34*, 288–305.

Strong, T., Lysack, M. and Sutherland, O. (2008). Considering the dialogic potentials of cognitive behavioural therapy. In *Against and for CBT* (R. House and D. Loewenthal, Eds.). Ross-on-Wye, UK: PCCS Press (pp. 156–168).

Tannen, D. (1998). *The argument culture: Moving from debate to dialogue*. New York: Random House.

Tomm, K. (1988). Interventive interviewing: Part III. Intending to ask lineal, circular, strategic, or reflexive questions? *Family Process, 27*, 1–15.

Vico, G. (2001). *New science* (D. Marsh, Trans.). London, UK: Penguin. (Original published in 1744.)

Volosinov, V. N. (1987). *Freudianism: A critical sketch* (I. Titunik, Trans; I. Tutunik and N. H. Bruss, Eds.). Bloomington, IN: Indiana University Press.

White, M. and Epston, D. (1990). *Narrative means to therapeutic ends*. New York: W. W. Norton.

Wittgenstein, L. (1953). *Philosophical: investigations* (G. E. M. Anscombe, Trans). New York: Macmillan.

Zahavi, D. (2007). *Subjectivity and selfhood: Investigating the first-person perspective*. Cambridge, MA: MIT Press.

Zeig, J. (1980). *A teaching seminar with Milton H. Erickson*. New York: Brunner/Mazel.

15

RELATIONAL AS THEORY? RELATIONAL AS A PRINCIPLE? RELATIONAL AS SYMBOL OF INTEGRATION?

Helena Hargaden

In this chapter, the author argues that since the relational approach became more explicit at the beginning of this century it has had, broadly speaking, a beneficial influence on the psychotherapeutic professions. The author proposes that the movement towards relational theory was given impetus particularly by the publication of Daniel Stern's The Interpersonal World of the Infant *(1985/1998), based on 30 years of research by scientists and clinicians in the field. Perhaps the most important influence of the relational approach, the author proposes, is that it has provided a principle of integration between different schools and modalities of psychological work. The term relational can also be understood as a symbol of the type of sensibility associated with the therapeutic task. Expanding on these ideas, the author explores the development of relational thinking within transactional analysis, describing its positive effects and identifying some potentially negative trends.*

Introduction

It is a complex matter to define my theoretical orientation, for whilst my training background is in transactional analysis and other humanistic therapies, I have been in Jungian analysis, and consulted with psychoanalysts and Jungians about my clinical practice over several decades. My philosophical home, though, is in humanism, the literary, political and philosophical context for humanistic psychologies. My journey into the relational approach began with my exploration of Daniel Stern's work in the early 1990s, which led to my making links between Stern's interpersonal world of the infant (1985/1998), Kohut's (1978) self-object theory and the transactional analysis model of ego states (Berne, 1986/1961). This line of enquiry led to collaboration with my colleague Charlotte Sills on the development of a theoretical model, wrought out of real case studies (Hargaden &

Sills, 2002), which sought to incorporate the nuanced relational understanding that Stern's research findings required of the potent therapist. It has since become clear that unwittingly we were part of a synchronous process of change alongside other modalities which were moving in a similar direction; seeking to find ways to integrate Stern's findings by reinterpreting and expanding their theoretical models.

Relational psychoanalysts have been leaders internationally in the field of relational thought, broadening relational ideas to include culture, politics, transgenerational trauma, gender studies and sexuality, and extending our use of language, enabling us to think about clinical 'unthought knowns' (Bollas, 1987). A fascinating example of their creative and positive influence on clinical thought is how they transformed our understanding of the Oedipus complex, which rarely found a theoretical way into humanistic thinking and anyway was discredited as a serious theory (Masson, 1984), into a meaningful accessible theory of the 'third' (Gerson, 2004; Aron, 2006). The original idea of the 'third' derives from an understanding of how the 'father' (father as metaphor for any other person or occurrence, such as the mother's work for instance, or a same-sex partner, or a grandparent) interrupts the oedipal process so that mother and child are separated by a 'third' other, enabling the child to move out of the symbiotic relationship with the mother. In the therapeutic relationship the 'third' could be many things – one of which could be the therapist's thoughts experienced as an intrusion into the empathic flow of the therapeutic relationship. We could even understand the impact of Stern's theory as a 'third' as it altered traditional understanding of child development and the nature of symbiosis.

In this chapter, I will trace the significance of Daniel Stern's work, it being one of the main reasons that relational psychotherapy became more explicit about the turn it has taken. I propose that the development of the relational has been valuable to the psychotherapeutic community as an integrating principle, enabling us to have a dialogue between modalities in a way that had previously not seemed possible. With a specific focus on transactional analysis, I will demonstrate how the mutuality and reciprocity encouraged by the development of the relational approach has broadened our collective understanding by encouraging the cross-fertilization of ideas; that the bonds of loyalty to the original creator of one's own modality, whether that be Freud, Jung, Berne, Perls, Rogers or anyone else, which seemed to oblige clinicians to follow a type of 'party line' of theory, have been loosened, and that we have all benefited from this. Curious and independent-minded therapists have been freed up to integrate new knowledge and go beyond the limiting constraints of their own schools of principles and methodologies. I will discuss potential theoretical misunderstandings of the term 'relational' and conclude that although there are some negative trends within relational approaches, ultimately the overarching relational principle is one of integration; it continues to open up the doors for continuing dialogue between the modalities of psychology in a way which enhances our work with clients and patients.

Relational as theory: The influence of Daniel Stern

Stern's *The Interpersonal World of the Infant* (1985/1998) caused a mini revolution in clinical thinking. He described a baby who has a separate mind thus providing a challenge to the concept of symbiotic attachment. In his delineation of four domains of self, he ushers in the idea of multiple selves in continuous evolution instead of just one self being stuck in a phase or fixated in time. Drawing on 30 years of medical and clinical experimentation by large numbers of researchers, Stern's findings obliged clinicians, of whatever ilk (taking into consideration of course that each modality has its own particular strengths and weaknesses), to engage anew with the complexity, mystery and subtlety of subjectivity. They had to acknowledge the predominance of non-verbal selves, recognize the scientific basis for an innate predisposition towards intersubjectivity, and concentrate more reflectively on how language can not only bring about meaning but has the capacity to obscure implicit meaning. By bringing us into the internal mind of the infant, when before it had only been possible to access early experience retrospectively, Stern showed us new ways to think about relational experience, and what the mind required for optimal development. Stern's contribution to our understanding of implicit relational knowing was one of the major drivers for a reconceptualization of the term relational. Across modalities, we began to integrate his extraordinary contribution to our understanding of the mind and the significance of these new observations for effective clinical work. It became incumbent upon psychotherapists and psychologists to formulate new ways of thinking by sharing their understanding and critiquing their own and others' models at the same time as working out how to develop clinical theory and methodology. The dialogue continues to this day.

Relational as a principle of integration: The impact of the development of relational psychotherapy on transactional analysis

The shift towards relational exploration was inherent in the humanistic theory of TA which already brought the intrapsychic world into the social one through an analysis of transactions. In setting up an interpersonal, transactional therapy Berne (1986/1961) inherently implies a two-person psychology, where the therapist's and client's subjective experiences can be further explored. Within TA literature there was an increasing focus, starting in the 1980s, on the interplay of intrapsychic and interpersonal worlds and of patterns of conscious and unconscious modes of communication within the therapeutic relationship, a theme which is identified in a compilation of papers from that period (Cornell & Hargaden, 2005). These ideas were further developed by Hargaden and Sills (2002), whose relational model of transactional analysis provided a theoretical base to explore the realms of uncertainty and the unknown, and the nuances of implicit relational experience, with theoretical assistance. These changes prompted a critical examination of traditional TA theory, stimulating many TA clinicians to re-examine their theory and practice. For instance, the International Association of Relational Transactional Analysts was set up in 2009 initially to provide a forum for advancement of relational thinking. IARTA has since provided colloquia, workshops and encouraged more writing, with a set of papers edited by Fowlie and Sills (2011). Manifest in these and other papers is the richness of clinical understanding developed as a result of an intensive period of cross-fertilization of ideas, in particular integrating ideas from psychoanalysis into the existing intersubjective framework provided by the TA model of ego states (Little, 2004).

This activity within TA is mirrored in other modalities and has enabled a breadth and depth of theoretical expansion from which to think about human suffering. Alas, everything has the defects of its qualities. The term relational has now been used so widely and frequently that it leads me to ask: who would not want to be relational? Does this term really offer a theoretical framework? Perhaps not. The term is maybe best understood as offering a principle of integration, not only of new research, but also the knowledge gained from the different schools of psychological thought. Nevertheless, a term which has become so ubiquitous is perhaps easily misconstrued so that meanings are ascribed to it that it does not have.

Some theoretical misperceptions of the relational

In the main, the relational approach in psychoanalysis has involved writers and theorists integrating humanistic theory into their models. Humanistic theory has similarly integrated psychoanalytic thinking. Hence it is hard to support the idea that there is a ready-made or pre-existing relational theory as such. Despite this, there has been an increasing tendency to suggest that there is a specific theory of relational psychotherapy, moreover a theory that has cast iron principles, as follows.

Relational means being empathic

An outstanding issue that probably should not be resolved but does cause difficulty is that the meaning of relational takes on different forms depending, it seems, on the subjectivity of the clinician. For example, a trainee therapist arrived in my practice, enthusiastic about relational thinking. This turned out to mean, for her, that I would always agree with her views, her experience and her perceptions. When this turned out not to be the case she accused me of being non-empathic and non-relational. Apparently I was not conforming to her interpretation of relational. Naturally, this was an interesting therapeutic impasse which we worked through but nevertheless it heightened for me an understanding of how easily the approach can be co-opted in meanings which are reductive and self-serving.

Empathy is easily equated with relational thinking for obvious reasons, and its 'rediscovery' in the writing of Rogers (1957) and others, alongside the considerable research to show that empathy is significant and works (Asay and Lambert 1999), has put empathy centre stage of relational thought. However, this requires further examination. For instance, Guggenbhul-Craig believes that empathy can be used to bind the patient more firmly to the therapist, since in the client's eyes the therapist 'has become someone who apparently sees the greatest value in something which might not appear so very valuable at first glance' (1971: 73). In a different but equally important critique, Hoffman (1992) believes that empathy can be experienced by the client as a self-protective strategy in which the therapist is hiding some aspect of himself. Thus the notion that one always has to be empathic as a therapist, meaning that the client must always feel understood, can become a straitjacket for a therapist who fears to disturb his client, or make a space for the client to feel the often devastating experience of rejection and other difficult feelings.

Another common theoretical misunderstanding is the blurring of empathy with attunement, yet a theoretical distinction needs to be made between the two. Empathy, although not without a feeling component, is essentially a cognitive function which the therapist uses to let the client know they have understood what they are saying and feeling (and sometimes this happens even if the therapist doesn't understand but can make it appear that they do). I think that empathy is mostly an intellectual performance albeit an extremely useful method to oil the wheels of the therapeutic alliance (or mis-alliance depending on what else happens in the therapy). A striving to behave empathically can be understood as the therapist consciously trying to be the 'good mother' whereas attunement is an involuntary reaction (countertransference) in which meaning only comes retrospectively.

Empathy and attunement go together

But do they? Attunement is a non-conscious deep feeling process. For example, Beebe and Lachmann (1992) observed how infants, in mutually affective relationships with caretakers, moved in and out of synchrony, contact, ruptures and repairs. They describe this non-verbal engagement as proto-conversations which are made up of gesture, rhythm and musicality. Such attunement in the clinical setting is a form of complex countertransference response where the therapist, for example, may find herself unconsciously attuning to the body position of the client, unexpectedly feeling tears well up, or righteous anger swelling within her. A deep-seated sigh might escape her lips or she may have somatic responses in the form of a stomach ache, or bodily itching and so on, none of which are cognitive responses but based on an evolving non-verbal conversation.

Relational means interpersonal

Another example of a misperception of the meaning of relational came to my notice when a disgruntled colleague (seeking reassurance that her therapeutic modus operandus did not require her to change her thinking in any way) explained that she had always been 'relational' but upon further inquiry it became clear that what she thought of as 'relational' was that she worked in an interpersonal way. This is a particular difficulty in humanistic therapy where we are used to responding verbally to the client, afraid, maybe, to allow for silence or space lest anxiety and disturbance be generated by our more quiet presence. Maybe our attitude is captured by the patient of psychoanalyst Ron Britton's who told him to 'stop that fucking thinking!' (Britton, 1998: 88). What if the therapist too finds herself intimidated by a version of relational that dictates she must always be in relationship with an other? She too might be unable to do any 'fucking thinking' with such a dogmatic version of what it means to be relational in her mind. James Hollis (2012) extols the virtue of solitude and self-reflection, implicitly challenging the notion that one must always be relating in order to be relational.

Relational as non-conflictual

This is another distortion of relational psychotherapy that I recently came across on a discussion forum: in the middle of a heated online debate between several participants, another member wrote in to reprimand them for not being 'relational', by which she meant unharmonious. From this perspective relational means harmony and is non-conflictual.

Overall, the negative trend I perceive here is to make a dogma out of an idea. The irony is that the impact of the relational approach has in the past, as I have argued, steered us away from the dogma inherent in a rigid view of one's own theory.

Relational as symbol: We cannot teach the relational, we can only learn it

I propose that we cannot teach relational theory. We can only learn it if we are prepared to go on the type of therapeutic journey where it is possible to develop a robust consciousness of our true authentic selves in all their infinite variety of aggressive impulses as well as loving ones. Only when we feel robust and resilient will we have the capacity to travel on a journey with our clients, where they too can become equally powerful in themselves. For many of us, perhaps particularly in the humanistic tradition, it is easier to be in touch with our loving than our hating parts. However, the co-creation of an empathic environment alone will not enable the development of the type of resilience which is linked to personal power. An example which illustrates this clinical point is when someone feels criticized by the therapist and expresses hurt about this. For a therapist who has to be always the 'good object', the temptation may be to reassure the client and soothe the pain away instead of allowing herself to be the 'bad' object so the client can learn what feels so troublesome to him at such times. In another scenario where the therapist is being attacked, if she is too anxious about conflict to draw her client's attention to what is going on at a feeling level within the relationship, then the repressed rage within the client will never be exposed nor the potential in it for transformation realized. Davies and Frawley emphasize the importance of 'familiarizing the patient with the sadistic introject' and point out that the analyst must interpret this sensitively 'without making the patient enormously guilty' (1992: 30). We cannot of course always control how our interventions will be heard but as a guiding principle this is useful to guard against the therapist's own sadism.

Most recent research reveals that it is the engine of the client that operates the therapy (Norcross, 2011). This makes intuitive sense. What makes therapy possible and potentially effective is a well-motivated client or patient and a therapist who continues to examine their psyche, not think they have 'done their analysis'.

In conclusion

The relational approach has essentially been a force for good in our psychological communities for all the reasons outlined above. In a recent online Colloquium of the International Association for Relational Psychoanalysis and Psychotherapy, based upon Hoffman's paper 'Therapeutic Passion in the Countertransference', Steven Cooper (2013) argued that relational theory is a meta-theory 'because it is not a theory of technique or metapsychology. Instead, it describes a set of overarching principles, tensions between old and new, discipline and spontaneity, principles that relate to an epistemological position and a different kind of interpretive authority characteristic of many psychoanalytic theories.' Cooper was of course referring to relational developments within psychoanalysis but the same can be said for all schools of psychotherapy that are engaging with relational developments. As I have argued, the term relational has provided an integrating principle both within modalities and across modalities, enabling a kind of conversation between us all that once would have seemed impossible. The relational psychoanalysts have worked hard to expand on psychoanalytic ideas by putting them into a humanistic context of relatedness and therefore making them more accessible. Humanistic psychotherapy has been deeply enriched by engaging with psychoanalytic ideas that previously seemed irrelevant (as in the Oedipus complex) or were denied (as in the function and extent of aggression in human relatedness).

In summary I think that relational thinking has made it possible for all of us who share a relational sensibility, but still retain deep-seated differences and work in quite different ways, to have an ongoing conversation, the ultimate goal of which is to make us better, more competent, more able to work with people who are suffering. It is through this ongoing conversation that we continue to learn about each other's clinical vulnerabilities. In particular this conversation has increased awareness that to make a mistake is not only human but a necessary part of therapeutic healing as the client or patient begins to understand that they are not the only hurt or vulnerable person in the room.

References

Aron, L. (2006). Analytic impasse and the third: Clinical implications of intersubjectivity theory. *International Journal of Psycho-Analysis, 87:* 349–368.

Asay, T. P. and Lambert, M. J. (1999). The empirical case for the common factors in therapy: quantitative finds. In *The heart and soul of change: What works in therapy* (M. A. Hubble, B. L. Duncan and S. D. Miller, Eds.). Washington, DC: APA Press (pp. 33– 56).

Beebe, B. and Lachmann, F. M. (1992). *Infant research and adult treatment: Co-constructing interactions.* London and New York: Routledge.

Berne, E. (1986/1961). *Transactional analysis in psychotherapy.* London: Souvenir Press (First published 1961, New York: Grove Press).

Bollas, C. (1987). *The shadow of the object.* New York: Columbia University Press.

Britton, R. (1998). *Belief and imagination – Explorations in psychoanalysis.* London and New York: Routledge.

Cooper, S. (2013). Therapeutic passion in the countertransference by Irwin Hoffman. IARPP Colloquium Series: No. 22, May 6–May 19.

Cornell, W. F. and Hargaden, H. (2005). *From transactions to relations: The emergence of a relational tradition in transactional analysis.* Chadlington, England: Haddon Press.

Davies, J. M. and Frawley, M. G. (1992). Dissociative processes and transference-countertransference paradigms in the psychoanalytically oriented treatment of adult survivors of childhood sexual abuse. *Psychoanalytic Dialogues, 2:* 5–36.

Fowlie, H. and Sills, C. (Eds.) (2011). *Relational transactional analysis principles in practice.* London: Karnac.

Gerson, S. (2004). The relational unconscious: A core element of intersubjectivity, thirdness, and clinical process. *Psychoanalytic Quarterly, 73:* 63–98.

Guggenbuhl-Craig, A. (1971). *Power in the helping professions.* Dallas, TX: Spring Publications Inc.

Hargaden, H. and Sills, C. (2002). *Transactional analysis: A relational perspective.* London: Routledge.

Hoffman, I. (1992). Some practical implications of a social-constructivist view of the psychoanalytic situation. *Psychoanalytic Dialogues, 2:* 287–304.

Hollis, J. (2012). *Finding meaning in the second half of life: How to finally really grow up.* Toronto: Inner City Books.

Kohut, H. (1978). *The search for the self: Selected writings of Heinz Kohut 1950–1978* (P. H. Ornstein, Ed.). Vol. 1. Madison, CT: International Universities Press.

Little, R. (2004). Ego state relational units and resistance to change 3: An integration of transactional analysis and object relations. *Transactions. The Journal of the Institute of Transactional Analysis, 1:* 3–10.

Masson, J. M. (1984). *The assault on truth: Freud's suppression of the seduction theory.* New York: Farrar, Straus, Giroux.

Norcross, J. C. (2011). *Psychotherapy relationships that work: Evidence-based responsiveness.* New York: Oxford University Press.

Rogers, C. R. (1957). The necessary and sufficient conditions of therapeutic personality change. *Journal of Consulting Psychology, 21:* 95–103.

Stern, D. N. (1985/1998). *The interpersonal world of the infant.* New York: Basic Books.

16
SHADOWS OF THE THERAPY RELATIONSHIP

Andrew Samuels

The author argues that the relational turn in psychotherapy has led to moralism, conformism and hypocrisy on the part of many clinicians. Relationality cannot engage with the phenomenon of solitude in a satisfactory manner leading to a potential flight from the unconscious. The author proposes that there is more than one therapy relationship to consider and that the key task is to hold their simultaneity in mind. He proposes a methodology by which this might be done. The author argues that what is being discussed will be incomprehensible in terms of the various approaches to psychotherapy proposed by the British government.

Introduction

This chapter probes the shadow of the relational turn in psychoanalysis and psychotherapy. By 'shadow', I mean the negative and undesirable aspects of an approach to practice that has achieved almost universal acceptance. It is significant that one plan to promote psychotherapy in the mental health field was going to use the slogan 'It's the relationship, stupid!' Hence, the chapter suggests that what was once cutting edge has become something worse than a cliché – actual harm might be being done.

My own clinical development has been markedly pluralistic (Samuels, 1997). I began in the Humanistic movement in the 1970s doing encounter groups, but changed direction to qualify as a Jungian analyst in 1977. From the 1990s onwards, I have become involved enough in American relational psychoanalysis to be on the founding board of the International Association for Relational Psychoanalysis and Psychotherapy.

If I were a humanistic therapist still, I'd be feeling aggrieved. For the relational turn in psychotherapy stems from the work of Carl Rogers and the person-centred approach (e.g. Rogers, 1996). What has been 'invented' in the United States could be termed 'humanistic psychoanalysis'. And anyone who has done even a basic course in person-centred psychotherapy and counselling may well know more deeply than many in the highly educated and over-trained psychoanalytic world about the therapy relationship (e.g. Tudor & Worrall, 2006).

The two things I want to discuss as shadow features of the relational are (i) its potential for conformism and moralism, and (ii) to say that, at its worst, relational psychoanalysis, and the relational turn in psychotherapy generally, can constitute a flight from the inner world and the relation to the self exemplified by the experience of solitude.

Moralism, conformism and hypocrisy

First, then, I propose that psychotherapy and counselling have overdone the stress on providing a secure container within which a therapy relationship can thrive (cf. Lazarus, 1994; House, 2003: 52–59). This leads to behavioural conformism and a corresponding moralism. What are the disadvantages of the current stress on the frame, on boundaries, on the container? Doesn't this lose the element of surprise, the risk inherent to psychotherapy (cf. Clarkson, 1995, on 'defensive therapy'), the exposure to danger that is involved in any process of self-understanding and/ or growth? Are we witnessing the decline of psychotherapy in the relational mode into a kind of monism, where it is all about an attuned simulacrum of nurture, safety and a secure parental base – therapist as parent or, more often, therapist as mother? Underpinning this is a valorisation of something called 'intimacy', or the capacity for intimacy.

Often, banally, intimacy is defined in terms of how long people can manage to stay together. Longevity is the acid test, apparently, of whether you can manage a relationship. Have you helped your client to 'settle down'? Many people don't want to settle down, and many therapists don't want to practice 'settled down' therapy! What gets missed in that kind of therapy are all the unruly, uncontrollable aspects of sexuality, not just literal sexuality, but sexuality in the mind as well (cf. Rosiello, 2000). We see ambivalence and even hypocrisy among contemporary practitioners as they address the sexual – a moralistic posture in relation to sexual experimentation and towards promiscuity.

Hypocrisy is the act of opposing a belief or behaviour while holding the same beliefs or performing the same behaviours at the same time. Hypocrisy is frequently invoked as an accusation in politics and in life in general. One key feature of hypocrisy is the refusal to apply to ourselves the same standards we apply to others. Hence hypocrisy is one of the central evils of our society, promoting injustices such as war and social inequalities in a framework of self-deception.

With these thoughts in mind, I want to turn to the professions of psychotherapy and counselling, both in and of themselves, and as representative of the wider culture. My accusation is that, when it comes to promiscuity, psychotherapy as an institution and many (but not all) psychotherapists as individuals are hypocritical. In terms of the etymology of the word hypocrisy, they are play acting or feigning something. As well as scoring points, I am interested in probing this phenomenon.

It is significant that sex outside of relationship is largely untheorised by analysts and therapists – or, if there is a theoretical position taken, it is invariably in terms of psychopathology, of an alleged fear of intimacy, problems in attachment ('ambivalent attachment') and relationship, perversion and so on. There is an absence of consideration of sex-as-force (but see Kahr, 2007). Actually, with some notable exceptions, there is very little contemporary psychoanalytic writing on bodily experience at all (but see Totton, 1998; Orbach, 2009). When Lyndsey Moon (personal communication, 2008; see Moon, 2007) was undertaking research focusing on the needs of bisexual clients, during which she interviewed 40 therapists (lesbian, gay male, heterosexual, queer and bisexual), only three (including the present writer) 'actually went anywhere near "sex" as having a meaning that needs to be talked about or talked through with clients'. Moon speculates that the bulk of the therapists were experiencing 'much fear of the sexual body and sexual behaviour'.

I think it is interesting to ask whether there might be something in the fundamental thinking or set-up of psychotherapy that leads to a carnality-averse conservatism. Certainly, the proliferation of schools in psychotherapy is a gorgeous metaphor for this whole topic: on the one hand, historically, most therapists have been monogamously wedded to one school (Feltham, 1997), yet the field itself is – or so it could be argued – becoming ever more, and ever more threateningly, promiscuous.

We have learned that, for every majority discourse, there is likely to be a subjugated minority discourse. In psychotherapy – as in society – the majority discourse is relational. Hence, the subjugated minority discourse will be the opposite of relational; in the language of this paper, promiscuous (see Barker & Langdridge, 2009). I have wondered if the silence of psychotherapists on the topic of promiscuity reflects a kind of sexual horror – so they translate everything into a discourse of relationality in which 'persons' get split off from 'sex'.

Putting these ideas – of hypocrisy and a subjugated non-relational discourse – together exposes the secret moral conservatism of numerous psychotherapeutic clinicians compared to their often very different sexual behaviour as persons. We could begin to understand this more deeply by seeing it as envy on the part of the therapist of the sexual experimentation and out-of-order behaviour related to them by their clients. Many psychotherapists are not overtly judgemental about promiscuous behaviour but tell us that it is a stage or phase of psychosexual development – usually adolescent. As such, the client should grow out of it because it cannot be sustained into middle or old age. It is not hard to see that, aside from whether it is true or part of a general cultural denial about the sexuality of older people (Gott, 2004), this is far from non-judgemental accepting and rules out any possibility that promiscuity might function as one template (in classical Jungian terminology, 'archetypal structure') for lifelong relational individuation. We don't talk much about the need to hold the tensions between the one and the many when it comes to relationships.

The matter comes to a head when psychotherapists engage with infidelity ('cheating') on the part of their clients. While not denying that some therapists, particularly couple therapists, understand cheating as a systemic phenomenon, the overall psychotherapeutic take on the matter is that it is a symptom of something else, some problem in the cheat, usually of a narcissistic kind. The cheated upon usually feels immense pain and the cheat often feels great guilt. These are strong affects for the therapist to engage with. Hence, unsurprisingly perhaps, what we see in the majority of instances is a counter-resistant valorisation of relational longevity and an utterly literal understanding of 'object constancy' at the expense of relational quality. Provided you are in a longstanding relationship, you are, to all intents and purposes, OK. (I take up this point in relation to persons seeking to train as psychotherapists in Samuels, 2006.)

However, when it comes to sexual desire, time doesn't have all that much to do with it. When I was a schoolboy, there was a joke about the theory of relativity: if you kiss a sexy girl for five minutes it feels like ten seconds; if you stick your hand in a flame for ten seconds it feels like five minutes. In the unconscious, time doesn't work the way it does at the conscious level.

The same is true in relation to sexual desire. One of the most compelling accounts of this is in Ernest Hemingway's *For Whom the Bell Tolls* (1941). Mortally wounded, the Spanish Civil War volunteer Robert Jordan is going to cover the escape of his comrades. Lying on the ground, weapon at the ready, he reflects on how he has lived a lifetime of sexual intimacy and a kind of 'marriage' with Maria, a girl living with the partisan band who has been raped by Franco's soldiers. He tries to recall: 'Well, we had all our luck in four days. Not four days. It was afternoon when I first got there and it will not be noon today. That makes not quite three days and three nights. Keep it accurate, he said. Quite accurate.' And earlier, in passion, 'there is no other now but thou now and now is thy prophet. Now and forever now ... there is no now but now.' And later, reflectively, 'I wish I was going to live a long time instead of going to die today because I have learned much about life in these four days; more I think than in all the other time.'

However, as I do not wish to create yet another foundational position, let me hasten to add that erotic time is no truer than any other form of time.

Solitude and flight from the inner world

The second shadow problem is a flight from the inner world. Where does relational psychotherapy stand on the questions of introversion and solitude? Not 'being alone in the presence of another' as Winnicott, whom it is so dangerous to challenge, said, but being alone, just being on your own, on your tod, being private, being a poet, being a mystic, being a solitary, 'just leave me alone', being a monk, being a hermit, or just being a person who wanders the streets looking at other people's bodies and getting turned on. This is not 'related', but may well be a royal road to the inner world. What about the relationship with one's self as revealed in dream and fantasy – what does relational therapy have to say about that? Not as much as it should. No, much of modern relational therapy is really turning into communication science – flat, grey, monochrome, dull, no images, no coruscations, no scratchy bits. Just flat. But maybe one can have interior depth and relationship at the same time. Jung taught that 'the soul is the very essence of relationship', and he also added that 'the mystery of life is always hidden between two' (Jung, 1946, paras 411 and 489). We will return to having it all, interior depth and relationship, when we discuss the many-ness of the therapy relationship, below.

For now, let's probe the idea of solitude a bit. Much is at stake here, clinically, for suicidal phenomena are often linked with isolation. There's an important gender angle to solitude as well: after bereavement, divorce or separation, Western men have terrible trouble with isolation, seemingly more than women. But we also know the incredibly valuable role of solitude in creativity (Storr, 1988), and also how necessary it is to be alone when things have got too much and a person needs quiet asylum.

However, we in the West live in a one-sidedly extroverted culture and being popular or being seen to be popular is very important, not only for young people. And being popular, or well thought of, is really rather important for therapists as well, isn't it, as the social organisation of the profession shows? Psychotherapists and counsellors do not spend much time on the therapeutic needs of what could be called 'natural introverts'. But what do we think their intimacy prospects might be? To enjoy an introverted self-state is not dissociation, is it?

Something relevant to this discussion came up at a joint conference in 2009 of the British Independent Psychoanalysts and Relational Psychoanalysts from New York. Listening to both sets of theorists, one could not avoid asking where the relation to the self had gone, given all the relational and intersubjective focus? How does the relation with oneself develop if not to a degree in isolation and solitude? What does a one-person psychology look like in an era of relational therapy? I'd like to suggest that working with the private, asocial imagery found in dreams and fantasies may be a special kind of attachment.

Freud was critical of 'oceanic feelings'; and these usually arise in a state of solitude. Jung had a different view and post-Jungians invoke the mythic image of the Uroborus (Samuels, 1985), the worm or snake that is depicted in a circular form, head in mouth. This suggests self-feeding (but not only a grandiose ablation of the breast) – and, crucially, there is the implication of self-impregnation, meaning the way in which new psychological patterns arise from the isolated depths of the solipsistic unconscious. Things in the unconscious arise and come on stream *sui generis*. They do not necessarily depend on a relation with another. Even if psychoanalytic science disputes this, it is how the phenomena of subjectivity present themselves to human consciousness and so cannot lightly be dismissed.

Conformism and state regulation of counselling and psychotherapy

There is more to this business of conformism than something on the personal level. Right now, as a profession, we are addressing the whole issue of state-imposed conformism (e.g. Parker & Revelli, 2008; King & Moutsou, 2010). And we know, academically and intellectually, how contemporary culture irradiates clinical work. We know that we cannot work in isolation from what is going on in the society within which we are working. If you work in education, you will have experienced the way government agendas have invaded education. We, as therapists, are going to see more and more pressure on us to conform and I worry that relational therapy may be less well equipped than other kinds to resist state pressure for conformity.

Note on politics and solitude

I want to take a further short detour into some of the connections between politics and solitude. These are ideas developed from my work as a political consultant (Samuels, 1993, 2001). In 'political clinics' worldwide on 'introverted politics', we find that we neglect or dismiss at our peril the private political engagements of poets, philosophers, mystics, shy people, the insane – and many women (who have been 'trained' not to speak out openly in politics). So – can a person be political or exercise social responsibility on their own, in solitude, in private? Is there an inner politician? Yes – the inner politician pours her or his inner politics into the zeitgeist, the collective, public fields of communication, the society itself.

One therapy relationship or many?

Psychotherapists and counsellors speak and write of 'the' therapy relationship. But this is not accurate; there are many therapy relationships in play at the same time (Clarkson, 1995). It can be very difficult to depict this simultaneity in a clear and compelling manner.[1]

In the Jungian and post-Jungian clinical world, an attempt to show how there are many therapy relationships going on at the same time, as opposed to there being several dimensions of one therapy relationship, has a long history stemming from Jung (Samuels, 1985). Consider Figure 16.1 with its double-headed arrows.

Arrow 1 indicates the conscious connection between therapist and client, where we can see the treatment alliance and the social linkages that make therapy possible. I think that Jung's insistence that analysis be carried out face-to-face, whether taken literally or more metaphorically as a kind of humane, relational principle, means this arrow is much more important than at first seems to be the case. This is the locale for confrontation with the other that was mentioned earlier

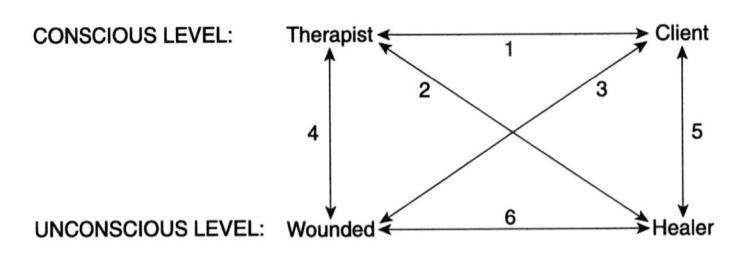

Figure 16.1 One therapy relationship or many?

and sits at the heart of any therapeutic encounter, whether in a consulting room or not. For me, it is an important tenet of psychotherapy that, in addition to the members of the nuclear family, the client can also be the therapist's ally, enemy, supervisor, therapist, fellow citizen, master/mistress and, on occasion, soul mate.

Arrows 2 and 3 refer to transference projections from the unconscious of therapist and client onto the consciously perceived figure of the other. The therapist projects his or her wounded parts onto the client. The client projects his or her healthy/healer parts onto the therapist. These benign projections seem to me to be the way that therapist and client come to recognise each other qua therapist and client. Without these projections, there would not be the heightening of relational tension that makes the therapeutic encounter, in some difficult to define way, different from an ordinary relationship.

But what happens in arrows 2 and 3 rests to a great extent on what happens in arrows 4 and 5. Arrow 4 signifies the therapist's connection to his or her personal wounds (Sedgwick, 1994). This should not be limited to whatever has gone on in the analyst's personal analysis (though it is significant that, as Freud noted [1912], it was Jung who was the first to call in 1910 [published in 1913 – CW4, para. 536] for compulsory training analyses, now a feature of almost every psychotherapy training in some form or other). Rather, we are referring to the therapist's whole apperception of his or her life. Arrow 5 is intended to refer to the client's gradual understanding of his or her potential to be other than a client. The client needs to get in touch, over time, with his or her healthy/healer parts, to not only be able to project them onto the therapist as part of an idealising transference. For there is also the important issue I mentioned earlier – helping and healing others as part of mental health.

Arrow 6 indicates the underlying unconscious connections between therapist and client.

I could have added arrows to show how the therapist, the client, and the various therapy relationships are linked to the outer world – the culture, society, and the specific positions of therapist and client therein.

Concluding thought

In attempting to discover the shadow aspects of relationality in therapy, we have travelled a long way, exploring moralism and conformism on the part of therapists, wondered if there is a flight from the unconscious itself carried by an eschewing of the virtues of solitude, and proposing that there is more than one therapy relationship to consider. What is being discussed here is far beyond the comprehension of the State apparatus, impossible for the bureaucrats and politicians – and any proposed regulatory authority – to understand (Parker & Revelli, 2008; Postle & House, 2009). Paradoxically, the one thing that therapists have proclaimed as their unique selling point may also make them uniquely ill-equipped to see off the intrusions of the State – namely, relationality and the fetishisation of the therapy relationship.

Note

1 At the conference where this paper was first presented, I addressed the problem of showing the simultaneity of the different therapy relationships as follows. I played the track *Duelling Banjos* from John Boorman's film *Deliverance*. In the film, rich bankers from the city take a wilderness trip in the poverty-stricken Appalachians. One of them has a guitar. They come across a group of hillbillies and among the group is a ten-year-old boy who is multiply handicapped and the implication is that somehow inbreeding is involved – he has special educational needs and possibly he is blind. The boy has a banjo. The man and the boy play together and gradually, as a kind of relationship develops, the musical passion increases. At the end, the boy cracks a smile. The locals stand and watch, expressionless. It is a conversation as much as a duel, and I have always seen this music as expressive of something profound about therapy. The boy with the banjo in my mind I see as the therapist and the man with the guitar I see as the client but it works just as well vice versa. Having played the track through, I played short segments of it to illustrate each of the therapy relationships (as illustrated by the double-headed arrows in Figure 16.1). I asked pairs of people from the audience to enact the two ends of all of the therapy relationships and gave them different coloured ribbons to play with so as to express their response to being in one or other of the therapy relationships – as well as their response to the music. Gradually, the lecture hall became criss-crossed by coloured ribbons, the more so as the outside world of society and culture was depicted. By the end of the exercise, the whole audience was involved in a therapy dance and many said the exercise did bring home something of what they experienced as therapist. Hence, it was a declarative and expressive exercise, and not an educational one. It was also, given the professional politics of that moment, right after a candidate (the author) critical of the government's plans for regulation of counselling and psychotherapy had been elected as Chair of the United Kingdom Council for Psychotherapy. Hence this was a moment of resistance as well. It might be interesting to play the track: www.youtube.com/watch?v=1tqxzWdKKu8

References

Barker, M. and Langdridge, D. (Eds.) (2009). *Understanding non-monogamies*. London: Routledge.

Clarkson, P. (1995). *The therapeutic relationship in psychoanalysis, counselling psychology and psychotherapy*. London: Whurr.

Feltham, C. (1997). Challenging the core theoretical model. *Counselling, 8*: 121–125.
Freud, S. (1912). Recommendations to physicians practising psycho-analysis. In *Standard Edition 12*. London: Hogarth.
Gott, M. (2004). *Sexuality, sexual health and aging*. Maidenhead: Open University.
Hemingway, E. (1941/1994). *For whom the bell tolls*. London: Arrow.
House, R. (2003). *Therapy beyond modernity: Deconstructing and transcending profession-centred therapy*. London: Karnac Books.
Jung, C. G. (1913) General aspects of psychoanalysis. *Collected Works of C. G. Jung*, Vol. 4. London: Routledge and Kegan Paul.
Jung, C. G. (1946). The psychology of the transference. *Collected Works of C. G. Jung*, Vol 16. London: Routledge and Kegan Paul.
Kahr, B. (2007). *Sex and the psyche*. London: Allen Lane.
King, L. and Moutsou, C. (Eds.) (2010). *Rethinking audit cultures: A critical look at evidence-based practice in psychotherapy and beyond*. Ross-on-Wye: PCCS Books.
Lazarus, A. A. (1994). How certain boundaries and ethics diminish therapeutic effectiveness. *Ethics and Behaviour, 4:* 255–261.
Moon, L. (Ed.) (2007). *Feeling queer or queer feelings? Radical approaches to counselling sex, sexualities and genders*. London: Routledge.
Orbach, S. (2009). *Bodies*. London: Profile.
Parker, I. and Revelli, S. (Eds.) (2008). *Psychoanalytic practice and state regulation*. London: Karnac Books.
Postle, D. and House, R. (Eds.) (2009). *Compliance? Ambivalence? Rejection? Nine papers challenging HPC regulation*. London: Wentworth Learning Resources.
Rogers, C. R. (1996). *A way of being*. Orlando, FL: Houghton Mifflin.
Rosiello, F. (2006). *Deepening intimacy in psychotherapy: Using the erotic transference and counter transference to facilitate treatment*. Northvale, NJ: Jason Aroson.
Samuels, A. (1985). *Jung and the post-Jungians*. London and Boston: Routledge and Kegan Paul.
Samuels, A. (1993). *The political psyche*. London: Routledge.
Samuels, A. (1997). Pluralism and psychotherapy: What is good training? In *Implausible professions* (R. House and N. Totton, Eds.). Ross-on-Wye: PCCS Books (pp. 199–214).
Samuels, A. (2001). *Politics on the couch: Citizenship and the internal life*. London: Karnac.
Samuels, A. (2006). Socially responsible roles of professional ethics: Inclusivity, psychotherapy and 'the protection of the public'. *International Review of Sociology, 16*(2): 175–190 [Taylor & Francis Online].
Sedgwick, D. (1994). *The wounded healer: Countertransference from a Jungian perspective*. London: Routledge
Storr, A. (1988). *Solitude*. London: Flamingo.
Totton, N. (1998). *The water in the glass: Mind, body and psychoanalysis*. London: Rebus.
Tudor, K. and Worrall, M. (2006). *Person-centred therapy: A clinical philosophy*. London: Routledge.
Winnicott, D. W. (1958). The capacity to be alone. *International Journal of Psychoanalysis, 39:* 416–420.

17

A CRITICAL COMMENTARY ON 'THE RELATIONAL TURN'

Keith Tudor

This chapter offers a critical commentary on Chapters 10–16 in Part II of this volume, and is a revised and expanded version of the author's previous commentary (Tudor, 2010a) on chapters which appeared previously as articles in a special issue of the European Journal of Psychotherapy and Counselling *(EJPC). On the basis of both a vertical and a horizontal reading of these chapters, this commentary offers some explication of the text of all seven chapters, including an analysis of citations and references to what Traue (1990) has referred to as 'ancestors of the mind'; some exegesis on 'the relational turn' in psychotherapy as presented in these chapters; and a critique of this relational 'turn'.*

Introduction

I am delighted to have been asked by the editors to reprise and extend my commentary (Tudor, 2010a) on original manuscripts. In the sense that a reprise is a return to an original theme, and as the theme has been enhanced by the addition to Part II of this volume of two chapters, by Loewenthal (Chapter 12) and Hargaden (Chapter 15), I also appreciate having the opportunity to read more and to offer some variations on that original theme and commentary.

A commentary is not, or should not be, simply another contribution. In part an explication of the text (from philology), in part criticism (as in literary criticism), in part exegesis (originally from theological studies), and in part political criticism, the purpose of a commentary is to offer some treatise on the text: an exposition of principles or a drawing out and summary of themes, commonalities and differences – and, in the context of and reflecting the topic of the relational, perhaps even a relational commentary.

Context

Just as we cannot not be relational, so we cannot not be contextual: we are, after all, political/social animals. One aspect of the context of this chapter and Part II of the book is the first special issue of the *EJPC* on 'Relational psychology in Europe', edited by Helena Hargaden and Joseph Schwartz (2007b), in the editorial of which the editors identified five key elements of relational psychotherapy:

- The centrality of relationship
- Therapy as a two-way street involving a bi-directional process
- The vulnerability of both therapist and client are involved
- Countertransference is used not merely as information but in thoughtful disclosure and collaborative dialogue
- The co-construction and multiplicity of meaning (Hargaden & Schwartz, 2007a, p. 4).

Perhaps unsurprisingly, these elements not only appeared in the articles in that issue but also in the articles in another second special issue, 'The relational turn in psychotherapy and counselling: Cutting edge or cliché?' edited by Del Loewenthal (2010). Moreover, and also unsurprising given the theme of the second special issue, the chapters in this part of the book have a (more) questioning and critical tone.

Another context is that the relational turn or, perhaps more accurately, plural relational turns are being discussed in a number of disciplines: in theology (Jansen, 1995); economic geography (Boggs & Rantisi, 2003); sociology (Donati, 2010); and professional and vocational education (Edwards, 2010).

A third context is my own journey with 'the relational' which, with regard to counselling and psychotherapy, has been influenced, first, by my own experience of life, 'the great co-therapist' as Karen Horney is attributed to have said; second, by personal therapy over a span of nearly 30 years, experience which has encompassed gestalt therapy, transactional analysis, Jungian analysis, psychoanalytic psychotherapy, and a humanistic psychotherapy informed by Hakomi, and in various forms: predominantly individual, but also group, couples, and family; third, by my own experience as a practitioner over nearly 30 years; and fourth, by my own training in different approaches to therapy: gestalt therapy and contribution training, transactional analysis, and the person-centred approach, as well as a number of short courses in other approaches.

These experiences have also been informed by my own research and writing both before and since the original commentary. My conceptual research and writing before 2010 on the relational includes work on co-creative transactional analysis (Summers & Tudor, 2000), which, together with other subsequent publications on this approach, have recently been collected into one volume (Tudor & Summers, in press); on the ethics of relational transactional analysis (Cornell et al., 2006); on person-centred therapy as relationship therapy (Tudor & Worrall, 2006); and on therapeutic relating (Tudor & Widdowson, 2009). Since the original commentary, published in 2010, I have written, perhaps more specifically, about the relational, in terms of: person-centred relational therapy (Tudor, 2010b), including a relational conceptualistion of Rogers' therapeutic conditions (Tudor, 2011a); extending Stark's (1999) taxonomy, a 'two-person-plus therapy' (Tudor, 2011d); and, most recently, our relationship with the earth (Tudor, 2013).

This context – and much more, known and unknown – has informed my vertical reading of all seven chapters in Part II of this volume and, like Ullman (Chapter 9), my 'horizontal' commentary, which I have organised into four themes: history, territory, and ancestors; language, meanings, and the symbolic; social, political and ethical relations; and dialogue.

History, territory, and ancestors

One of the aspects of current debates about the relational which particularly interests me is the authors and theorists that people cite and reference. The 'current' 'relational turn' is often dated back to 1983 and ascribed to the work of Greenberg and Mitchell who first used or coined the term 'relational psychoanalysis'. However, therein lies another turn or twist – or two. First, I and others who inhabit and draw more on the humanistic than the psychoanalytic tradition would argue that 'the relational' dates back to the work of Jessie Taft (1882–1960) who coined the term 'relationship therapy' (Taft, 1933) and whose work influenced Carl Rogers. As Samuels (Chapter 16) acknowledges:

> If I were a humanistic therapist still, I'd be feeling aggrieved. For the relational turn in psychotherapy stems from the work of Carl Rogers and the person-centred approach . . . What has been 'invented' in the United States could be termed 'humanistic psychoanalysis'.
> (p. 184)

To some extent this is simply a matter of who you read and where you train; problems arise, however, when people claim primacy and territory.

The second problem or twist is that, when colleagues refer to 'relational . . .' (as an adjective describing a noun) and especially to '*the* relational', they often make an elision from these as generic terms of reference to the more specific 'relational *psychoanalysis*'. For example, the theme of the first special issue of the *EJPC* on 'Relational psychotherapy in Europe' (Hargaden & Schwartz, 2007b) becomes, in Ullman's commentary, 'relational psychoanalysis'. This is not only inaccurate, it is partial, and, at worst, privileges one theoretical approach or tradition over others and, in doing so, perpetuates a turf war mentality between different theoretical orientations of psychotherapy and counselling and 'forces' of psychology which ignore our common heritage and present interconnectedness. Moreover, and perhaps most ironically, it is neither mutual nor symmetrical – or relational! In his introduction to the first special issue of the *EJPC* on the relational, Loewenthal commented that: 'For some, the relational is most apparent in the psychoanalytic traditions of Freud, Klein and object relations theories as well as Jung' (2007, p. 1) which, as it stands, is accurate; however, he followed this by stating that: 'the increased interest in relational psychotherapy *now* includes a whole range of humanistic, existential, integrative and other approaches' (ibid., my emphasis) which implies that these approaches are only 'now' turning to the relational, which patently is not the case. In his original article (commentary) in the first special issue, Aron wrote about this: 'There was never any question, within the circles in which I was associating, that this burgeoning of interest in relational theory and practice was a development within psychoanalysis rather than outside it' (2007, p. 91). Reading this again, I am not sure whether Aron was extolling this non questioning or making a comment about the insularity of psychoanalysis.

Orbach (Chapter 2), like Aron, focuses on psychoanalysis, but represents the history somewhat differently; she names a number of different tendencies which focus

> on the actual experience of patients, their history and the ways in which intrapsychic development was a development of the internalizations of relationships they had experienced from the earliest moments of their entry into the world ... [and] was always the basis, in the United States, of the work of the interpersonalists, the intersubjectivists *and of latterly* what has become known as the relational school.
>
> (p. 12, my emphasis)

Hargaden and Schwartz (2007a) have acknowledged the humanistic roots of relational psychoanalysis and specifically Rogers' contribution and work. As they put it: 'This type of listening is very skilled, deeply empathic, yet retaining the therapist's subjective sense of self. It is the very essence of a relational approach to working with clients.' (2007a, pp. 3–4). Similarly, in his foreword to a recently published book celebrating 50 years of humanistic psychology in the UK, Samuels (2013) has commented:

> Taking the field as a whole, I think it is reasonable to say that humanistic psychotherapists are *the* experts in the therapy relationship – and maybe in the therapeutic/working alliance as well. I must add that to achieve this they have had to learn from relational psychoanalysis with regard to therapist self-disclosure, acknowledgement (of therapist mistakes) and enactments. It's a good example of cross-fertilization.
>
> (p. xi)

Whilst I agree with Samuels' overall assessment and sentiment, and despite having experienced the therapeutic eras of eclecticism, integration, and now pluralism, we have some way to go before we have wide-scale cross-fertilisation with much informed hybridity.

I have always been interested in ancestry (and not simply because of my family name!), in the history of ideas and the lineage of influence on clinicians through therapists, trainers, and supervisors. In the spirit of an historical review and, specifically, to trace our theoretical and intellectual ancestry and to ascertain what we have or claim in common by means of an analysis of citations and references, for the original commentary, I read both special issues of the *EJPC* (Hargaden & Schwartz, 2007b; Loewenthal, 2010). For the textual analysis of citations and references, I included those original articles which made specific reference to relational influences and sources and, therefore, excluded Anderson (2007) (Chapter 6 in the present volume), and noted the relational theorists and authors that each contributor cited or specifically acknowledged as an influence on their understanding of the relational. I also excluded the commentaries, as to include them would have unduly weighted the data. Having identified 74 citations or references to authors or key figures, I then excluded those who had been cited or referenced by only one contributor. The results of this analysis are noted in Table 17.1.

Three points of interest strike me about this citation/reference analysis:

1   That Fairbairn and Winnicott are the most cited (each by five contributors), followed by Rogers, Mitchell, Stern, Aron, Hoffman, and Benjamin (each cited by four contributors).
2   That, given that there were a further 55 single references to other authors, nearly three quarters (74%) of citations and references to relational 'ancestors' were to those unique to that/those particular author/s, a finding which suggests that there is less cross-fertilisation with regard to those by whom we are influenced than Samuels was ascribing to that potential between psychoanalytic and humanistic psychotherapies.
3   That the analysis reveals a predominance of psychoanalytic/psychodynamic influences.

In terms of history, there is in Part II of this volume a distinct 'back to the future' flavour, especially in Blass and Carmeli's contribution (Chapter 10) in which they question the newness of the relational. In his then 'newer psychotherapy', Rogers (1942) used the term 'relationship therapy' to distinguish it from other viewpoints which included advice, suggestion, reassurance and encouragement, catharsis, and intellectual interpretation. In using this term, Rogers acknowledged its source in the work of Jessie Taft (1933), a pioneering social worker and therapist, and the influence of others in the 'Philadelphia School' (including Frederick Allen and Virginia Robinson), who had studied with Rank – which puts Rogers, who himself attended a workshop with Rank, only two handshakes away from Freud. Rogers' (1942) relationship therapy was characterised by: a focus on the independence and integration of the individual; a greater stress (than previously) on the emotional elements or feeling aspects of a situation, and on the immediate situation; and 'upon the therapeutic relationship itself as a growth experience' (ibid., p. 30). He continued: 'this type of therapy is not a preparation for change, it *is* change' (ibid.). With regard to the development of Rogers' work, as readers may be more

Table 17.1 Analysis of authors cited and referenced by contributors

Authors (in chronological order) cited or referenced by more than one contributor	Hargaden & Schwartz (2007)	Orbach	Haberlin	Nodelman	Cornell	Cowan-Jenssen	Carmeli & Blass	Parker	Sanders	Strong	Samuels	Loewenthal	Hargaden
	Chapters in Part I						*Chapters in Part II*						
Freud	x						x						
Ferenczi					x		x	x					
Buber									x			x	
Fairbairn	x	x			x	x	x						
Sullivan					x			x					
Winnicott	x			x	x	x	x						
Rogers	x								x		x		x
Bowlby	x					x		x					
Balint			x				x						
Orbach			x					x					
Greenberg & Mitchell	x				x		x						
Mitchell	x	x					x	x					
Stern		x	x				x						x
Aron		x			x		x						x
Hoffman						x	x			x			x
Fonagy (including Fonagy et al.)	x								x				
Benjamin		x	x	x			x						
Gerson				x	x								x
Tudor & Worrall									x	x			
	Articles in *EJPC* Issue on Relational Psychotherapy in Europe (Hargaden & Schwartz, 2007b)						Articles in *EJPC* Issue on The Relational in Psychotherapy and Counselling: Cutting Edge or Cliché? (Loewenthal, 2010)						

familiar with the terms 'non directive' (1939), 'client-centred' (1951), and 'person-centred' (1961), it is worth remembering that in the beginning was 'relationship'.

Some of the territorial claims to 'the relational' derive from certain allegiances, for example, to self psychologists to Kohut rather than to Kohut *and* Rogers; a certain ignorance and misunderstanding of the literature outside a particular approach, for instance, of Rogers' *six* therapeutic conditions, or of the complexity of countertransference; and certain commercial – and colonising – interests, such as the establishment of a relational 'school'. In their preface to *Relational psychoanalysis*, Mitchell and Aron stated that: 'Over the past two decades, a distinctly new tradition, generally associated with the term relational psychoanalysis has emerged within American psychoanalysis' (1999, p. x). They write about this 'tradition'; 'institutions' (the Washington School of Psychiatry, and the William Alanson White Institute); a 'Division' (39 – Psychoanalysis) of the American Psychological Association); a 'relational track' (in the Postdoctoral Programme in Psychotherapy and Psychoanalysis at New York University); and others refer more generally to a relational 'school': all of which in some way institutionalise what many may understand as relational (see Chapter 10). Such claims for the relational are all too reminiscent of colonisers who, in claiming territory for their particular colonial power, defined the existing land as '*terra nullius*', a perspective which, in Australia, was only overturned as recently as 1992 (in the Mabo judgement; *Mabo v Queensland*, 1992). Clearly, the 'relational' existed before 1979; the naming of it as a tradition, institute, track or school, however, may not have been formalised by some until more recently.

Language, meanings and the symbolic

This history, or histories, and such territorial claims are manifested and mediated through language and it is clear that the 'relational', let alone '*the* relational', has many meanings. Sanders (Chapter 13) makes the point, from a person-centred perspective, that psychotherapy is rooted in and inseparable from relationship; and, this being so, he – and others – can wonder what all the fuss is about. Furthermore, to claim that a particular therapy is relational is to imply that other therapies are not. Elsewhere (Tudor, 2008), I have critiqued cognitive behavioural therapy (CBT) for its claim on – or its attempt to claim – the territory of the cognitive and the behavioural, as if other therapeutic approaches do not address cognition or behaviour, a point Strong (Chapter 14) also implies. (I should say that I am equally critical of the person-centred approach [PCA] for its implied claim to exclusivity in centring on the person.)

However, as with cognition and behaviour within CBT and 'person-centred' within the PCA, the 'relational' has a particular meaning, especially from a psychoanalytic perspective. Greenberg and Mitchell's (1983) relational model in psychoanalysis offered a fundamental alternative to classical drive theory. Others, such as Blass and Carmeli, take issue with this, viewing the relational 'turn' in psychoanalysis simply as an extension of Freud's conceptual methodology; and yet others view the relational as offering new and alternative theories that sit alongside drive/defence theory. However, it is clear that many relational psychoanalysts view the relational as a different paradigm – and the relational turn as a paradigm shift (see Mitchell, 1988). Mitchell and Aron put it clearly: 'relational concepts do not provide understandings of different phenomena from those explored by the drive/defence model; relational concepts provide *alternative* understandings of the *same* phenomena' (1999, p. xiv), a point with which Blass and Carmeli take issue, arguing that Freud took a dialectical position.

Herein lie some of the differences about the relational: its definition, its position, and its significance, and, again, it is not surprising that different contributors to this volume view the relational differently. Here, on the basis of my horizontal reading of the chapters in Part II, I outline a number of different ways in which I consider that the term 'relational' is used.

1. The relational refers to relationship which is the therapy itself

This is represented by the work of Taft (1933) and Rogers (1942) amongst others. For Blass and Carmeli, and for Sanders, psychoanalysis or psychotherapy, respectively, *is* relational and cannot not be relational; both use 'relational' as a synonymous adjective to describe therapy, albeit different forms of therapy, and Hargaden (Chapter 15) refers to the relational as 'a symbol of the type of sensibility associated with the therapeutic task' (p. 176).

2. The relational describes human nature and systems of human relations

Sanders puts this bluntly in a passage that bears repetition:

> Relationality is a human capability so fundamental and essential, I do not wish to waste time debating whether it is innate. It is not difficult to achieve. It happens. All human beings recognise that there is a serious breach of functioning when relationality is absent or fails.
>
> (p. 153)

Many wisdom traditions, thinkers and writers describe our human need and urge for relationship. In the West it is a specific consequence of Cartesian dualism that we have to emphasise holism and relationship in order to make it clear that we are inherently relational. For most people who draw on indigenous wisdom traditions, the view that human beings are relational is simply a tautology.

This meaning of the term relational catches something of the organismic and holistic view of the person as an inherently social – and political – animal that cannot be understood outside of her/his environment (see Tudor & Worrall, 2006). Whilst Blass and Carmeli are somewhat dismissive of this aspect of the relational, this view of the person is explicit in the contributions of Sanders (Chapter 13), who refers to the significance for primates of attachment, and of Parker (Chapter 11), who refers to the Marxist concept of man as 'an ensemble of social relations'.

3. The relational refers to a particular form of psychoanalysis

This more specific definition of the relational describes a convergence of interpersonal psychoanalysis (from Sullivan, Fromm, and Thompson), object relations (from Klein, Fairbairn, Guntrip, Winnicott, and Bowlby), self psychology (Kohut), and psychoanalytic feminism (Dinnerstein, Chodorow, Gilligan, and Benjamin), and is particularly associated with the work of Greenberg, Mitchell, and Aron. In this context the term relational is used specifically to bridge the traditions of interpersonal psychoanalysis and object relations (see Mitchell & Aron, 1999).

4. The relational encompasses the symbolic 'non relational'

This is another specific and technical use of the term 'relational' within psychoanalysis. Language is a significant aspect of Lacanian psychoanalysis and, therefore, of Parker's contribution to this issue. Lacan incorporated into psychoanalysis linguistics (from Saussure) and anthropology (from Lévi-Strauss), and emphasised the symbolic as he viewed psychoanalysts as 'practitioners of the symbolic function' (Lacan, 1977, p. 72). For Lacan and Lacanians, the symbolic is one of three orders that structure human existence (the others being the imaginary, and the real). In addition to attachment and the intersubjective, Parker identifies language as a third tradition of work on transference in psychoanalysis, and that it is the symbolic (order) that touches the real. Using the example of sex, Parker argues that a sexual encounter is conceptualised as impossible and, in this sense, a *'non-relation'*. He describes four conceptual elements – the human being as 'an ensemble of social relations', negativity, power, and prefigurative aspects of analysis – by which what Lacanians refer to as 'non relation' is nevertheless embedded in a kind of relational model of human subjectivity. (In her contribution [Chapter 15], Hargaden also uses the symbolic with reference to the relational but does so to refer to the sensibility associated with the therapeutic task and the way of engaging with this work.)

5. The relational refers to traditions or lenses in other therapeutic approaches

In developments which overlap with this convergence in psychoanalytic thinking and which also draw explicitly on other, humanistic sources, there has been a resurgence of interest in the relational in other approaches to psychotherapy and counselling: in dialogical psychotherapy (Friedman, 1985; Hycner, 1991); gestalt therapy (Hycner & Jacobs, 1995); transactional analysis (Hargaden & Sills, 2002; see also www.relationalta.com); and interpersonal psychotherapy (Stuart & Robertson, 2003), with the result that 'the relational' is used to describe both specific developments (the 'turn' of 'relational turn') as well as a broad approach which is more relational than instrumental, mechanistic, directive, or manualised. Strong (Chapter 14) picks up on this when he refers to certain forms of CBT, and the way in which certain people translated principles of practice into technical, skills-based approaches.

6. The relational refers to ways of conceptualising the therapeutic relationship or relationships, of working through, in, and with relationship

There are a number of conceptualisations of this aspect of the relational. Gelso and Carter's (1985) seminal work offered a tripartite analysis of the therapeutic relationship comprising: the 'working alliance', the 'real relationship' and, interestingly, what they referred to as the 'unreal' relationship i.e. the transferential/countertransferential relationship. To Gelso and Carter's (1985) three therapeutic relationships and Barr's (1987) concept of the developmentally needed relationship, Clarkson (1990) added a fifth, the transpersonal relationship, and developed this as an integrative model of understanding different therapeutic relationships. DeYoung (2003, p. viii) argued that a relational approach 'provides a strong foundation for responsible, coherent eclecticism.' Stark's (1999) work, in which she identified one-person, one-and-a-half-person, and two-person psychologies – to which I have added a two-person-plus psychology (Tudor, 2011d) – is a useful framework which informs different modes of therapeutic action. In his contribution, Samuels (Chapter 16) takes issue with the notion of '*the* therapeutic relationship' (see also Summers & Tudor, 2000), arguing for 'the many-ness of the therapy relationship', and offering a model which catches several dimensions of one therapy relationship.

7. The relational describes an integrating principle

This is most explicit in Hargaden's contribution (Chapter 15) in which she suggests that the most important influence of the relational approach is that it has provided 'a principle of integration between the different schools and modalities of psychological work . . . enabling us to have a dialogue between modalities in a way that had previously not seemed possible' (p. 177). She draws specifically on the work of Daniel Stern (1985, 1998) as having facilitated this and traces the significance of his work 'as one of the main reasons that relational psychotherapy [has become] more explicit about the turn it has taken' (p. 177). This represents the view that integration is – and relational theory could be viewed and developed as – meta-theory.

8. The relational describes a particular ethics

Relational ethics are concerned with an ethics of care, in this case the therapeutic relationship between client and therapist, and, as such, are useful in qualitative research and research in any area of intimacy e.g. in palliative care, as well as close professional and/or personal relationships. Drawing on the work of Emmanuel Lévinas, Jacques Derrida, and Paul Ricœur, Orange (2012) has discussed the implications of their work for what she referred to as 'the discourse of hospitality' (p. 165) and for understanding what some people are referring to as an 'ethical turn' in contemporary psychoanalysis, a turn or development which both echoes and extends the relational turn. In his contribution, Loewenthal (Chapter 12) also draws on Lévinas, and raises some important questions for therapeutic practice when we put the other, i.e. the client, first. I would extend this point, and wonder also about the practice and implications of putting 'the Other' first. Schmid (2002) made this point well when he suggested that Buber's (1923/1937) 'I–Thou' should perhaps be expressed as 'Thou–I'.

Social, political and ethical relations

In her contribution, 'Democratizing psychoanalysis', Orbach (Chapter 2) argues that 'Relational psychoanalysis has a democratic, co-created view of the therapeutic relationship' (p. 13). Three other contributions in Part II (Parker's, Sanders', and Samuels') also pick up the politics of the relational and focus explicitly on the personal and social/political nature of the relational in psychotherapy; and, in his contribution, Loewenthal (Chapter 12) does this with a focus on ethics.

Parker (Chapter 11) discusses three examples of ensembles of power. In his second example he critiques the model or metaphor in psychoanalysis – and, I think, more generally in psychotherapy and counselling – of the therapeutic relationship between therapist and client as that of or as analogous to the relationship between a caregiver and child. This parental metaphor is a ubiquitous one (for critiques of which see Lomas, 2001; Tudor, 2009a), and one which, according to Parker, brings with it a particular conception of power and, therefore, of power relations. This analysis adds a useful dimension to concerns about the infantilisation of clients, trainees, and supervisees.

In much of his writing, Sanders is overt about his political concerns about and stance towards therapy, and activism. In his contribution to this volume (Chapter 13) his political perspective appears more subdued; however, he picks up his early reference to 'medicalised, reductionistic, dose-oriented, mechanistic, psychotechnologies' towards the end of the chapter when he comments briefly about the politics of such 'technologies'. In his contribution, Strong (Chapter 14) refers to what has become known as 'the Layard agenda' (Layard, 2005, 2006), by which the exclusive use of CBT has become the therapy of choice, at least as far as some governments are concerned. The Layard agenda is based on an economic analysis, although it has been presented as based on 'evidence-based' research; Sanders reflects – and invites us to reflect – on the politics and political psychology of this agenda.

In his more polemical piece, Samuels (Chapter 16) argues that the relational has a Shadow side which has led to a certain conformism and moralism, and that, at worst, the relational 'can constitute a flight from the inner world and the relation to the self' (p. 185). He proposes that we pay more attention to solitude. Samuels' argument echoes Mitchell and Aron's (1999) concern with interpersonal theorists and 'their dialectical swing away from classical intrapsychic theory [which] tended to deemphasize the internal world and internal psychic structures' (p. x).

Of course, when we emphasise something or one thing, such as interpersonal, social or political relations, there is always a danger of polarisation: politics *or* the couch, and so Samuels' question – 'What does a one-person psychology look like in an era of relational therapy?' (p. 188) – is an important one. The answer to this particular question or, at least, the task is to find ways of bringing together internal, object relations and interpersonal, social or political relations into the therapy, thus, politics *and* the couch (see Tudor & Hargaden, 2002).

In her contribution Hargaden (Chapter 15) suggests that the relational approach or, perhaps in this sense, the relational project, which demonstrates more mutuality, reciprocity and even respect between practitioners, has broadened our collective understanding and loosened bonds of loyalty to a particularly modality, founding fathers and mothers, and dogmatic 'party line' approach to theory and succession – a point which has strong political undertones and implications for a more genuinely relational and integrative future for theory, dialogue and organisation. However, lest we get too excited and/or complacent about a bright, united 'one nation' integrative relational future, Hargaden warns of the hegemony and ubiquity of the relational and of '*the* relational', as well as some of the misunderstandings of both the term and the theory. This is one of the great strengths of Hargaden's work, both here and elsewhere, in which she invites and challenges us to reflect consistently and to invite and challenge others to do so, and, thereby, to turn over a particular 'turn' or trend and, thus, to stay reflexive, that is, critically reflective. Loewenthal, too, promotes reflection, arguing that, thinking relationally, psychoanalysis has had to reconsider its theory – and its status as theory. Hargaden and Loewenthal also share a philosophical and methodological stance of giving primacy to practice and theory derived from and very much informed by practice. As Rogers and Wood (1974) put it: 'First there is experiencing, then there is a theory' (p. 216).

In his chapter Loewenthal (Chapter 12) discusses ethical relations, considering that ethics is not separate from practice and not extraneous to transformative practice. He bases this on post-existential human relations and post-existentialism (see Loewenthal, 2011) which itself represents a relational turn from the somewhat individualistic and inherently narcissistic concerns of (a modernist) existentialism. He raises significant questions for ethical practice – or a practice of ethics – in psychoanalysis, if not psychotherapy, for example, what it would mean for the client to put the therapist first. Orange (2012) has discussed the concept of clinical hospitality. Loewenthal's question challenges us to think about the clinical guest. Significantly, in many Romance languages, the words for host and guest are the same, for example, *ospite* in Italian, the understanding of which is determined by the context. Loewenthal also usefully extends the application of such relational ethics to other relationships in education, management, and research.

With regard to politics and the state of the *polis*, given the current climate in parts of Europe and elsewhere I would have expected in these contributions more than a brief reference to the politics of professional regulation and registration, and some discussion of this from a relational perspective. Samuels mentions this in a note about state conformism, and warns us about how this can invade the clinical space; and Loewenthal does question whether theories and disciplines are being policed by economic licensing arrangements 'which, in turn, attempt to control language and thought' (p. 140) as well as organisation. In Aotearoa New Zealand, in response to lobbying from the profession, the state has regulated psychotherapy in the form of the registration of the title 'psychotherapist'. Now the consequences are being felt and analysed (see Tudor, 2011c, 2012), consequences which include a regulatory board which is largely out of relationship with the profession that it governs, and which has consistently sought to extend its spheres and scopes of influence. What appears to have upset most psychotherapists (or at least those who are upset) is that the board is 'out of relationship' with them, which is of interest for our present concern as, I think, this confuses personal relations/hips with social, political and ethical relations/hips. In this analysis, moves towards statutory regulation and state registration may be understood – and experienced – as attempts to regulate from an external and parental position, as distinct from an encouragement for practitioners to organise around self- and co-regulation. As such, it is indicative of a profession out of relationship with itself in a society which is regressive rather than progressive (see Tudor, 2011b). The statutory regulation of psychotherapy and the state registration of psychotherapists thus represents a modernist rather than post-modernist response to the regulation of professional relationships and of those between psychotherapists and the public.

Dialogue

The fourth theme apparent in Part II of this volume is that of dialogue. This is especially apparent in Strong's contribution (Chapter 14) which is less about the relational (he uses the word only three times), and more about the dialogic, and specifically a dialogue with CBT, inspired by the publication of a particular book: *Against and for CBT* (House & Loewenthal, 2008). Interestingly, the subtitle of the book is '*Towards a constructive dialogue?*' and Strong certainly offers this in his contribution. Drawing on the writings of Mikhail Bakhtin, the Russian philosopher, literary critic and semiotician, Strong considers CBT as, at best, dialogic practice. However, given Strong's analysis, and his identification of diverging traditions in CBT, I would suggest that his argument is that CBT needs to be practised dialogically. Strong's emphasis is on the conversational and dialogic nature of therapy (he refers to 'relational encounters'). He writes about immediacy, responsiveness, and 'relational coordination' – which sounds or reads like empathic attunement – and presents a social constructionist perspective in which differences between therapist and client are part of the conversational work and, therefore, the co-constructed dialogue and meaning (see Summers & Tudor, 2000). Strong's use of language is significant in shifting views of CBT. In Table 17.2 I have summarised what I understand as Strong's dialogues with and within CBT.

Table 17.2 Summary of dialogues in Strong's chapter 'Staying in dialogue with CBT'

From a CBT based on . . .	. . . to a CBT based on
A biomedical discourse	Conversational challenge
A therapy using medical metaphors	Therapy as conversational practice
Diagnosis and intervention	Therapy with no predetermined structure
Centripetal ('scientifically-defined' CBT)	Centrifugal (new hybrids of practice)
Conversational management	Therapeutic dialogue
A conversation based on a manual and protocol	A negotiation of words and ways of talking
A conversational script	A delicate conversation
Prescribed monologue (led by the therapist)	A dialogic approach
A 'presumed grammar' (Wittgenstein)	A conversation heuristic (Anderson)
Conflicting and uncoordinated speech genres	Talking – and listening – which is generative and collaborative
Client's 'ineffective meanings'	Collaborative efforts to overcome the 'linguistic poverty' of those meanings

Of course, this 'from . . . to' analysis is an 'either . . . or' construction, and the challenge of dialogue is to stay dialogic, when within or with CBT or any other modality, especially when confronted with the non-relational and the lack of the dialogic: in other words, to adopt a 'both . . . and' perspective which is reflected in viewing therapy, as Strong does, as both a science and an art.

In its emphasis on mutuality and reciprocity between practitioners of different theoretical orientations or modalities, Hargaden's contribution (Chapter 15) is also about dialogue, specifically about empathy and the contribution that different traditions bring to understandings of empathy (see also Tudor, 2011d). I particularly appreciate her distinctions about relational not simply being interpersonal and certainly not meaning non conflictual.

Drawing on Orange's work (in Frie & Orange, 2009; see also Orange, 2011), which views relatedness as our primary human condition and ethics as a way of understanding and mediating this condition, Loewenthal (Chapter 12) also extols the place of and space for dialogue and what emerges in the between. Drawing also on ideas which he and others refer to as 'post-modernist' and which he has referred to as 'post-existential' (see Loewenthal, 2011), he discusses such space as a place to think about ways in which we are alienated. In a passage about postmodern ideas about being 'subject *to*' as distinct from being subject/s, he implies that therapy is a place of dialogue about this. He also discusses Martin Buber (1878–1965), the philosopher of dialogue, contrasts Buber's conceptualisation of the 'I–It', and 'I–Thou' relationships (originally with the divine), and applies them to the therapist's relationship with the client. However, whilst Loewenthal attributes a 'continuous dialectics' to the 'I–Thou' relationship, I would argue that the 'I' of the 'I–Thou' still represents a one-and-a-half person psychology, whereas the additional conceptualisation of a 'Thou–I' relationship (after Schmid, 2002) speaks to two-person relational dialogue in which the therapist may put the client first and, as Loewenthal acknowledges, the client may, appropriately, put the therapist first.

The relational turn: Cutting edge or cliché?

When I first came across the phrase 'the relational *turn*' I must admit to having somewhat grumpy/cynical and sectarian reactions: 'So, what's new?', 'Aren't we all "relational"?', 'So "relational" is the new "integrative"', 'It's the new brand', etc., and, when I heard that psychoanalysts were 'claiming' to be the instigators and authors of 'the relational turn': 'Oh, yeah. Haven't they read Rogers, Taft, or a whole heap of practitioners and theorists outside their immediate circles?', etc., etc. I'm not particularly proud of these reactions, but I do think they reflect some truths and tensions in the field, as reflected not least in the pages of this current volume.

As I read more I became more concerned about the lack of relationship and dialogue between approaches, schools and forces of psychology and therapy, and between counselling, psychotherapy, and psychoanalysis. Winston Churchill (1874–1965) wrote that 'history is written by the victors' and it seems to me that unless we want to perpetuate a dynamic of winners and losers, of privileged and underprivileged therapies, and of exclusive and excluded therapies (along the lines recommended by the UK's National Institute of Health and Clinical Excellence), it is important to reflect on, meet, and dialogue about our history, common ancestors and roots, and the cross-fertilisation and interrelationship of ideas, language, and politics – on common ground as well as disputed territory.

As I read more I also became somewhat concerned about which way the relational was turning: inwards to a more theorised one-person psychology or outwards to a genuinely two-person or even two-person-plus psychology, one which could include a 'social turn' (Tudor, 2009b) and/or 'intermateriality' (see Loewenthal, 2010)? In undertaking the background research for this chapter, I came across a conference on 'The Relational Turn' held (in June 2013) at Esalen, California under the heading 'The Practice of Sustainability' the intent of which was 'to provide opportunities for dialogue and sharing best practices toward building empathic communities' (Esalen Institute, 2013). If 'the relational' was or is 'turning', is it turning to the Right, to the Left, or to the Green – or, perhaps, the relational's not for turning!

Is the relational cutting edge? Insofar as the cutting edge refers to something that is state of the art, then clearly it should be, though I'm less sure that it is. Insofar as something which aspires to be cutting edge keeps therapists alert to and mindful of how we relate to and with clients and with each other and is 'a type of sensibility', as Hargaden puts it, then it is a good thing. Is the relational a cliché? Insofar as '*the* relational' has become reified (as Blass & Carmeli, and Samuels suggest), and 'the therapeutic relationship' is often cited as *the* most important factor in therapeutic outcome (when, in fact, according to Asay & Lambert, 1999, it is 'extra therapeutic factors'), then, yes, the relational has become overused and unoriginal. Insofar as something which has become a cliché had an original meaning and effect, then perhaps we should remind ourselves of that original meaning. Interestingly, when I first wrote the heading of this part of the chapter I wrote 'The relational turn: Cutting edge *and* cliché?' Perhaps my unconscious got the better of me and it is both.

References

Anderson, J. (2007). Forgiveness – A relational process: Research and reflections. *European Journal of Psychotherapy and Counselling, 9*(1), 63–76.

Aron, L. (2007). Relational psychotherapy in Europe: A view from across the Atlantic. *European Journal of Psychotherapy and Counselling, 9*(1), 91–103.

Asay, T. P. and Lambert, M. J. (1999). The empirical case for the common factors in therapy: Quantitative findings. In *The heart and soul of change: What works in therapy* (M. A. Hubble, B. L. Duncan and S. D. Miller, Eds.). Washington, DC: American Psychological Association (pp. 33–56).

Barr, J. (1987). The therapeutic relationship model: Perspectives on the core of the healing process. *Transactional Analysis Journal, 17*(4), 134–140.

Boggs, J. S. and Rantisi, N. M. (2003). The 'relational turn' in economic geography. *Journal of Economic Geography, 3*, 109–116.

Buber, M. (1923/1937). *I and thou* (R. G. Smith, Trans.). Edinburgh, UK: T. & T. Smith.

Clarkson, P. (1990). A multiplicity of psychotherapeutic relationships. *British Journal of Psychotherapy, 7*(2), 148–163.

Cornell, W. F., Hargaden, H., Allen, J. R., Erskine, R., Moiso, C., Sills, C., Summers, G. and Tudor, K. (2006). Roundtable on the ethics of relational transactional analysis. *Transactional Analysis Journal, 36*(2), 105–119.

DeYoung, P. A. (2003). *Relational psychotherapy: A primer*. London, UK: Brunner-Routledge.

Donati, P. (2010). *Relational sociology: A new paradigm for the social sciences*. London, UK: Taylor & Francis.

Edwards, A. (2010). *Being an expert professional practitioner: The relational turn in expertise*. New York, NY: Springer

Esalen Institute. (2013). *The relational turn*. Retrieved from www.relationalturn.com/index2.html

Frie, R. and Orange, D. (2009). *Beyond postmodernism: New dimensions in clinical theory and practice*. London, UK: Routledge.

Friedman, M. (1985). *The healing dialogue in psychotherapy*. New York: Jason Aronson.

Gelso, C. J. and Carter, J. A. (1985). The relationship in counselling and psychotherapy: Components, consequences, and theoretical antecedents. *The Counseling Psychologist, 13*(2), 155–243.

Greenberg, J. and Mitchell, S. (1983). *Object relations in psychoanalytic theory*. Cambridge, MA: Harvard University Press.

Hargaden, H. and Schwartz, J. (2007a). Editorial. *European Journal of Psychotherapy and Counselling*, 9(1), 3–5.

Hargaden, H. and Schwartz, J. (Eds.) (2007b). Relational psychotherapy in Europe [Special Issue]. *European Journal of Psychotherapy and Counselling*, 9(1).

Hargaden, H. and Sills, C. (2002). *Transactional analysis: A relational perspective*. London, UK: Routledge.

House, R. and Loewenthal, D. (2008). *Against and for CBT: Towards a constructive dialogue?* Ross-on-Wye, UK: PCCS Books.

Hycner, R. (1991). *Between person and person: Towards a dialogical psychotherapy*. Highland, NY: Gestalt Journal Press.

Hycner, R. and Jacobs, L. (1995). *The healing relationship in gestalt therapy*. Highland, NY: Gestalt Journal Press.

Jansen, H. (1995). *Relationality and the concept of God*. Amsterdam, The Netherlands: Rodopi.

Lacan, J. (1977). *Écrit: A selection* (A. Sheridan, Trans.). London, UK: Tavistock.

Layard, R. (2005). *Happiness: Lessons from a new science*. London, UK: Penguin.

Layard, R. (2006). *The depression report: A new deal for depression and anxiety disorders*. Centre for Economic Performance, London School of Economics, London, UK.

Loewenthal, D. (2007). Introduction to the special issue. *European Journal of Psychotherapy and Counselling*, 9(1), 1.

Loewenthal, D. (Ed.) (2010). The relational in psychotherapy and counselling: Cutting edge or cliché? [Special Issue]. *European Journal of Psychotherapy and Counselling*, 12(3).

Loewenthal, D. (2011). *Post-existentialism and the psychological therapies: Towards a therapy without foundations*. London, UK: Karnac Books.

Lomas, P. (2001). *The limits of interpretation*. Harmondsworth: Penguin (original work published 1987).

Mabo v Queensland (1992). (No 2) [1992] HCA 23; (1992) 175 CLR 1. 3 June.

Mitchell, S. (1988). *Relational concepts in psychoanalysis: An integration*. Cambridge, MA: Harvard University Press.

Mitchell, S. A. and Aron, L. (Eds.) (1999). *Relational psychoanalysis: The emergence of a tradition*. Hillsdale, NJ: The Analytic Press.

Orange, D. (2011). *The suffering stranger: Hermeneutics for everyday clinical practice*. New York: Routledge.

Orange, D. (2012). Clinical hospitality: Welcoming the face of the devastated other. *Ata: Journal of Psychotherapy Aotearoa New Zealand*, 16(2), 165–178. DOI: 10.9791/AJPANZ.2012.17

Rogers, C. R. (1939). *The clinical treatment of the problem child*. Boston, MA: Houghton Mifflin.

Rogers, C. R. (1942). *Counseling and psychotherapy: Newer concepts in practice*. Boston, MA: Houghton Mifflin.

Rogers, C. R. (1951). *Client-centered therapy*. London, UK: Constable.

Rogers, C. R. (1961). *On becoming a person*. London, UK: Constable.

Rogers, C. R. and Wood, J. K. (1974). Client-centered theory: Carl Rogers. In *Operational theories of personality* (A. Burton, Ed.). New York: Brunner/Mazel (pp. 211–258).

Samuels, A. (2013). Foreword. In *The future of humanistic psychology* (R. House, D. Kalisch and J. Maidman, Eds.). Ross-on-Wye, UK: PCCS Books (pp. x–xiv).

Schmid, P. F. (2002). Presence: Im-media-te co-experiencing and co-responding. Phenomenological, dialogical and ethical perspectives on contact and perception in person-centred therapy and beyond. In *Contact and perception* (G. Wyatt and P. Sanders, Eds.). Ross-on-Wye, UK: PCCS Books (pp. 36–51).

Stark, M. (1999). *Modes of therapeutic action: Enhancement of knowledge, provision of experience, and engagement in relationship*. Northvale, NJ: Jason Aronson Inc.

Stern, D. N. (1985). *The interpersonal world of the infant: A view from psychoanalysis and developmental psychology*. New York: Basic Books.

Stern, D. N. (1998). *The interpersonal world of the infant: A view from psychoanalysis and developmental psychology* (Rev. Ed.). New York: Basic Books.

Stuart, S. and Robertson, M. (2003). *Interpersonal psychotherapy: A clinician's guide*. London, UK: Arnold.

Summers, G. and Tudor, K. (2000). Cocreative transactional analysis. *Transactional Analysis Journal*, *30*(1), 23–40.

Taft, J. (1933). *The dynamics of a controlled relationship*. New York: Macmillan.

Traue, J. R. (1990). *Ancestors of the mind: A Pakeha whakapapa*. Wellington, Aotearoa New Zealand: Gondwanaland Press.

Tudor, K. (2008). Person-centred therapy, a cognitive behavioural therapy. In *Against and for CBT: Towards a constructive dialogue?* (R. House and D. Loewenthal, Eds.) Ross-on-Wye, UK: PCCS Books (pp. 118–136).

Tudor, K. (2009a). 'In the manner of': Transactional analysis teaching of transactional analysts. *Transactional Analysis Journal*, *39*(4), 276–292.

Tudor, K. (2009b). Psyche and society: The contribution of psychotherapy to community wellbeing. Keynote speech at International Public Mental Health Symposium: Toward Global Wellbeing, Auckland University of Technology, Auckland, Aotearoa New Zealand, 7 November.

Tudor, K. (2010a). Commentary: Turning over 'the relational'. *European Journal of Psychotherapy and Counselling*, *12*(3), 257–267.

Tudor, K. (2010b). Person-centred relational therapy: An organismic perspective. *Person-Centered and Experiential Psychotherapies*, *9*(1), 52–68.

Tudor, K. (2011a). Rogers' therapeutic conditions: A relational conceptualization. *Person-Centered and Experiential Psychotherapies*, *10*(3), 165–180.

Tudor, K. (2011b). There ain't no license that protects: Bowen theory and the regulation of psychotherapy. *Transactional Analysis Journal*, *41*, 154–161.

Tudor, K. (Ed.) (2011c). *The turning tide: Pluralism and partnership in psychotherapy in Aotearoa New Zealand*. Auckland, Aotearoa New Zealand: LC Publications.

Tudor, K. (2011d). Understanding empathy. *Transactional Analysis Journal*, *41*(1), 39–57.

Tudor, K. (2012). Ebb and flow: One year on from *The Turning Tide: Pluralism and Partnership in Psychotherapy in Aotearoa New Zealand*. *Psychotherapy and Politics International*, *10*(2), 170–177. DOI: 10.1002/ppi.1271

Tudor, K. (2013). Person-centred psychology and therapy, ecopsychology and ecotherapy. *Person-Centred and Experiential Psychotherapies*, *12*(4), 315–329.

Tudor, K. and Hargaden, H. (2002). The couch and the ballot box: The contribution and potential of psychotherapy in enhancing citizenship. In *What's the good of counselling and psychotherapy?: The benefits explained* (C. Feltham, Ed.). London, UK: Sage (pp. 156–178).

Tudor, K. and Summers, G. (in press). *Co-creative transactional analysis: Papers, responses, dialogues, and developments*. London, UK: Karnac Books.

Tudor, K. and Widdowson, M. (2008). From client process to therapeutic relating: A critique of the process model and personality adaptations. *Transactional Analysis Journal, 38*(3), 218–232.

Tudor, K. and Worrall, M. (2006). *Person-centred therapy: A clinical philosophy*. London, UK: Routledge.

18

THE RELATIONAL

A postmodern meta-narrative

Alistair Ross

In this chapter the author identifies common themes that form a relational postmodern meta-narrative emerging from the thinking of eight of the authors who contributed the previous chapters in Part II. While taking different perspectives they agree that the relational is a vital subject and identify the value of the 'other' within social and political contexts. The relational as intellectual discourse has philosophical foundations expressed through overlapping narratives and there is a desire for a distinctive identity for therapeutic modalities, whilst seeing the potential of the relational as an integrative symbol. Yet there are areas where the relational does not sufficiently address issues of power or evil. There are depths in us and our wider narratives that need to be confronted. The author argues that both Levinas and theological discourses on evil have something to offer our understanding of the relational in addressing its symbolic potential and its necessary shadow.

Climbing to the summit of any mountain is exhilarating, especially in the company of friends where there have been shared excitements and dangers on the journey, both up and down. Afterwards, as we sit around a table enjoying a well-deserved meal, we share our recollections, and it is always surprising how different the experiences have been. Given that five people have journeyed on the same granite massif, sharing the same time and space, it is always astonishing that the individual accounts vary so widely. Climbing for me is less about the achievement of reaching a summit, enjoyable as it is, and more about the relationship that goes on between my inner and outer worlds, the embodied relationship I have with the physical demands of the journey, as well as the time and relationship I have with my friends.

My opening metaphor of different journeys, on the same mountain, enhancing relationship in often unexpected ways, summarizes the contributions made by Carmeli and Blass, Parker, Loewenthal, Sanders, Strong, Hargaden, and Samuels. To set their work in context, the last decade has seen counselling and psychotherapy in the UK dominated, for good or ill, by the issue of statutory regulation. Running parallel with this has been the government-funded, evidence-based initiative to increase access to psychological therapies through adopting multiple forms of cognitive behaviour therapy (CBT). By contrast, the USA has seen a spotlight on the 'relational' best illustrated in the work of Stephen Mitchell and other like-minded analysts, who established the International Association for Relational Psychoanalysis and Psychotherapy in 2001. This has focused on developing new initiatives, opening out psychoanalytic and therapeutic understandings on the basis of relational engagement. A key figure, Manny Ghent, believed as early as 2002 that relational psychoanalysis marked a sea change in the analytic and therapeutic worlds. The links of IARPP with such influential British figures as Samuels and Orbach has contributed to a focus on relational psychotherapy. In the opening chapter of this volume, Loewenthal notes the key themes of relational psychoanalysis identified by Hargaden and Schwartz (2007). My reading of Hargaden and Schwartz is broader and I see the relational themes held across different theoretical traditions as:

1   Use of the therapist's own subjectivity
2   The phenomenology of the co-created transference
3   Recognition of a patient's worth
4   Accountability for a therapist's own countertransference
5   The vitality of present-centred relatedness
6   The vulnerability of therapist and client
7   Thoughtful disclosure and collaborative dialogue
8   Co-construction and multiplicity of meaning (ibid., p. 4).

The preceding chapters represent an emerging British engagement with the relational sea-changes that have crossed the Atlantic, whilst also identifying the philosophical foundations to a relational approach already existing in European thought. Each author has a distinctive voice offering fresh insights, thoughtful reflections, clear challenges, and uninhibited critique of the subject, the recent focus on the relational in psychotherapy. These eight nationally and internationally known figures bring with them expertise, standing and authority and offer us the opportunity through creative dialogue to engage further in this exploration of the relational. Samuels is concerned; Carmeli and Blass are critical; Parker is challenged; Sanders is bemused; Hargaden is creative; Loewenthal is philosophical; while Strong addresses the different issues raised by CBT, but is linked by his focus on relational dialogue.

My intention is to give a brief critique of each chapter, to then identify themes that run across their contributions, and to add a concluding reflection.

Zvi Carmeli and Rachel Blass (Chapter 10) offer a very tightly focused chapter on the 'supposedly' relational turn found in psychoanalysis. To set them in context Carmeli is a clinical psychologist and a candidate at the Israeli Institute of Psychoanalysis. He is the Head of the Department of Education at Herzog College and an Adjunct Lecturer at the Hebrew University of Jerusalem. He has researched and written on the underpinnings of the theory of mind of relational psychoanalytic theories and on the negative impact of introducing neuroscientific metaphors into psychoanalytic and psychological discourse. Blass is a psychoanalyst in private practice in London, a professor at Heythrop College, and a visiting professor at University College London, as well as sitting on the Board of the International Journal of Psychoanalysis. Blass has established a substantial publishing record of engaging and critical debate concerning psychoanalysis. Carmeli and Blass challenge the contention that there has been a relational revolution in psychoanalysis. They identify a traditional psychoanalytic understanding of the 'ontological isolation' of each person, apart from relationship but vitally influenced by relationship. Consequently, the 'mind has an objective existence' where there are truths 'to be described, interpreted, discovered, independent of the context (the relationships) in which they are realized and expressed' (p. 123). The therapeutic process is one where the client finds himself, discovers her inner truth and becomes integrated with it through the knowing of the analyst and the client's experience of the analyst transferentially.

This contrasts with the relational psychoanalytic view that each person 'is his or her relationships' and that meaning is derived from the 'cultural-relational system in which he develops' and 'cannot be understood apart from that system' (p. 123). A relational approach sees the mind as 'an interactive phenomenon whose contents are not present within it but are rather created within the interactive context in which it is realized' (p. 124). The therapeutic process becomes one of change brought about by the relationships that are formed between the client and analyst. They become partners to a new transforming relationship where the analyst adopts a non-authoritarian stance of equality, respect, humility and doubt. This relationship repairs or corrects harmful relationships from the past.

Carmeli and Blass, while identifying the polarized stances adopted in the current debates, believe that there is room for consensus and arbitration. They argue the central 'bone of contention' is a view of human nature which is inherently relational, where 'experiences, motivations, and meanings ... are formed anew, time and again, in various relational contexts in which the individual finds himself' (p. 125), including the analytic relationship. Carmeli and Blass counter this view by arguing that the relational approach is less revolutionary because traditional psychoanalysis is more relational than it is made out to be. Drawing on object-relations theories they suggest that relationship has always been central to the psychoanalytic task, where Freud adopted a dialectical view including both drive and relationship. They add that relational psychoanalysis is also more traditional than it is sometimes willing to acknowledge. What relational psychoanalysis contributes is a clearer focus on the 'diverse and complex ways in which interpersonal interaction affects the patient's experiences' (p. 126). What relational psychoanalysis detracts from the analytic encounter is a corrective dimension that Carmeli and Blass view as a regression to pre-Freudian times. In this regard they identify the shadow side of relationality mentioned by Samuels, that of a dominant discourse that knows best, a form of apparently benign paternalistic benevolence offering a corrective relationship, advice, suggestion, guidance, even cure.

By contrast, Ian Parker (Chapter 11) explores psychoanalysis from a Lacanian perspective. Drawing on Ferenczi and Sullivan, he first discerns a 'trajectory from the interpersonal to the intersubjective to the relational' (p. 131) before leading to his own 'bone of contention' – the nature of transference and the actual relations that inform this. Parker identifies two traditions in psychoanalysis related to transference. In attachment-based psychoanalysis, the transference arises out of the mother/infant bond, which influences all later relationships 'as a special kind of glue holding people together' (p. 132). In intersubjective-shaped psychoanalysis, the transference, and by implication the counter-transference, acts as 'conduit for feelings' (p. 132) accessed by both partners in the therapeutic relationship. Parker locates relational psychoanalysis as an oscillating dynamic between these transference polarities. It is this oscillation that Parker examines in further detail using the language of Lacan. He therefore offers a third form of transference related to language. In a Lacanian world, transference is identified by signifiers in the language of the patient that form representations of them. The analyst's role is to understand the conscious and unconscious aspects of such signifiers, which inhibit or entrap the client and their ability to be. The words 'relation' or 'relational' Parker understands to be 'empty signifiers' which offer the potential for 'fullness and universality' as well as 'sites of conflict, division and political struggle' (p. 137). Parker offers the clearest view of the relational which includes a relation between:

1   Analysand and analyst
2   Infant and caregiver
3   Self and other
4   Individual and collective
5   Personal and the political
6   The clinic and the world

Parker disentangles 'the way these six different binary oppositions are woven into each other' (p. 134) through a reflection on power (we shall return to this subject later), the dialectics of authority and the politics of the personal. His ideas go beyond the territorial debates over the origin and use of the relational in psychoanalysis and psychotherapy and offer some ideas that paradoxically are more inclusive and elusive at the same time. Parker's intention is to stimulate more reflection on the language of the relational that encompasses the individual, the other, the community, the social and the political without reducing it to a simple binary equation.

Loewenthal (Chapter 12) offers Levinas as an example of how we can hold together philosophy, ethics, ideas of truth and justice rooted in the relational engagement with an 'other'. Living human engagement therefore impacts both our thinking and our clinical practice. Loewenthal turns to Levinas, rather than Buber, in developing a form of post-existentialism that overcomes the limitations of Buber and existentialism. Hargaden offers a 'subject to' post-existential approach that moves beyond the subject/object divide inherent in many therapeutic modalities. The challenge is to keep ourselves open to the 'other' in an ontological way and to do this Loewenthal drawing on Levinas advocates 'heteronomy' rather than 'autonomy'. The challenge is always to put the other first, recognizing the Otherness of the Other. This brings us into a radical form of relationship that spans justice, truth, ethics, and care that Loewenthal argues should influence not just therapeutic practice but wider organisational, educational, managerial and social structures. The ability to recognize and meet the other avoids the theoretical violence that has been done in the name of defending positions and instead offers well-being by a relational experience of being in the moment with another.

After the vigorous Lacanian and Levinasian gymnastic workout led by Parker and Loewenthal, Sanders (Chapter 13) offers a more relaxed narrative account that utilizes stories to communicate the vitality of the relational. Steeped in a person-centred tradition Sanders states: 'It did not occur to me that psychotherapy could be anything other than an activity rooted in, inseparable from, relationship' (p. 152). Like other contributors Sanders focuses on our primary understanding of what it is to be human. Drawing on attachment theory, the intrinsic desire to communicate through language and symbols, and a recognition of the other for the psyche/mind to function, Sanders states that 'relationality is a human capability so fundamental and essential . . . in the service of flourishing, love and peaceful co-existence' (p. 153). He identifies how difficult it is to function when 'relationality is absent or fails'. Sanders identifies the importance of the relational in the context of other views of being human that are reductionist, medicalized, mechanistic or technocratic. He then re-emphasizes the vital, dynamic core of person-centred therapy that privileges the relational without the pressures to mend, cure, heal or spiritually connect. Relational therapy 'sets the client free to construct experience and understand their process of change in any way they can' (p. 153). Sanders reaffirms the vital place of relationship in current research of psychotherapy, including CBT, in online meeting and in difficult non-verbal and silent encounters with clients. Examining this in more detail Sanders offers that at the heart of relational encounter is a form of connection and knowing that speaks of 'self-with-other encounter' that requires 'involvement, reciprocity and co-creation' (p. 157) in a way that challenges and changes us as therapists. He uses a story of abuse occurring in a religious context to describe how the abused person touched him emotionally as 'something ultimately precious, her very immortal soul, changed me' (p. 158). The point Sanders makes as he moves beyond the individual to the social and political dimensions of psychotherapy is that the reason agencies or governments deny the relational is because they do not wish to be challenged or changed. Sanders concludes that 'relational therapy is not about only doing what works; it is also about doing what is right' (p. 159).

Building on Sanders' critique of CBT research that identifies the place of the relational, Strong (Chapter 14), a Canadian psychologist, academic and CBT therapist, examines it as a dialogic activity. While primarily addressing issues raised in House and Loewenthal's (2008) *Against and for CBT*, Strong has valuable comments to make on the relational. Strong's view of CBT is strikingly different from the way it is presented in many other contexts (Westbrook, Kennerley & Kirk 2011). He begins by describing CBT as 'a fascinating conversational work-in-progress' (p. 161) and it soon becomes clear that Strong offers an alternative vision of CBT: 'good therapy, from a dialogic perspective, is a delicate negotiation with clients, not a well-administered conversational script' (p. 162). Strong draws from the work of Wittgenstein, and more especially the Russian philosopher and cultural theorist Mikhail Bakhtin. Bakhtin's ideas on the dialogical self have more recently been related to psychotherapy, especially object-relations and Lacan (Pollard, 2008). Strong addresses the question of how therapeutic dialogue is 'different from the conversations clients have been having with themselves and others' (p. 165). A dialogic approach requires a responsiveness in the client and the therapist to each other but 'when dialogue wanes or gets ideologized, speakers default to restrictive language games or genres' (p. 163). He adds 'clients and therapists bring different interpretive histories to their dialogues and this extends to how they make meaning in and from their dialogues' (p. 167). The challenge for relational psychotherapy is to avoid being ensnared in the language games of each other and 'to find ways of talking and listening that are generative and collaborative' (p. 168). Strong offers further insightful reflection on the nature of the language and communication that happens in therapeutic settings, and this applies to all psychotherapy not just CBT. For example, 'a spiritual language game of bereavement is clearly different from a biomedical one focused on depression, yet these two dialogues could clearly be about the same phenomenon' (p. 168). He concludes with a comment by Bakhtin, 'there is no final resting place for the word. There are only negotiated responses and where they next take us' (p. 172).

Strong's contribution is important but it reads as a cut-down version of a longer, more complex text. It is however refreshing to hear a view of CBT that is generative and dialogic, one which adds another stream to the river of relational psychoanalysis and psychotherapy.

Helena Hargaden (Chapter 15) is an integrative psychotherapist, transactional analysis psychotherapist, supervisor, trainer and coach, and has written specifically about the relational in terms of transactional analysis. Hargaden roots the relational broadly within the humanistic therapies, particularly transactional analysis, and in the interpersonal research of Stern. As Stern's ideas have arisen from observational research rather than a specific philosophical position (although there are always implicit philosophies at work), this has allowed his work to be used widely by different modalities. Hargaden and Sills (2002) see their work in relation to transactional analysis as part of a wider trend focusing on the relational, which Hargaden argues is a central integrating principle. In true integrative fashion Hargaden finds commonalities and views co-operation rather than completion as healthy for therapy whether as a client or a practitioner. Loewenthal helpfully identifies some of the misconceptions that have arisen around the term relational, including that being relational means being empathic. Clearly being relational involves empathy, as well as attunement, but Hargaden identifies how empathy as a cognitive structure can be a straitjacket inhibiting the work for both client and therapist. Similarly, being relational involves the interpersonal, but Hargaden argues that some people conflate the two leading to the diminishing of both. She sees the problem in an idea being made into a dogma rather that her approach, which is to see the relational as a symbol that cannot be taught, only learnt, through our own life and in the lives of other people, some of whom are our clients.

Andrew Samuels (Chapter 16) does what he does best by offering illumination and irritation in equal measure. His writing is never dull and he brings a spark of creativity to the subject as he examines the shadow side of therapeutic relationships. Samuels adopts a broad-ranging panoramic approach, examining the subject from different vantage points, however, at times his ideas are rather too sweeping. The relational turn, especially as currently understood and summarized in the bullet points above, does not, in my opinion, solely stem from Rogers and the person-centred approach, important as they are. The subject under discussion is complicated enough without Samuels adding 'humanistic psychoanalysis' as another category, although some analysts have adopted a humanistic value base. I disagree that potentially a basic course in person-centred therapy more deeply informs someone in therapeutic relationships than many 'highly educated and over-trained' analysts (p. 185). There is a plethora of counselling courses run primarily in the FE sector in the UK which adopt person-centred principles, but which often fail to deliver the depth required to move beyond a formulaic use of person-centred therapy. Yet, when Samuels's moves into the substance of his chapter he touches on three issues that vitally influence all of us concerned with therapy.

First, Samuels is critical of an implicit relational conformity or forms of standardization that militate against creativity, intimacy, and difference. This conformity fails to equip therapists with the ability to offer resistance in the face of the pressures to adopt a party line, as seen in previous debates in the UK concerning different responses to regulation. Further, a focus on relationality can imply that there is one set of appropriate or ideal relations that are being sought. If these ideals are invested with power and become the 'majority discourse' it always leads to voices being ignored or silenced. Samuels contends that there are many therapy relations all in play at the same time and so to focus on one is to neglect the others.

Second, he is concerned with hypocrisy, 'one of the central evils of our society' (p. 185), which infects the therapeutic world where there is a great deal of talk about relationality, but in a disembodied, split-off way where we do not live this out in practice. At the conference where Samuels first presented his ideas he used an experiential exercise to respond to a visual and musical excerpt, *Duelling Banjos* from the film *Deliverance*. From this Samuels drew out the interrelatedness and the multiple forms of relating that we exist in as therapists. To privilege one kind of relationality above another would be hypocritical. Samuels helpfully warns us that hypocrisy is to be found in our profession and within each of us. Like other forms of evil, it does not announce its existence, but simply is.

Third, Samuels identifies the need for inner depth, often expressed in and through solitude, where the relational can be 'a flight from the inner world' (p. 185). He also explores the isolation found in people and in the wider trends in our society. While isolation is a central concern for many, especially men, it can be a place of creativity. To my mind what makes solitude different from isolation is the degree to which it is a chosen act rather than an outcome of life events, some of which we have no control over. Here Samuels offers a unique insight that requires further reflection and development. He is to be commended for his courage and his ability to shine light into shadow places – in us, our work, our profession and our society – that can too easily hide behind the comforting idea that everything is relational.

In responding to these engaging explorations of the relational, what themes emerge across the various contributions that form a prototype postmodern meta-narrative? These can be identified as:

1   The relational, however defined, is vital
2   The relational is problematic, especially in relation to power
3   The relational has social and political dimensions
4   The importance of narratives that are negotiated
5   The importance of philosophical foundations
6   Confronting depths and touching on evil

First, the relational is perceived to be vital. What becomes immediately apparent is just how elusive the whole notion of the 'relational' is. Something that is so obvious, real and known, Sanders thinks does not need definition. He adds: 'relationality is not difficult to achieve. It happens. In fact you have to actively prevent it from happening by putting things in between the two selves involved' (p. 158). Yet it still becomes difficult to capture the relational within the static limitation of words. It reminds me of the difficulties experienced by BACP, UKCP and other therapeutic organizations in defining what the words 'counselling' and 'psychotherapy' mean in a way that fully captures the nuances understood by a wide range of differing practitioners. It is certainly a factor that has complicated and confused the discussions around statutory regulation, a theme touched on by Samuels. Yet words are all we have and so they must be utilized, imperfect as they are, to capture the sense of the 'relational'. Strong's emphasis on the dialogic and how such conversations are negotiated, if they are to be therapeutic, is vitally important. The relational has acquired a central place in therapeutic thought and practice in such a relativity short time (in the time-scale of ideas) that, as Hargaden suggests, it plays a symbolic role. The relational captures something that had either been lost in a pursuit of dogma or orthodoxy, or is newly emerging as seen in Loewenthal's post-existential approach. Relationality encourages co-operation across modalities that most sees as vital for a healthy profession. It is as if we have seen the emergence of a postmodern meta-narrative, paradoxical as that statement is, with all its attendant issues and complexities.

Second, the relational is problematic, especially in relation to power. Each contributor has emphasized this in different ways. Blass and Carmeli see relational psychoanalysis generating such a focus on the relationship that some forms of therapeutic engagement become restrictive and regressive rather than liberating. All new ideas and practices, no matter how relationally inclined, need to heed this warning. We are only ever one decade away from evolution/revolution becoming a dogmatic form of orthodoxy. Parker believes that relational psychotherapy based on attachment draws on an understanding of power that shapes future engagements. This makes it difficult to anticipate other forms of relating beyond our understanding of attachment and seeks to avoid being trapped in one way of being. Loewenthal underlines this by focusing on ethical practice as an expression of justice and truth through ongoing encounter with the other. Sanders' stories illustrate the abuse of power, a factor still often neglected in therapeutic traditions (Khele, Symons & Wheeler 2008). He fears the relational as merging both therapist and client leading to the difficulty of managing the differences between them. Hargaden cautions how the relational brings with it power-laden attitudes that hinder, rather than help relationship. Samuels sees a shadow side to all-encompassing relational approaches that generates a new orthodoxy with the power to include and exclude, or set new norms for conformity.

Third, the relational has social and political dimensions. There is a clear desire within the psychotherapy world to connect the personal with the political. Samuels' pioneering text *The Political Psyche* (1993) broke new ground when first published. In 1995, the organization Psychotherapists and Counsellors for Social Responsibility was formed to provide a forum to debate, and a vehicle to influence, wider social, cultural, environmental and political issues beyond the therapeutic space. The push for regulation in the UK in the last decade has further focused this development. So, one vision for relational psychotherapy (that incorporates the multiple connections identified by Parker) is that it 'promises to connect the personal and the political'. In the past, psychoanalysis has been viewed as a purely clinical encounter with no connection to the world beyond the consulting room; now, relational psychoanalysis or psychotherapy are described by Loewenthal, Samuels, Parker and Sanders as instruments of social change. This links back to the previous reflection related to the nature of power. Who owns or has access to the power to make decisions, often by a minority on behalf of the majority, is an ongoing tension in a democratic society. Yet, what we are also discovering is that psychotherapy and counselling organizations face the same tensions, make the same mistakes and fall into the same traps. Our privileged access to the psyche and gaze on our inner world and the inner worlds of others does not prevent us from falling down a large hole in the road, if we are not looking up, as well as looking in.

Fourth, there is the importance of narratives that are negotiated. Even a traditional psychoanalytic stance incorporates levels of negotiation, trial and error conversations and tentative interpretations (Lemma, 2003) allowing a narrative to emerge. Carmeli and Blass write that 'analysts will normally use the experience of the relationship, their feelings and sensitivities, to struggle to understand what is going on and on the basis of this offer interpretations, not God-given truths but rather as attempts to formulate what can be seen at this moment, recognizing that the interpretation may be influenced by relational factors that may help and/or hinder getting a better grasp of the truth of the matter' (p. 126). This does mark a change where therapists are willing to embrace not knowing, humility and doubt. Parker believes that relational knowledge is 'incomplete, evanescent, lost again after it appears in analysis as the truth of the subject' (p. 135), which can be recovered by adopting Strong's Bakhtinian dialogic approach, requiring a re-discovery of aliveness where the therapist and client fall in and out of 'coordinated conversations'. Yet it is much more than a 'democratic synthesis of shared perspectives' (p. 136). Other therapeutic terms that convey such an encounter are to be found in Mearns and Cooper's (2005) *Working at relational depth* and Stern's concept of attunement (Wright, 2009). Hargaden sees how the relational can be used in embodied and creative ways to enhance the narratives told by specific modalities (transactional analysis) but that it can also be symbolic for others.

Fifth, there is the importance of philosophical foundations. One of the long-standing problems of counselling and psychotherapy training is the inadequate attention often paid to philosophical and theological understandings of what it is to be human, concepts of the mind, the origin and status of truth, the nature of evil and the ontology of being. Yet in addressing what relational means, and to bring out the nuances of understanding, each contributor has utilized philosophical categories, ideas or theorists (implicitly or explicitly). Carmeli and Blass discuss the relational within the context of relational psychoanalysis, helpfully focusing on the philosophical roots of traditional psychoanalysis. Parker writes from a Lacanian perspective (although his thinking spans many areas), and for me understanding Lacan is as much a philosophical as a psychoanalytic task. Lacan utilizes ideas that require a philosophical understanding to fully understand his unique use of these to his own psychoanalytic ends. Loewenthal draws insights from existentialism and Buber (which he critiques) and post-existentialism and Levinas (which he also critiques). While I have affinities with Levinas' ideas, they can be elusive and alienating, so it is important that Loewenthal and others immerse themselves in his thought and advance his ideas in order to enhance the relational. While Sanders doesn't define relational he does identify the assumptions, drawn from Bakhtin and Wittgenstein, that underpin his thinking and practice. Understanding the role philosophical thinking plays in how we understand the relational would seem essential.

Sixth, the relational offers us the opportunity to confront the depths of the psyche in both the individual and society. The relational is no panacea, no nirvana and needs an ongoing critical engagement and reflexivity on the behalf of its participants to avoid the dangers of complacency or hypocrisy. Earlier we considered where power is situated in the relational, however, there is another dimension. We can be caught up in actions, relational or otherwise, that Samuels goes as far as to suggest could be termed evil and this takes us into the realm of complex areas of thought and behaviour evoked by the term 'evil'. Samuels does not shy away from this and in so doing opens up another intriguing area of thought. If we are to confront the shadow side of any relational dimension to our humanity we also need to address when it goes wrong. The shadow side of Modernism was that it neglected the theological and philosophical traditions, with the exception of a few, such as Riceour and Levinas. While Loewenthal introduces us to transcendence as found in Levinas, it would be rewarding to take this further by engaging with his ideas in *Transcendence and evil* (Levinas, 1987). Levinas invokes the name of God and it is a reminder that theological traditions have long addressed the nature of evil as found in Surin's (1986) *Theology and the problem of evil* and Fiddes' (2000) *Participating in God*. The advent of post-modernism offers space for old and new narratives including a return to the depth of engagement with the human condition. It is precisely this engagement that theology has offered in the past, and still has something to offer in our understanding of the relational as long as old dogmas and narratives can be overcome.

The relational emphasis now found in some forms of psychoanalysis and psychotherapy may be viewed as a contemporary and postmodern meta-narrative consisting of the categories identified earlier by Hargaden and Schwartz (2007). It is also clear that any ongoing focus on, and use of, the term relational requires a correspondingly greater awareness of its complexities, contradictions and concerns. Understanding the depth of human-to-human encounter, expressed through the term relational, can take us to the very heights of visionary potential in others and ourselves. Yet at the same time it requires us to enter into the very darkness, a shadow side experienced as a form of existential or ontological isolation that shapes our being, our lives, our truths and meanings, and even our destiny.

References

Fiddes, P. (2000). *Participating in God: A pastoral doctrine of the trinity*. London: DLT.

Hargaden, H. and Schwartz, J. (2007). Editorial. *European Journal of Psychotherapy and Counselling*, 9(1): 3–5 [Taylor & Francis Online].

Hargaden, H. and Sills, C. (2002). *Transactional analysis: A relational perspective*. London: Routledge.

House, R. and Loewenthal, D. (Eds.) (2008). *Against and for CBT: Towards a constructive dialogue?* PCCS Books: Ross-on-Wye.

Khele, S., Symons, C. and Wheeler, S. (2008). An analysis of complaints to the BACP, 1996–2006. *Counselling and Psychotherapy Research*, 8(2): 124–132.

Lemma, A. (2003). *An introduction to the practice of psychoanalytic psychotherapy*. Chichester: John Wiley.

Levinas, E. (1987). Transcendence and evil. In E. Levinas, *Collected Philosophical Papers* (A. Lingis, Trans.). Dordrecht: Martinus Nijhoff Publishers.

Mearns, D. and Cooper, M. (2005). *Working at relational depth in counselling and psychotherapy.* London: Sage.

Pollard, R. (2008). *Dialogue and desire: Mikhail Bakhtin and the linguistic turn in psychotherapy.* London: Karnac.

Samuels, A. (1993). *The political psyche.* London: Routledge.

Surin, K. (1986). *Theology and the problem of evil.* Oxford: Blackwell.

Westbrook, D., Kennerley, H. and Kirk, J. (2011). *An introduction to cognitive behaviour therapy: Skills and applications.* London: Sage.

Wright, K. (2009). *Mirroring and attunement: Self-realization in psychoanalysis and art.* Hove: Routledge.

19

AFTERWORD

The personal equation

Andrew Samuels

This afterword reviews the human and personal aspects of practice and theory in the therapy field. The author touches on 'the personal equation' as somewhat neglected in the forging of people's professional positions. He also discusses aspects of the image of the Wounded Healer as these relate to the spectrum of thinking about therapy's relational turn.

The first part of this book celebrated and detailed what relational therapy might look like and incorporated two commentaries on what was offered. The second part was more critical in nature and also included two commentaries. My job is to say something useful about the whole thing, which strikes me as a massive task.

The 'personal equation' is the bias that the observer brings to his or her observation, and to subsequent thinking and theorising. As Jung put it, 'One sees what one can best see oneself'.

What personal equations are at work to make a therapist enthusiastically adopt, or noticeably and critically refrain from adopting, or take a measured and judicious view ('the middle way') in connection with therapy's relational turn? These enquiries, which are not focused on any particular one or more of our stellar contributors, inform my afterword. They chime with issues raised by my co-editor Del Loewenthal in his opening chapter where he asked 'is it possible that these different psychotherapeutic methods have really come about in order to deal with different types of "psychopathologies" in people who are psychological therapists?'

These are subsets of a wider question about why people become therapists in the first place, which, unless I am much mistaken, is not really addressed in this, a book that addresses so much. Hence, infused with a sense of the book as a whole, we can usefully look into the personal and human motivations surrounding and driving what has been written. Does this not take us into Wounded Healer territory? Perhaps we need to revisit what Atwood and Stolorow (1979) suggested when they took up and massively elaborated Jung's idea that 'every psychology is a personal confession' and suggested that our theories are driven by who we are and by our wounds. And wasn't this the very kernel of Ellenberger's 'creative illness' (1970)?

Let's see. It could be a profound personal *fear* of relationship that drives a person to become a relational therapist. In this reading of it, the therapist-to-be manages their fear by self-administering measured doses of relationship. But an equally profound *need* for relationship, never satisfied in life, might be at work – the lonely therapist. Those other therapists who urge caution regarding the possible idealisation of the therapy relationship, lest it collapse into a jelly of false equality and ignorance of the nitty-gritty of socio-political reality, well, they might be caught up in an extensive rationalisation of a problem they have with others. The algebra is, of course, endless, and these are just a few possibilities.

The relation of the therapist to their work (the work) as a whole is much discussed in private but rarely in public, and our book is no exception. We have read much about power and its management, about mortality, vulnerability and illness, a bit (but not a lot) about sexuality in the therapy encounter, and many pages about the routes to relationality that the authors have taken or not taken. But not much about why they are therapists in the first place.

Can it be taken for granted that all therapists are wounded and that this inflects their choice of career? If so, can it also be taken for granted that therapists get something for themselves out of doing the work, call it 'healing' if you will? In which case, the work is more than constituting 'the desire of the therapist' or being an answer to the question 'what do therapists want?' What do the writers of our chapters want? Why are they writing in the way that they do? Of course, it is more than personal idiosyncracy or the working out of the author's personal myth. One is not born Kleinian. Nor should we be reductive without an admixture of irony and admission that this way of thinking grossly over-simplifies why people do anything at all.

Then there is the context of each author, which must surely partially explain why they have different views? The time and location in which he or she is writing. The socioeconomic and cultural context. Let's not forget the pattern of friends and enemies within their profession that they have created over the years. I have long ago (1989) suggested that the best way to understand much psychoanalytic and Jungian writing is to ask: 'Whom is this a polemic against?, who is the writer's enemy here?' And I remembered to cite Heraclitus to reassure us that polemic is OK, lies at the heart of pluralism, because *Polemos* (Greek for strife) is the 'king of all, the father of all'. This means that polemic is the parent of creativity.

Many therapists would agree that we suffer from a range of wounds that somehow fit us for our jobs. We do our best to stay in contact with these wounds ('integrate' them). But this leads to two big problems. The first is that we sometimes use our wounded status to excuse bad behaviour inside and outside the consulting room. Inside, things like sexual misconduct, financial exploitation (deliberate or incidental) and theoretical rigidity come to mind. But there is a lot that goes on in the therapy world outside the consulting room that should not be facilely wished away by reference to our being Wounded Healers: personalising of professional issues, splits within therapy organisations, and (still, sometimes) indifference to wider arcs of suffering in the world – to list a few. We can add to this list of the consequences of woundedness: collusion by groups of therapists with the state and its interests regarding the 'mental health' of citizens and the *trahison des clercs* (betrayal by the intellectuals) that has gripped sections of the therapy industry.

The collusion I am referring to, in which some of us seek the job and income security that attaches to practising 'state therapy', is that of a slavish desire to be in the good books of the powerful. Many have accused psychoanalysis of losing its radical edge to gain such approval and advantage. But this is really only a part of the picture. There is another kind of woundedness, the opposite kind. This takes the form of a perpetual adolescence and rebelliousness against all authorities, leading to self-congratulation for one's independence and critical posture – but to little effect in the world. So there is a spectrum of wounds to consider ranging from deference and bowing and scraping on the one hand to meaningless defiance on the other.

Another problem is created by the temptation for therapists to over-control and compensate for being wounded by adopting a fixed persona of 'The Healer'. I did detect, or thought I detected, this from time to time in the book. Such exotic self-idealisation is not only potentially dishonest; it can also cut the client off from their own healing potential. Only the therapist does that! We may need to recover the image of 'the client as healer', something theorists such as Jung and Harold Searles introduced but which has perhaps got lost these days. Does the client not have a responsibility for the therapist, as Hoffman asks (2006)? And, I would add, wider responsibilities to self and others and world.

This reader, with a privileged position, was struck by how little there was in the book about the role of the client, whether as healer to him or herself, or as healer to the therapist, or as healer to the wider society. This strikes me as odd at a time when psychotherapy researchers are demonstrating how important it is to consider the stage and state the client has attained when considering, not only the outcome, but also the experience and flavour of the work. Could it be that the client is getting lost, and might it be worthwhile exploring that a bit?

If you go for intersubjectivity, then there is a risk that the components of it might be lost, might not be given the separate scrutiny that their particularity deserves. If you demur from an intersubjective approach, then there is equally little to be said about the client's role. I realise that it may seem iconoclastic to say it, but the client seems to have gone missing both when the focus is on the relationship with the therapist *and* when this relation is refused. But those critical therapists writing here who are more sceptical about relationality may also have 'lost' their clients too. They seem more concerned with their interpretive role, or their pre-determined ideas about the limits of the client, the client's lack, the client's rupture.

This is not to turn the client into the driver of everything. But something is going on within this fascinating and important problematic of 'the client', wherever one situates oneself in the relational spectrum. And it is a power issue.

Power is one of the red threads that run though the book. It is definitely not overlooked herein, whether in terms of power in the therapy room or power in the world. However, the client's power in relation to the therapist, and the client's power in relation to themselves, remain interesting topics to pursue.

The client's power is delimited by what has come to be called 'the diversity agenda' in the therapy professions. This means the specific nature of the client's position: age, money, sex and sexuality, health, nationality, ethnicity, religion. These specifics also exist in the therapist of course and we know that the interactive alchemy that the two 'lists' of specifics generates is both a gift to the therapy, making it real, and also the main source of blockage, impasse and hatred. I am wondering if this question of diversity has been dealt with adequately in these pages. It is not quite the same as discussion of the political sources, outcomes and limitations of the therapy process. Have we broken the client down sufficiently, pun intended? Has the monolithic version of 'client' been allowed to dominate our thinking and writing? Is there actually a client? Or a therapist?

Recently, when considering myself both as therapist and client, the question of my being a Jewish man came up. This was on one of those interminable internet forum discussions. Someone told a joke: 'There's a Jewish castaway on a desert island. And he builds two synagogues, the second being the one he does not attend.'

I responded that the way I had heard the joke was that there were *two* Jews on the island and they built three synagogues so that, as one said to the other, 'Now we can both boycott that *schmuk* over there.' The pull in the joke – and the pull in this book – is to alliance as well as to exclusion, and to relationality as well as to solipsism and fantasies of superiority. Therapists are like other people – only more so.

References

Atwood, G. and Stolorow, R. (1979). *Faces in a cloud: Subjectivity in personality theory*. New York: Jason Aronson.

Ellenberger, H. (1970). *The discovery of the unconscious*. London: Alen Lane; New York: Basic Books.

Hoffman, I. (2006). The myth of free association and the potentials of the analytic relationship. *International Journal of Psychoanalysis, 87*, 43–61.

Samuels, A. (1989). *The plural psyche: Personality, morality and the father*. London and New York: Routledge.

INDEX

A

abstinence 43, 96, 111, 131
Acquarone, S. 41
'Addiction to near-death' 89
Akhtar, S. 67, 68, 69, 70, 71
American Psychoanalytic Association (APsaA) 97
American Psychological Association (APA) 97
Amphitryon 38 84
analytic frame 84–6, 102, 103
analytic stance 14–16, 111–13
ancestry of articles 196–7
Anderson, H. 68, 165, 167, 170
Anderson, J. 65, 72, 167, 170
anonymity 96, 111, 112
Aotearoa, New Zealand 205
Aron, L. 3, 56, 57, 58, 94, 101, 103, 109, 112, 141, 196, 198t, 199, 199–200, 201, 203
arrows of therapy relationship 189–90
attachment theory 5, 16, 23, 83
attunement 221; and empathy 180
Atwood, G. 126, 224
authenticity 4, 22, 108, 109
authority, location of 112
autonomy 148; vs. heteronomy 146–7, 148

B

Bakhtin, M. 9, 161, 163, 166, 168, 171, 172, 217
Balint, E. 48, 49, 68, 198t
Barlow, D. 162–3
'the basic fault' 68
'to be or not to be' 146
Beck, A.T. 166
Becker, C. and Becker, L. 143, 144
Becker, E. 81, 84
Beebe, B. 13, 69, 103, 111, 180
'beloved' case study 27–38; countertransference 30–1; disassociation of patient 30–2, 33–4, 103; haunting by dead sister 32; masturbation within the session 33–4; meeting outside consulting room 31–2, 33–4; patient aggression 35–6; racial dyad 28, 103; reading social services case file 37; self-disclosure of pregnant therapist 33, 35, 36, 103; unlocking the impasse 29–30
Benjamin, J. 23, 37n, 45, 76, 110, 116, 131, 198t
Bentall. R. 154–5
Berne, E. 176, 178
bespoke analysis techniques 14–15, 100, 104
Beyond Post-modernism 141
bi-directionality of therapeutic relationship 4, 21
birth trauma 40, 50, 83–4; and disruption of infant–mother dyad 40–1, 47, 114
bisexual clients 186
blank screen, therapist as a 24
Bleuler, E. 5
body: anxieties 28, 51, 83, 89, 90, 102, 110; drawing on countertransferential bodily experience of analyst 46–7; earliest relationship with self and other through 50; engaging with bodily self 49–50; infant experiences registered on a 87; mind splitting off from 28, 44; as an object 87; psychosomatic 87
Bowlby, J. 5, 16, 82, 153, 198t
Bromberg, P. 49
Buber, M. 41, 47, 48, 68, 69, 110, 112, 143, 144, 157, 198t, 203, 206–7

INDEX

C
Carmichael, K. 67
Carter, J.A. 202
Cartesianism 122–3, 200
case reports, reviewing with patients 59, 104–5
castration anxiety 82
Against and For CBT 161, 162, 172, 173, 205, 216
centrifugal approaches to therapeutic dialogue 161, 163–4, 172
centripetal approaches to therapeutic dialogue 161, 164, 172
changing of therapists, relational psychoanalysis and 90, 157–8, 216
citation/reference analysis 197, 198t
Clarkson, P. 189, 202
client, role of 226–7
cognitive behavioural therapy (CBT): criticism of territorial claims of 199; evidence-based approach to practice 162, 163, 203, 212; research on 154; UK government endorsement of 162, 172, 203, 213
cognitive behavioural therapy (CBT), dialogic practice of 161–74, 205, 213; content negotiations 165–7; conversational resources and resourcefulness 169–70; dialogic approach to practice 164–5; diverging conversations 162–4; 'going on together' in turn by conversational turn negotiation 167–9; manuals 162, 163, 164, 169; moving forward with 172–3; rigor in dialogic practice 170–2; Ross' critique 216–17; science issues 162, 172; summary of dialogues 205–6, 206t
Cognitive Realignment Therapy 154
computer-mediated relationships 155
conformism 185, 218; and state regulation 189
'continuity of being' 40–1, 48, 50
'conversational realities' 171
Cooper, J. 68, 69
Cooper, M. 152, 221
Cooper, S. 182
countertransference 4, 56, 109, 213; attunement as a form of 180; in 'beloved' case study 30–1; evaluation of 14, 18, 62, 63, 132; 'Hate in the countertransference' 89–90; obstacles of 55; in 'primal silence' case study 45–7, 49
couples therapy 68–9, 187
cross-fertilisation of ideas 177, 179, 196, 197

D
de Masi, F. 81
death: drive 133; fear 83; instinct 81, 82 *see also* mortality; mortality in consulting room case study
defensive rage 68
Deliverance 218
democratizing psychoanalysis 13–16, 98–101, 111–13, 136, 137, 203; and democratization of fee structures 23–5; examples in consulting room 14–16; and Lacanian analysis 136; relational routes to 12–13
dependency and recognition 22–3
Derrida, J. 67, 142, 146, 202
desire 123, 136; sexual 187
dialogic practice of cognitive behavioural therapy (CBT) 161–74, 205, 213; content negotiations 165–7; conversational resources and resourcefulness 169–70; dialogic approach to practice 164–5; diverging conversations 162–4; 'going on together' in turn by conversational turn negotiation 167–9; manuals 162, 163, 164, 169; moving forward with 172–3; rigor in dialogic practice 170–2; Ross' critique 216–17; science issues 162, 172; summary of dialogues 205–6, 206t; UK government endorsement 162, 172, 203, 213
dialogue, themes of 205–7
The Differend: Phrases in Dispute 168
disruption and repair 69, 103–4, 116
dreams 188
drive model 99, 123, 126, 133, 199, 214

E
ego psychology 97, 100
Eichenbaum, L. 13, 15, 23
email relationships 155
empathy: and attunement 180; and the relational 179–80, 206, 217–18
empty signifiers 133–7, 215
end of analysis 135

229

INDEX

Erickson, M. 165, 169
ethical theme 204–5
ethics of relational psychoanalysis 140–50, 202–3; autonomy vs. heteronomy 146–7, 148; Buber and 143–4, 206–7; as distinct from practice 142–3, 150; Levinas and 147–50; from a post-existentialist perspective 140–3, 145, 215–16; post-modernism and implications for 145–6; 'to put the client first' 142–3; space for dialogue 145, 206–7; and vested interests 148
European Journal of Psychotherapy and Counselling 4, 98, 193
evidence-based approach to practice 162, 163, 203, 212
evil 221–2
existentialism 102, 141, 143–4, 145

F

Fairbairn, R. 5, 16, 23, 62, 82, 117, 127, 198t
fantasies 131, 188
fee structures, democratization of 23–5
feminism 13, 99, 131, 201
Ferenczi, S. 55–6, 57, 62, 100, 101, 103, 131, 198t
Fiddes, P. 222
Fonagy, P. 12, 37n, 69, 111, 132, 153, 198t
forgiveness 65–79, 103–4, 115–16; in consulting room 69–70; in couples relationships 68–9; development origins of capacity for 69, 115; 'Ealing Vicarage case' 74; evolutionary perspective on 70; finding true 116; literature review 66–72; as a negative 71, 74, 75, 116; neuropsychological research 70; as a positive 70–1; psychoanalytic writing on 67–9; psychology texts on 70; recognition for need for 116; reconciliation and 67, 71; religious and cultural ideas on 66–7; research conclusions 75–6; research study methodology 72–3; research study results 73–5; and revenge 72; self-forgiveness 74–5; therapist's personal benefits from research on 76; for victims of trauma 71, 116
Frankfurt School 130
Freud, S.: on anxiety 82; citations by contributors 198t; on death 81–2; dialectical position including drive and relationship 126, 214; early dialogue with Ferenczi 103; on forgiveness 67, 75; impossible professions 149; on interminable nature of analysis 135; on 'oceanic feelings' 188; Oedipus complex 13, 69, 122, 177; Rat Man 123; on subjective factor 100; unlocking impasses 5; view of individual 122, 123, 125, 126
Frie, R. 141, 206

G

Gelso, C.J. 202
gender-conscious therapy 23, 103
Gerson, S. 46, 60, 111, 114, 177, 198t
Gestalt therapy 167, 201
Gilbert, H. 68, 69
Giraudoux, J. 84
Goffman, E. 165, 168–9
Goldman, D. 90
Gottlieb, R.M. 67, 69
Greek vs. Hebraic 146–7
Greenberg, J. 3, 57, 62, 93, 99, 100, 104, 126, 195, 198t, 199
guilt 68, 83

H

Hamlet 146
Hargaden, H. 4, 5, 176, 178, 194, 195, 196, 197, 201, 204, 213, 217–18, 222
'Hate in the countertransference' 89–90
Heidegger, M. 4, 145, 170
Hemingway, E. 187
heteronomy: vs. autonomy 146–7, 148; Levinas on truth in terms of 147–8
history of relational psychoanalysis: development of different versions 97–9; early dialogue between Freud and Ferenczi 103; in Europe 5, 62; origins of terminology 195–6, 197; roots in radical movements 13, 98, 99; in UK 12–13, 62, 97, 100; in US 4–5, 62, 93–7, 99–100, 184–5
Hoffman, I.Z. 81, 84, 90–1, 102, 126, 127–8, 170, 180, 182, 198t, 226
Horsfield, P. 71
hour, therapy 84, 85–6, 102
House, R. 161, 164, 166, 172, 173, 185, 191, 205, 216
human, becoming 16
human nature, relational view of 122–3, 125, 133, 153, 200, 214, 216

INDEX

humanistic psychoanalysis 182, 184, 194, 195, 196, 197, 218
humanity, confirmation of client's 49, 50, 156–7
Husserl, E. 145
hypocrisy 185–7, 218, 221–2

I

'I–It' and 'I–Thou' 144, 203, 206–7
impasses, unlocking 110–11; 'beloved' case study 29–30; Freud on 5; mortality in consulting room case study 88–91, 110; in primal silence case study 44–6, 110, 114–15
infant–mother dyad 12–13, 111, 215; attunement and proto-conversations 180; birth trauma and disruption of 40–1, 47, 114; bonding difficulties 41, 47, 87; connections between analyst/analysand relationship and that of 131, 135; relevance in understanding capacity to forgive 69, 115
infants, internal world of 178
infidelity 187
integration, relational to describe a principle of 62, 97–8, 177, 178–9, 182, 201, 202
International Association for Relational Psychoanalysis and Psychotherapy (IARPP) 94, 95, 107, 213
International Association of Relational Transactional Analysts 179
International Psychoanalytic Association (IPA) 97
interpersonal psychoanalysis 62, 97, 201, 203; relational bridging gap between object relations and 62, 97–8, 131–2, 201, 204; relational psychoanalysis emanating from 4–5, 200
interpersonal, relational as 180–1
The Interpersonal World of the Infant 176, 178
interpretation 17, 26n, 96, 113, 126, 220–1
intersubjectivity 37n, 111, 132, 178, 201; space for 44, 48, 49; in trajectory of psychoanalysis 131, 215
intimacy 185
isolation 188, 218

J

James, H. 144
James, W. 5

Joseph, B. 89
Jung, C.G. 66, 188, 189, 190, 195, 224

K

Kantrowitz, J.L. 104
Kernberg, O.F. 68, 69, 74
Klein, M. 68, 82, 125–6
Kleinian psychoanalysis 83, 86, 98, 113
knowledge 112, 124, 135
Kohut, H. 68, 113, 176, 198
Kriegman, D. 57, 89, 90

L

Lacan, J. 85, 89, 217
Lacanian psychoanalysis and relational turn 130–9, 215; desire 136; dialectics of authority 135–6; end of analysis 135; and Left 130, 134, 137–8; politics of the personal 131, 137, 220; power ensembles 135, 203; relations and empty signifiers 133–7, 215; signifiers of transference 132–3, 135, 215; symbolic in 133
Lachmann, F.M. 103, 111, 180
Laclau, E. 134
Langs, R. 85
language: client's 166–7, 170–1; flexible and resourceful 170; games 165, 168, 170, 217; internal and external 166–7; meanings and the symbolic 199–203; and obscuring of meaning 178; regulation and controlling of 205; as a tradition of work on transference 132, 201, 215
Latour, B. 169
Layard agenda 161–2, 172, 203
Lea, M. 155
Levinas, E.: on autonomy 148; background 145; critiques of 149, 221; ethics of 8, 141, 142, 143–4, 146, 147–50, 203, 215–16; on *Hamlet* 146; on heteronomy 147–8; as post-existential 145; on transcendence 222
'life' fear 83
living as enactment 17
Loewenthal, D. 3, 142, 143, 145, 146, 149, 150, 161, 166, 172, 173, 184, 194, 197, 203, 204, 205, 206, 207, 216
Lyotard, J.-F. 147–8, 149, 168

M

Marx, K. 133
McDougall, J. 41, 87

231

McLaughlin, J.T. 55, 56, 62
Mearns, D. 221
A Meeting of Minds 93, 100
mentalization 37n, 69, 111, 115
Merleau-Ponty, H. 4, 141, 146
mind: splitting off from body 28, 44; and truth, relational view of 123–5, 214
Mitchell, S. 3, 4, 117, 123, 126, 127, 199–200; background 99, 102; citations by contributors 197, 198t; concerns over flight from inner world 203; early development of relational psychoanalysis 93–4, 95, 195; efforts to integrate object relations and interpersonal psychoanalysis 62; on email therapy 155; influences on work of 98–9, 102; Orbach's critique of 13, 98, 99; on profound changes in conception of person 125; relational matrix 94, 102; response to patient's repeated attacks 124–5
Modernism 222
Moon, L. 186
moral imagination 70
moralism, conformism and 185
mortality 80–92; confronting death in therapy 60–1, 84–6; and death instinct 81, 82; existential approaches to anxiety of 102; literature review 80–6; Rank's theory on 83; religious beliefs and 84; violence arising out of fear of 81
mortality in consulting room case study 86–91; analytic frame for confronting 84–6, 102; anxieties of therapist 80, 90; overcoming an impasse 88–91, 110
mother–infant dyad 12–13, 111, 215; attunement and proto-conversations 180; birth trauma and disruption of 40–1, 47, 114; bonding difficulties 41, 47, 87; connections between analyst/analysand relationship and that of 131, 135; relevance in understanding capacity to forgive 69
Muran, J.C. 3, 103–4
Murphy, L.J. 155
'mutual analysis' 56, 62, 131
mutual recognition 37n, 116
mutuality 62, 100, 111–12

N
narcissism 68, 74, 91, 141, 145
narratives, negotiated 219, 220–1
'negativity' 133, 134

neuropsychological research 70
neutrality, therapeutic 17, 18–21, 22, 112
New York University Postdoctoral Program in Psychotherapy & Psychoanalysis 94, 95, 97, 199
non-conflictual, relational as 181
non-verbal analytic work 47–9, 101, 102, 155–6
non-verbal conversation 180

O
object relations 5, 12, 131, 217; relational bridging gap between interpersonal psychoanalysis and 62, 97–8, 131–2, 201, 204; UK development of 62, 97, 98
Object Relations in Psychoanalysis Theory 62, 93
Oedipus complex 13, 69, 122, 177
off the shelf techniques 14–15, 100, 104
one-person psychology 113, 117, 127, 188, 202, 204; and shift to two-person psychology 125, 202, 207
Orange, D.M. 115, 141, 202, 204, 206
Orbach, S. 13, 15, 23, 46–7, 50, 99, 130, 131, 136, 186, 196, 198t, 203
original morality 70
outside the consulting room, meeting clients 16, 31–2, 33–4, 111

P
Pain and Pleasure 87
parent–child interactions 116
Participating in God 222
pastoral counselling 68
'The patient's experience of the analyst's subjectivity' 58
Patton, J. 68
person-centred relational therapy 152–60, 199, 216; assumptions of 153; changing of therapist through 157–8, 216; moments of connection 156–7; a rejection of psychotechnological therapies 153, 158, 203; research on effectiveness of 154–5; unpopular with governments 158
personal equation 224–6
phantasies 125–6
phenomenology 141, 145–6, 168, 213
Philadelphia School 197
philosophical: foundations 10, 122, 219, 221; traditions, Western 146–7
Piontelli, A. 40
'poetic wisdom' 166, 168

INDEX

Poland, W. 56–7
political: social and ethical relations 203–5; and social dimensions of relational 219, 220
The Political Psyche 220
politics: connection between clinic and activism 130–1; dialectics of authority 135–6; of the personal 131, 137, 220; of psychotechnologies 158, 159, 203; of regulation and registration 140, 189, 191, 204–5, 207, 212–13, 219, 226; and solitude 189
post-existentialism 140–3, 145, 215–16
post-Jung 189
post-modern meta-narrative 219–22; confronting depths of psyche with relational 219, 221–2; and importance of philosophical foundations 219, 221; negotiated narratives 219, 220–1; political and social dimensions of relational 219, 220; relational as problematic 219, 220; relational as vital 219
post-modernism 141, 145–6, 206
post-phenomenology 141, 142, 146
power: of client 226–7; ensembles of 135, 203; illustrating abuse of 157–8; of past relationships, relinquishing 20–1; relational as problematic with regard to 219, 220; tensions in democratic society 220
power of therapist 85, 86, 89, 111, 134, 136, 167–8; deferring of client to 168, 169; and maintaining of analytical frame 85–6, 102; surrendering of 86
'primal silence' case study 39–52, 101–2, 114–15; accessing of birth records 46, 115; countertransference in 45–7, 49; early trauma theoretical considerations 40–1; engagement with bodily self 49–50; family history 42–3; re-birthing sessions 50; relational unconscious and enactment of key issues 46–7, 51, 101; separation anxiety 51; silent regression in supportive presence of therapist 47–9, 101; unlocking impasse in 44–6, 110, 114–15; vulnerability of therapist 46, 101
promiscuity 186
psychoanalysis/psychotherapy relationship 95–7
Psychoanalytic Dialogues 94–5
psychosis 5, 81

psychosomatics 39, 41, 87
psychotechnological therapies 153, 158, 203

R

radical empiricism 6
radical movements 13, 98, 99
Rank, O. 81, 83, 84, 90, 197
Ransley, C. 67, 71, 73
Rat Man 123
re-birthing sessions 50
The Real Thing 144
reconciliation and forgiveness 67, 71
regression: differences in American and British use of term 101; in 'primal silence' case study 47–9, 101
Relational Concepts in Psychoanalysis 13, 62, 94
relational matrix 94, 102
Relational Perspectives Book Series 94, 95
relational, post-modern meta-narrative of 219–22; confronting depths of psyche with relational 219, 221–2; and importance of philosophical foundations 219, 221; negotiated narratives 219, 220–1; political and social dimensions of relational 219, 220; relational as problematic 219, 220; relational as vital 219
relational turn in psychotherapy 121–8, 213–14; changing of therapists 90, 157–8, 216; claims for 121–5; cross-fertilisation of ideas with other modalities 177, 179, 196, 197; cutting edge or cliché 207–8; key elements of 4, 213; leading field in relational thought 177; man as inherently relational, view of 122–3; many versions of 97–9, 189–90; as a meta-theory 182; mind and truth, view of 123–5, 214; as a principle of integration 62, 97–8, 177, 178–9, 182, 201, 202; as revolutionary 125–8; teaching 100–1, 181–2; theoretical misperceptions 179–81; theory 178, 182
relational turn in psychotherapy, shadows of 184–92, 203–4; critique of 218–19; hypocrisy in addressing the sexual 185–7, 218, 221–2; moralism and conformism 185, 218; solitude and flight from inner world 187–8, 218
relational unconscious 46–7, 51, 101
'relational,' use of term 199–200, 200–3; change in 93–4; to conceptualise

therapeutic relationship 202; to describe a particular ethics 202–3; to describe an integrating principle 62, 97–8, 177, 178–9, 182, 201, 202; to describe human nature and systems of human relations 133, 153, 200; to encompass the symbolic 'non relational' 133, 181–2, 201; to refer to a particular form of psychoanalysis 200–1; to refer to lenses in other therapeutic approaches 201; to refer to relationship which is therapy itself 200

relationship, psychoanalysis/psychotherapy 95–7

'relationship therapy' 195, 197

relationships: connection in childhood and analysis 131, 135; different types of 5; many relationships of therapy 189–90; relational as referring to ways of conceptualising therapeutic 202; research on effectiveness of therapeutic 3–4, 154–5; between therapist and mode of working 5–6; traditional vs. relational view of 122–3

religious: beliefs and practice on mortality 84; teachings on forgiveness 66–7

research, on effectiveness of therapeutic relationship 3–4, 154–5

restorative justice 70–1

revolutionary view of relational psychoanalysis 125–7

Rey, J.H. 70

ritual 84; of therapy hour 84, 85–6

Rogers, C. 5, 152, 165, 179, 184, 195, 197, 198t, 200, 204

Rozmarin, E. 141

rupture and repair 69, 103–4, 116

S

Safran, J.D. 3, 103–4

Samuels, A. 70, 114, 132, 136, 184, 187, 188, 189, 195, 196, 220

schizophrenia 5, 83, 154

Schneiderman, S. 5, 85

Schwartz, J. 4, 5, 82, 194, 195, 196, 197, 213, 222

Searles, H. 81, 83

self-disclosure 22, 57, 124–5; of pregnant therapist 33, 35, 36, 103

self-disclosure, clinical example of: benefiting patient 55, 57–8, 59, 104, 108–9; discussion of case report with patient 59, 104–5; elements of good relational technique 109; reversing of traditional patient/therapist role 55, 108; vulnerability of analyst in 55, 58, 59, 104

self-disclosure, clinical example of decision against: impasse in therapy 60–1; reasons for decision 61–2; vulnerability of therapist 61

self-psychology 68, 98, 113

self, relation to 188

self-with-other encounters 33, 41, 50, 157, 216

'separated attachments' 23

separation anxiety 51, 82, 83–4, 114

sex, as non-relational 133

sexual: desire 187; fantasies 131; hypocrisy in therapists addressing the 185–7, 218, 221–2

shadows of relational turn 184–92, 203–4; critique of 218–19; hypocrisy in addressing the sexual 185–7, 218, 221–2; moralism and conformism 185, 218; solitude and flight from inner world 187–8, 218

Shlien, J. 153, 156–7

Shotter, J. 171

signifiers: empty 133–7, 215; of transference 132–3, 135, 215

silence in psychotherapy sessions 155–6; silent regression in supportive presence of therapist 47–9, 101

Sills, C. 177, 178, 179, 201, 217

sin 67, 74

Slavin, M.O. 57, 89, 90

social and political dimension of relational 219, 220

social, political and ethical relations 203–5

SoCRATES project 154

solitude 187–8, 218; and politics 189

South Africa 70–1

Spears, R. 155

Spy, T. 67, 73

Stark, M. 202

state regulation 140, 189, 191, 204–5, 207, 212–13, 226; denial of relational and 158, 216; in New Zealand 205; and problems of definitions 219

Stern, D.B. 35, 54, 57, 63, 126, 132, 176, 178, 198t, 202, 217, 221

Stolorow, R. 69, 113, 124, 126, 224

Strange Situation Test 69

subjectivity: of client 36, 109; politicising 130, 137; of therapist 13–14, 21, 24, 58, 62, 100–1, 136, 178, 213
Sullivan, H.S. 4, 5, 62, 131, 198t
Surin, K. 222
symbolic 133, 181–2, 201
symbolic, language meanings and 199–203
symmetry between therapist and patient 100, 110, 112
Szasz, T. 87

T
tacit knowledge 4
Taft, J. 195, 197, 200
Target, M. 37n, 69, 111
teaching relational theory 100–1, 181–2
technique, relational perspective as a 108; crucial elements of good 109; disclosure of analyst's life as a marker for 108–9; no 'off-the-shelf' approach 14–15, 100, 104; unlocking impasses between therapists and patients 110–11
terminology 93–4, 95–7
territorial claims 198–9
Theatres of the Body 87
theology 66, 67, 194, 221, 222
Theology and the Problem of Evil 222
'theory of mind' 69
theory, relational as 178; as a meta-theory 182; misconceptions of 179–81
therapeutic stance 14–16, 111–13
'third' 177
time allotted to therapy sessions 84, 85–6, 102
training programs 94, 95, 190; differences between UK and US 96–7; inadequacies in 221; teaching without a prescribed technique 100–1
transactional analysis (TA) 178–9, 201, 217
Transcendence and Evil 222
transference 17, 30, 55–6, 122, 128; 'disclosure' shaping 109; Geson on 60; signifiers of 132–3, 135, 215; theme across theoretical traditions 213; traditions in psychoanalysis related to 132, 201, 215
trauma: birth 40–1, 50, 83–4, 114; forgiveness for victims of 71, 116
truth: mind and 123–5, 214; in terms of heteronomy 147–8
Truth and Reconciliation Commission, South Africa 71

Tudor, K. 193, 194, 195, 198t, 199, 200, 202, 203, 204, 205, 206, 207
Tutu, D. 70, 71
two-person psychology 125; beyond a 142, 202, 207; shift from one-person psychology to 125, 202, 207; in transactional analysis 178–9

U
unentitlement, sense of 23
United Kingdom: development of object relations 62, 97, 98; government endorsement of CBT 162, 172, 203, 213; history of relational psychoanalysis in 12–13, 62, 97, 100; relationship between psychotherapy and psychoanalysis 96; training programs in US and 96–7
United States of America: history of relational psychoanalysis in 4–5, 62, 93–7, 99–100, 184–5; relationship between psychotherapy and psychoanalysis 95–7; training programs in UK and 96–7
Uroborus 188

V
Vico, G. 166, 168
violence arising out of fear of mortality 81
vital, relational as 219
vulnerability of therapist 46, 61, 101, 102; areas of danger and 56–7; of benefit to patient 55, 58, 59, 104; making use of 63

W
Wallerstein, R.S. 124
well-being 142–3, 146, 148, 149, 150
White, M. 170
White, W.A. 4–5
For Whom the Bell Tolls 187
Wiesenthal, S. 71
will, individual 102
'will,' to 83
Williams, R. 66
Winnicott, D. 5, 40, 47, 48, 58, 69, 89, 187, 198t
Wittgenstein, L. 165, 166, 168, 169
Women's Therapy Centre 13, 24
Working at Relational Depth 221
Worrall, M. 152, 153, 185, 194, 198t, 200
Wounded Healer 224
Writing About Patients 104